BRINGING SPIRITUALITY INTO BUSINESS

DONALEE GASTREICH

Published by Complete Solutions Press
St. Charles, MO
www.complete-solutionsllc.com

Printed in the United States of America
First Printing: 2022
ISBNs: 979-8-9864563-0-0 (paperback)   979-8-9864563-1-7 (ebook)
Library of Congress Control Number: 2022912936

TABLE OF CONTENTS

ACKNOWLEDGMENTS

To my sons for your love, acceptance, and belief in me and for being my greatest teachers. You taught me unconditional love, and I love you beyond words, beyond measure.

To my friends who supported me, trusted me, and believed in me even when I didn't—you know who you are.

To all my teachers, mentors, and guides along the way who are by far too many to mention here, so I shall share a few of the most impactful ones from over the last two decades.

Dr. Joe Dispenza, your personal healing story at age 26, when numerous doctors told you you'd need a Harrington rod surgery, you chose to heal yourself by thought and belief alone. You helped me heal from three back surgeries and a grand mal seizure when the doctor's prognosis was I'd always live in pain and be back in a year for a fusion.

Mary Morrissey, who added the spiritual side to coaching and reinforced my belief in my spiritual intelligence to guide and direct me in all that I do. You had me when you said you had two black belts—one in success and one in failure.

Oprah Winfrey for the *Super Soul Sunday* that introduced me to Eckhart Tolle's work, which set me on journey to slow down the freight train of thoughts in my head and led me to meditation.

Tony Robbins, who taught me the power of state, the fire walk, and how we strive to protect our identity.

Dr. Bruce Lipton, who introduced me to HeartMath Institute and the heart's intelligence and added the science to support all that I was learning.

The whole Hay House community and the beautiful work of Louise Hay.

Debbie Ford and her courageous work on our shadows.

David R. Hawkins for his work in the fields of consciousness and spirituality.

Tasha Eurich for her work in awareness, which became the A in my ABCs.

Byron Katie for "The Work" and the "Judge-Your-Neighbor Worksheet."

Daniel Goleman for introducing the world to emotional Intelligence.

To all the Life Mastery Consultants and Dream Builder coaches who joined me in my first Mastermind: Alan, Barbara, Summer, Gail, and Fiona, and then Deborah and Randy. I love you all so much. Thank YOU!

To all those who are unique and different to what our society calls normal and who boldly and bravely proclaim yourself with dignity, honor, and respect, I love you and support you.

And to this consciousness in which we all exist. This amazing planet we call home. To Mother Nature and all the bountiful resources she provides. To the natural healing plants and resources available to us.

Thank you to all the resources that have aided my journey and contributed to the material in this book.

INTRODUCTION

It is with exceptional pleasure and excitement that I share with you my greatest learnings in life. My oldest son asked me if I had one thing, one life lesson, to share with others, what would it be? I answered by telling him that I learned the value of other people in my life—that everyone comes into your life for a reason, a season, or a purpose, and that we are here to invite them in with open arms, without knowing why, and allow their purpose, reason, and value to unfold over time. I learned that other people increase my life by adding value, love, connection, and wisdom. They bring advancements, both ones I'd been seeking and those I had no clue were possible. It's through our connections with others that we truly prosper and grow beyond measure. Little did I know that this question stayed with me and became the basis and reason for this book. This book is filled with many of the lessons and learnings my life has unfolded.

Prior to knowing the value of others, I had a much different approach. As a single mom with three young boys (and all that comes with that—homework, sports, friends, etc.), a career, and a household to run, I had a system for everything. I loved meeting new people, but with an already busy life, I quickly tried to fit them in or out. I would ask a series of questions to see how I might fit them in, and when there was no evident way for seeing them more often and really getting to know them, I simply let them go. I would look to see if they had kids the same ages as mine or if their kids played the same sports that mine did. I would ask where they worked and what they did there to see if they might need my services. I would find out what part of town they lived in so I would know if it would be easy to see one another. Looking back, it seemed like I had 50 questions I drilled them with to fit them in or toss them out. No more. I now know that everyone has a message, meaning, or a magnificent contribution to my life.

Bringing Spirituality into Business is a compilation of my life's learnings and lessons that have brought much increase, advancement, and joy to my life and others. Little did I know the value in that one question asked of me so long ago. Every human being is here to grow, to prosper, and to become more of who they are. You are here to increase, advance, and prosper, and it's my intention that this be your result in reading and engaging in the words and invitations that follow.

Through the years, I've concluded that life is comprised of mastering one skill, one practice, and one process. We try to make it complicated and difficult, but it's really much simpler than we can fathom. The one skill is **A**wareness and the A in the ABCs to master you and your results. The one practice is **B**eing, which gives us the B in the ABCs. And the one process is **C**uriosity, which concludes the ABCs.

Bringing Spirituality into Business is my contribution to the world, to humanity, to you, to aid you in living an empowered life. This book is a collection of what it took me decades to realize, shift, and align with to allow myself to recognize my worth, value, and purpose. My life lacked meaning, purpose, and direction before I did the work to heal the wounded and hurt aspects within.

The real joy in life comes when you know yourself, when you embrace all that makes you *you*—all your quirks, secrets, fears, and uniqueness. When you stop avoiding the dark shadow aspects of yourself and painful memories, you'll begin to fully merge all of yourself together as a whole and complete being with acceptance, love, and gratitude. As you do, you will unlock greater gifts and potentials you never knew you had. You see, to resist anything, is like putting the brakes on life and slowing or stopping your growth and your life from blossoming. As you love and accept all parts of you, you step into your greatness and will live your life empowered.

Bringing Spirituality into Business is your guide to know yourself, grow yourself, and live life empowered. You'll learn the ABCs to master you and your results, with every step broken down into bite-size chunks for you to understand, work with, utilize, and integrate into your life.

Allow *Bringing Spirituality into Business* to be your owner's manual to living your best life possible, to connecting the dots, stepping into your greatness, and finding purpose and greater meaning in life. Allow it to be the pathway home to happiness, peace, and abundance. It is a collection of all the wisdom spirit brought to me and through me along my journey, and it is what I am here to share with you now. May it prosper you in ways you've never imagined.

Allow yourself time to go through the book because at the end of each chapter is an invitation to go deeper into what that chapter brings. Going deeper requires reflection, contemplation, and inquiry. It's in the Invitations at the end of each chapter where the magic happens. If you are reading this in the workplace, form a structure of support around reading together as a department, division, team, or group. If you don't work or work alone, form a book club with friends and family or join a book club via the website. It's in your weekly meetings that you'll be able to share, discuss, incorporate, and apply the messages and invitation in each chapter. Plan and make time for these weekly meetings and form them in a way that allows every voice to be heard and all to be empowered. It's in your weekly meetings that you will expand your awareness to see more within yourself, your abilities, and your weaknesses; you'll notice new ideas, insights, and intuitions. It's in your weekly work that you will learn to know yourself and how you're hardwired to connect with your Inner Wisdom in order to understand your intuition and to be able to trust it. It's in your weekly work where you will be growing yourself and beginning to live life empowered.

How to get the most out of *Bringing Spirituality into Business*:
- Allow time for the Invitation at the end of each chapter.
- Organize your group or book club or join one via the website link below.
- Meet weekly to share your insights, questions, and growth.
- Share and celebrate yourself and others along the way.
- Keep a journal or purchase the Companion Workbook to get even more out of this work and go deeper into knowing yourself.
- Do the Pre-Start Assessment found in the Companion Workbook or on the website linked below. This will provide you a tool to measure your progress and results.
- Have fun—you are about to learn more about yourself!

More support can be found at *https://complete-solutionsllc.com/Bringing-Spirituality-into-Business/*.

Support available on the website includes:
- Pre-Start Assessment

- Companion Workbook
- Weekly Book Club Support Group
- Winner's Circle – Group Support Beyond the Book
- Inquire/Schedule Business Training
- Inquire/Schedule Speaking Engagement
- Finish Assessment

Visit *https://complete-solutionsllc.com/Bringing-Spirituality-into-Business/* or scan the QR code with your smart device to access the *Bringing Spirituality into Business* bonus material.

SECTION I: EDUCATE

LAYING THE FOUNDATION

In this first section of *Bringing Spirituality into Business,* you'll learn:
- Terms, like spirituality
- Tools, or skills to master
- Value, in knowing yourself

It is in your knowledge and understanding that you will be able to lay a strong foundation to your growth and development and to your success. It's in your knowledge and understanding that you will gain the power to look at yourself through the lens of love and see things without the bias of your conditioning, social norms, and expectations.

Bringing Spirituality into Business is a tool to empower every individual to tap into their greatness, to unlock their inner genius and share their gifts and talents in the workplace, allowing the workplace to be a space where people advance and express more of their unique gifts and talents.

You are encouraged and invited to experience the words on these pages. You'll be invited to accept the **Invitation** at the end of each chapter. The Invitation offered is for you to explore, examine, and bring to your awareness anything and everything that that chapter brings up for you. It's an Invitation to go deep within and, in the process, get to know yourself intimately and with compassion and kindness. It's an Invitation to peel back layers upon layers of conditioning, beliefs, stories, and limitations that block you from your greatness.

Your human experience comes with conditioning. Your conditioning often brings up resistance. Resistance is thinking it isn't so. It's where the ego, in its attempt to keep you safe or the same, will counter what is said. This countering may look different for you. I invite you to notice how it shows up for you. It can show up as a story in your mind.

It can show up as a feeling in your body. It can show up as chaos in your system. It can show up as fear: fear of change, fear of what others will think, fear of the unknown. This is your opportunity to simply notice how it shows up for you.

You might be an individual who thinks this doesn't apply to you. You might be an individual who feels your core values are being challenged. You might be an individual who is scared to death of losing yourself in the process of change. You might be an individual who struggles to see beyond the cultural norms and ways. Or you may have a different experience. Know that whatever shows up is for you to see, to recognize, and to bring to the light. This "bringing to the light" allows you to know yourself more clearly, to understand what makes you YOU.

One thing you should remember is that there is greatness in YOU and *Bringing Spirituality into Business* will allow you to bring it forth and share it.

When businesses around the globe encourage and support every individual's greatness, people will be living their lives empowered. When we live life empowered, we are able to see and recognize the greatness in others. We will embrace our interconnectivity. We will find value in one another and invite others into our circles because we will see how much we need and value their gifts and talents in the co-creation process.

This first section will remind you that you are a spiritual being here on this planet at this time having a human experience. You may focus on your bodies and believe the body is all that you are, with all its limitations, faults, thoughts, feelings, and behaviors, and then get caught up in all the dramas, traumas, and problems that surface. In your focus on the body, you forget the bigger picture and all that you are.

Everything you experience in this life is just that—an experience. Yet you try to make everything so serious and detrimental to who you are. A tragedy does not define you. An illness does not define you. A job does not define you. Nor does a divorce or an addiction or the loss of a child. And yet all of these experiences are painful. They cause you to suffer and getting out from underneath the limited thinking and pain they bring is not something you are skilled at doing.

Please know that your pain and suffering are real. No one can tell you they are not. But in all of your life experience, they are but a tiny fragment of the bigger picture of all you are here to experience.

Donalee Gastreich

This first section aims to educate you and connect you to your divine nature, the higher self, and those aspects of yourself that you may have become disconnected with.

CHAPTER 1:

WHAT IS SPIRITUALITY?

Spirituality is that sense or belief that there is something bigger than you, something more to being a human than just your five senses. Spirituality invites you to see your connection to everything, everyone, to Universal Laws, and to the wisdom and intelligence within you. Spirituality reminds you that you are here to grow, to advance, and to prosper. It summons you to recall that the energy on this planet is cosmic or divine in its nature.

Spirituality is a broad concept of belief in something beyond oneself. Exploring spirituality is individual and personal, yet deeply connecting to others.

Spirituality offers a worldview that suggests there is more to life than what people experience on a sensory and physical level.

Not only does spirituality suggest that there is something greater that connects all beings to one another and to the universe itself, it proposes there is ongoing existence after the human experience and strives to answer our bigger questions. The questions all people ask and ponder at some point in their life include: Who am I? What is the meaning of life? How are we connected to one another? What's my purpose? We also ponder the truths and mysteries of the human experience.

Spirituality helps one know oneself, grow oneself, and live life empowered.

The word "spirit" comes from the Latin word *spiritus,* meaning "breath." It is defined as "the vital principle or animating force traditionally believed to be within living beings." The concept of spirituality is often confused with religious beliefs. Spirituality has nothing to do with religion. Religion exists outside of you, when you join others in believing or following a set of practices.

Spirituality, on the other hand, exists within you. It is an experience that one harbors inside and is extremely personal to each individual. It involves looking within and defining a system of beliefs that takes root within your own disposition. No one can instruct you on the perfect way to practice spirituality because, ultimately, only you know what is right for you.

Spirituality can bring a source of comfort and relief from the hurts and pains of life, like loss, rejection, and loneliness. While many people find their way to spirituality through religion or seeking God, others find their way to spirituality through a "dark night of the soul." The well-known author and spiritual guide Eckhart Tolle describes the "dark night of the soul" as an inner state that looks like depression, a collapse of your perceived meaning of life, that feels like an eruption into a deep sense of meaninglessness that affects all areas of life and consumes one's thoughts, feelings, and sense of self. It is said to be a stage in personal growth and development when a person undergoes a difficult and challenging time, often deeply miserable, to find themselves moving through the experience and coming out the other side more conscious of their perception of life and their place in life. This can be the beginning of one's spiritual growth.

There is no one way to develop your spirituality; in fact, there are many paths to spirituality. How you find your way will be personal and unique. Know that the road you take is your choice. No one is forcing people to wake up to spirituality. When you are ready, there will be an inner pull to more, which results in a curiosity to what you don't know. Let's face it: there is more that you don't know than what you do know. Allow this book to show you, to awaken your own inner pull to knowing more—more about you, more about yourself, more about your purpose and the meaning of your life.

Some say that spirituality feels like coming home—a beautiful homecoming to feel comfortable and connected with life, oneself, and others, to be truly present, comfortable with your choices, and alive to the possibilities and potentials of conscious change. In this coming home, you find peace, an inner balance, and connection, honoring yourself, your needs, and your boundaries while opening your heart to yourself and those you love. It's where self-love, self-respect, and integrity flourish.

Spirituality empowers you to radiate your natural beauty, your essence, and your light and love. Spirituality empowers you to heal, to mend your wounds, and to end self-perpetuated suffering. Spirituality allows you to commit, to devote yourself to the One Power and One Presence. This power is love and emotes compassion and inner peace. It reminds you of the Universal Laws: the laws of advancement, attraction, vibrations, cause and effect, and your oneness with all things.

Spirituality is living in the present moment with curiosity, acceptance, and grace. Spirituality is a brain state we can all reach. For the purpose of our general understanding of the term *spirituality*, it is expressed here as a higher state of consciousness.

The father of Western psychology, William James, defined spiritual experiences in 1902 as states of higher consciousness that are induced by efforts to understand the general principles or structure of the world through one's inner experience. At the core of his view of spirituality is what we might call "connectedness," which refers to the fact that individual goals can be truly realized only in the context of the whole—one's relationship to the world and to others.

Traditionally, this spiritual state has been described as divine, achievable through contemplative and embodied practices, such as prayer, meditation, rhythmic rituals, psychedelics, and other plant medicines. Indeed, this higher state of consciousness and connection has been reported in many spiritual traditions, ranging from Buddhism to Sufism and Judaism to Christianity. However, recent neuroscientific research shows that the same state can be achieved through secular practices as well.

Scientific and creative epiphanies with their accompanying ecstatic states are characterized by a sense of unity and bliss similar to religious experiences, with both involving a higher state of presence and observation. Geniuses, such as Isaac Newton, Louis Pasteur, Albert Einstein, and Nikola Tesla, reported spiritual-like states during their revelations or breakthroughs. These don't have to be the rare experiences of a chosen few. They can be reached in your everyday life.

We see athletes reaching higher states of peak potential and performance. We see leadership, executives, and influencers claiming states of flow, where they watch themselves achieving more in a few hours than they had been able to achieve in a week. We see our technological development exceeding even our own expectations. We see humanity evolving to higher states of consciousness. We see a rise in those flocking to experience psychedelics in an attempt to fast-track or biohack their way to spirituality and higher states of consciousness.

You have the ability to reach these states in your daily life; they are your inner nature. As the musician, singer, and songwriter Billy Corgan puts it:

> **I think a spiritual journey is not so much a journey of discovery. It's a journey of recovery. It's a journey of uncovering your inner nature. It's already there.**

Spirituality—call it what you will: pure consciousness; the power of the universe; the power of the creator or creation; the breath of life, the life force energy that sustains me and you; God, Abba, or a myriad of other labels. While spirituality is not a religion, many faith practices can lead to spirituality and thus recognize this power and presence.

In neuroscience, studies show us the way that spiritual states are reflected in the brain and other parts of the body. Spiritual practices have been shown to be closely linked to self-awareness, empathy, and a sense of connectedness, all of which can be correlated with the frequency of brain waves as measured by electroencephalogram (EEG). Studies using EEG have demonstrated how fragmented or out of step our whole brain activity can be much of the time, suggestive of conflicts between our behavior, thinking, feeling, and communication. Alternatively, expert meditators demonstrate more "harmonious" brain waves, which could be indicative of greater synchrony or connectivity within and across different neural areas. In short, **spirituality, similar to love, has physiological effects in the brain and body,** and EEG provides a view on these changes.

In addition, advancements in neuroscience and neuroplasticity show us that we can do more than just measure this kind of activity. We can also train our brains to behave in a more aware state by engaging in activities that facilitate greater connection or neural synchronization. Higher synchronization looks like a large group of brain cells singing together. Some practices known to create higher synchronization are meditation, prayer, breath work, yoga, and qigong (allowing a state of growing calmer). One interpretation is that neuronal synchronization enhances our brain harmony or integrity, thus achieving a state in which the brain works in a more congruent way, adopting a more global perspective. Yet other findings point to the psychological consequences of this state in which greater neuronal synchronization tends to enable a greater ability to make moral judgments and problem solve creatively.

Neuronal synchronization also correlates with feeling more self-connected, which in turn can further increase empathy, creativity, and social effectiveness. Big benefits in the workplace, right? In other words, it's associated with greater *self-awareness*, which has many practical benefits that will be discussed in other chapters.

From a business perspective, the self-aware leaders are those who receive more promotions, have more satisfied employees, and achieve more profitable results.

The awakening of consciousness is the next evolutionary step for mankind. ~ Eckhart Tolle

You might think taking a neuroscientific approach to spirituality to be absurd, profound, or even ineffable. But another perspective is that in the scientific exploration of such experiences, we can reveal the mechanisms enabling us all to achieve these states even in the most mundane moments, such as going to work or waiting in traffic. Scientific discovery could turn seemingly subjective experiences into a more unified understanding. Simply put, I've seen how spirituality can be experienced in business and in everyday tasks, allowing more meaning and purpose in all experiences.

Remember, spirituality is not a belief system and will be unique to you. There are many ways to experience spirituality and the benefits it brings. Some signs of your spiritual growth or insight to spirituality include:
- An ongoing desire to know yourself and grow yourself
- Deepening relationships and connections with others
- Experiencing compassion and empathy for yourself and others
- Experiencing feelings of interconnectedness
- Exploring deep questions on topics such as suffering, reality, and disease

- Feeling a sense of awe and wonder
- Seeking meaning and purpose
- Seeking happiness beyond external reward and material possessions
- A desire to make the world a better place

While specific spiritual views are personal and a matter of faith, research validates and shows us some of the many benefits of spirituality. The results are noteworthy in that they demonstrate the many measurable benefits in a scientific way. So, with an open mind and receptive heart, I invite you to explore some of these scientific findings for yourself.

The following are a few of the many positive discoveries related to spirituality and its influence on physical and mental health and well-being:

- Reduction in stress
- Reduced blood pressure
- Decrease in depression and anxiety
- Improved functioning of immune system
- Increased longevity
- More positive feelings
- Increased resilience and ability to handle challenges and change
- Greater psychological well-being
- Calm and peaceful state of being

In summary, spirituality is a personal journey that has a profound and lasting effect on your well-being as well as your perceptions, interactions, and relatedness with yourself, the world, and others. It validates that you are here to advance, to grow, and to become more.

You probably can see by now that *Bringing Spirituality into Business* is really about bringing spirituality into the lives of all through business. But WHY?

In my view, spirituality, or higher consciousness, is a huge **value add** for every individual in their personal and professional growth and development. To know oneself leads to growing oneself, and both of these lead to living life in an empowered state. And this is what businesses need—more empowered humans to unite together and share their amazing talents, wisdom, and awareness.

Steve Jobs gave the world a powerful message on hiring and management of people in the workplace when he said:

It doesn't make sense to hire smart people and tell them what to do; we hire smart people so they can tell us what to do.

Let's unite and rally together in *Bringing Spirituality into Business*.

INVITATION

Explore your thoughts and beliefs about spirituality and why you are reading this book.

_____

_____

In your words, what is spirituality to you?

_____

_____

What does it mean to you that you are a spiritual being here having a human experience?

_____

_____

What do you want to gain from reading this book?

_____

_____

CHAPTER 2:

WHY BRING SPIRITUALITY INTO BUSINESS?

In the first chapter, we summarized that spirituality is a personal journey that has a profound and lasting effect on your well-being as well as your perceptions, interactions, and relatedness with yourself, the world, and others. And it validates and acts as a magnetic pull to advance you to become more.

So *why* is spirituality important in business? Obviously, many reasons exist, and this book aims to bring many of them into your awareness. I am certain that a few ideas and reasons are coming to your mind right now. Every thought, idea, and reason coming to your mind is important in your journey. Take a moment to ponder this question and answer it for yourself before reading on.

The spiritual journey is one of learning to trust yourself and to question and grow in your understanding and knowledge. One of the first things that spirituality teaches you is the value and importance of your uniqueness and individuality. It says, "*You matter.*" You matter, and your contribution matters.

Talent can't be taught, but it can be awakened.
~ Wallace Stegner

Dynamic leaders like Steve Jobs believe that their employees' matter. Jobs hired them with the belief and understanding that they offered an enormous benefit to the company, and he allowed them to demonstrate their uniqueness and talents and share their contributions.

Bringing Spirituality into Business echoes this belief at its core. It asks all organizations, all management, all leadership to embrace the fact that every individual matters and what they bring to the organization is valued and appreciated, and to demonstrate this in every new hire and every employee. And yet, it only works and becomes relevant if you also align with and know that you matter.

So many adults struggle with worthiness, a sense of value and importance. Judgment, ridicule, criticism, and competition are common in the workplace. Engagement in the workplace is at an all-time low. Turnover in the workplace is at an all-time high.

If you are a manager, reflect on your department or team and discern if you are delivering this message. If you are not impacting your team with their value, look at the message you are sending. How you feel is the energy you are sharing, whether spoken or not. Reflect on your level of comfort and your feelings around sharing your viewpoint, ideas, improvements, and feeling heard and valued.

In 2020, workplaces around the globe saw drastic and unimaginable shifts, changes, and disruptions. When an existing workplace was already weak in its structure, these disruptions could be devastating, even crumbling. Some businesses did not make it. Even the firmly structured and developed workplaces felt the wobble and experienced the need to adapt quickly. Normally change is thought through, evaluated, analyzed, and adapted within a methodical and calibrated process. But in the pandemic, change happened quickly and without much reasoning and evaluation of options as many changes were the results of others' decisions.

Let's face it: We all experienced one of the most impactful, unanticipated, and previously unimaginable reactions and responses to a current event in our lifetime. As with all devastation or change, a pattern emerges: out with the old and in with the new. Through nature, we see the cycles of death and rebirth, a letting go and trusting in the renewal of life. There is so much to learn from Mother Nature. Look at the caterpillar, who spins a cocoon to serve as protection during its time of transformation. The transformed butterfly then fights and struggles to get out, to free itself, and to gift the world with a new beauty. It's a time of evolution.

You are in a time of transformation. You are evolving. Astrologers call this time the Aquarian Age. It is a time for new beginnings for each and every human being as new awareness, insights, and developments are brought forth. Even while many are focused on fear, worry, lack, and limitations, an expansion of consciousness is going on. This new human consciousness is beginning to take effect and has already affected hundreds of thousands of people and affects more every day.

This new awareness allows us to see everything and understand everything differently. Here are some examples:

- Have you ever thought you were more than a mind and a body?
- Have you thought that the world is not random but full of beauty and meaning?
- Have you thought that you are supported by something outside of your current awareness?

These thoughts are made real in the **new consciousness**. This new consciousness is an expansion in our perception beyond the abilities of the five senses; your five senses deal only in your physical reality. This new consciousness is expanding your perception beyond your five senses and beyond the physical reality.

We have new sensory perceptions being activated and coming online, allowing us to engage as the multisensory beings we are. All of this is aided by and advanced with our digital technology explosion, which accelerated in 2020. This digital transformation is causing organizations to create new, or modify existing, business processes, cultures, and employee and customer experiences to meet the changing business and market requirements. It's changing the way we see not only ourselves, the world, and our universe, but it's also changing more than that. It's changing relationships, communities, cultures, social structures, and *business*—how we run our business, how we operate our business, everyone in it, and the customers the business serves.

This new consciousness is new potential,
new possibilities.

Power in the old consciousness was exerted through control and manipulation; maybe you've noticed these structures being challenged, struggling, or even crumbling. In the new consciousness, power is found in the alignment of your personality with your soul, your ego with your spirit. We are being called to grow spiritually. Your multisensory abilities are recognized in your spiritual growth.

Bringing Spirituality into Business is about acknowledging every individual and their contribution. It's about recognizing our interconnectedness. It's about engagement, interactions, and teamwork that focus on individual strengths, not weaknesses. It's about creating a culture within the organization that is supportive of every individual feeling safe, valued, and supported as they share and contribute to the greater good. Its aim is unity, growing and developing individual talents, and all sharing in the mission and vision of the organization, as well as encouraging personal visions.

Spirituality is being present, realizing you are more than this present moment. It's understanding there is greatness in you and in every human being. It's getting to understand your purpose, meaning, and value, and it's seeing there is more to life than the material world.

While we are highly evolved, multidimensional beings, we are also primitive and stupid. Allow me a moment to explain: We are destroying our planet and, at the same time, inventing countless ways to heal her. We have great difficulty getting out of emotional depression, exercising regularly, or eating nutritiously. Yet there are mountains of research that informs us how to be healthy, strengthen our immune system, and support our mental well-being. We know what we ought to do but don't. We are overwhelmed by the screaming demands for change, and we are terrified of it.

Businesses everywhere are beginning to inspire a different future and doing great work, while many government agencies are dinosaurs resisting the new ideas. The world economy is changing. We are depleting our resources. The value of our currency is shifting. Environmental concerns are growing. Yet we want to maintain business as usual, pretending all is well.

Businesses are now greatly affected by this global mental health pandemic brought about by forced shutdowns, mask mandates, social distancing, working remotely, and the fear that has been the main media message for way too long. The individual effects fall upon businesses as they have the greater investment in the individual worker.

This is why *Bringing Spirituality into Business* matters.

A Gallup poll from May 2021 indicated that one-third of the population was diagnosed with some form of clinical depression, anxiety, or other form of mental illness, and seven out of 10 people were suffering or struggling.

This is why *Bringing Spirituality into Business* is so critical now.

In a time when so many new age principals tell us to stay positive at all times—not to think about the negative—I am asking you to do the opposite. Let's face the truth about the way each one of us lives, acknowledge where we aren't living in integrity, and then step away from any negative judgment so we can change—not through shame or blame but through love and compassion for ourselves and the human condition. In honoring our human nature without judgment, we can live from a more authentic place. As we begin to address the elephant in the room, as we have those courageous conversations, we will start to heal the wounds of our humanity and thus grow in our spirituality.

This is why *Bringing Spirituality into Business* is so important.

Never before have we experienced such massive extremes: division among the people and separation of values defining what's right and what's wrong. Then there is the judgment on those who don't comply and agree with your beliefs. Everywhere you look, there is another divide. Many are questioning their human rights. Their freedom of speech is being censored, their voices deleted, and their opinions buried. People's rights to what they put in their body are brought to the forefront as vaccine mandates are popping up across the globe. Businesses are struggling to employ reliable and competent people to run their organizations, hindering their ability to function at the necessary level. People are no longer tolerating the demands put upon them. Human rights and core values are being brought into awareness.

This is why *Bringing Spirituality into Business* is necessary now.

Every organization already has a vested interest in their staff. They hired them to serve and support their organization, and the business provides its employees a wage to do so. They have already invested time in hiring them, onboarding, and training. They have invested money in providing benefits in the form of life insurance and health, dental, and/or vision coverage. They already offer vacation, time off, sick days, maternity leave, and more. Many progressive organizations offer even more perks and benefits like childcare, help with college debt, gym memberships, or workout facilities. Some are beginning to offer personal and professional growth and development dollars to support the employee in learning new skills, advancing soft skills, and giving them the means to truly invest in themselves.

Spirituality reminds you that your body, your central nervous system, is hardwired for comfort, but your soul, your very essence, is hardwired for growth.

All of this and more is why *Bringing Spirituality into Business* will be the greatest reward for your organization, everyone in it, and everyone it serves, creating the biggest win/win/win.

INVITATION

What might you gain by bringing spirituality to work with you?

_____

_____

Can you recognize and list the ways in which you matter and how what you offer is valued?

_____

_____

How well do you trust yourself, on a scale of 1–5? Where might you do a better job at trusting yourself?

_____

_____

Are you fearful? of what? Why?

_____

_____

How critical are you? of yourself? of others?

_____

_____

How does it make you feel to criticize?

_____

_____

CHAPTER 3:

KNOW YOURSELF

You are comprised of 84 minerals, 23 elements, and 8 gallons of water spread across 38 trillion cells.

You have been built up from nothing by the spare parts of the Earth you have consumed, according to a set of instructions hidden in a double helix and small enough to be carried by a sperm. You are recycled butterflies, plants, rocks, streams, firewood, wolf fur, and shark teeth, broken down to their smallest parts and rebuilt into our planet's most complex living thing.

You are not living on Earth. You are Earth.

~ Aubrey Marcus

Reflect for a moment to ask yourself, How well do you know yourself?

The story of the Monkey and the Fish is a perfect example of how we really don't know ourselves. The story goes like this:

The fish loved the river. It felt blissful swimming around in its clear blue waters. One day while swimming close to the riverbank, it hears a voice say, "Hey, fish, how is the water?"

The fish raises its head above the water and sees a monkey seated on a branch of a tree.

The fish replies, "The water is nice and warm, thank you."

The monkey feels jealous of the fish and wants to put it down. It says, "Why don't you come out of the water and climb this tree with me? The view from here is amazing!"

The fish, feeling a little sad, replies, "I don't know how to climb a tree, and I cannot survive without water."

Hearing this, the monkey makes fun of the fish, saying, "You are totally worthless if you cannot climb a tree!"

The fish swims away and starts thinking about this remark non-stop and becomes extremely depressed. "Yes, the monkey is right," it would think. "I cannot even climb a tree; I must be worthless."

A seahorse sees the fish feeling all depressed and asks it what the reason was. Upon knowing the reason, the seahorse laughs and says, "If the monkey thinks you are worthless for not being able to climb the tree, then the monkey is worthless too because it cannot swim or live under water."

Upon hearing this, the fish suddenly realized how gifted it was, that it had the ability to survive under water and swim freely, which the monkey never could!

The fish feels thankful to nature for giving it such an amazing ability.

The moral in this story takes from Einstein's quote, "Everybody is a genius. But if you judge a fish by its ability to climb a tree, it will live its whole life believing that it is stupid."

Take a look at our education system that judges everyone based on the same criteria. Coming out of such a system, it's easy for many of us to start believing that we are actually less gifted than others. But this reality is far from the truth.

There is greatness inside of you.

I don't know about you, but I was never taught how to know myself. For most of my life, I didn't even know what I truly wanted. I didn't know what made me tick. I didn't know much about myself. I guess I felt life was a mystery, and I should stop trying to figure it out. Sure, I thought I knew what foods I liked, but I didn't know which foods were best for me. I knew my body needed exercise but didn't know which exercises were best for me. I knew I didn't feel complete and thought I needed to find a partner to complete me. I knew I wanted and needed friends, but I didn't know how to be a good friend. I didn't know what I brought to a friendship. I knew I had happy moments, but I had more sad moments that left me feeling alone and separate from the world. I didn't know why I felt that way. I didn't know I had options. I knew I had to find a job, to make money and provide for myself, but I never knew I could follow my dreams or my deepest desires.

I would notice qualities in others and wish I had that too. I would notice more of what I lacked, noticing all that I did not have. I spent a big part of my life noticing what was missing and feeling inadequate. I often entertained the thought of wanting more. I wasn't taught in my childhood that I could do, be, or have anything I wanted. I wasn't instructed or guided to believe in myself. I didn't know that I should go for my dreams. I spent a big part of my life playing small, feeling less than, and constantly focused outwardly to what others thought about me or what they had that I didn't. Little did I know, all of this was forming my identity.

You will strive to hold yourself true to the identity with which you believe is you. Your Identity becomes the most influential driver to the results you will achieve in all areas of life. Shaped and formed from your childhood, your identity governs your self-worth, relationships, work life, finances and achievements.

I was brought up going to church, with beliefs in Catholicism and Christianity; my family mostly feared God, making my focus on the suffering and pain that life brings. I noticed fears in others, but I also noticed some of those fears I shared and some I did not. I learned to keep quiet so as not to appear different from others. Whenever I did speak up and question anything, like the fears I did not share, I was called naive, stupid, or ignorant of the reality before me. This is just one example of how our identity is formed. For many, religion brings faith, trust, and clarity, but for me, it brought questioning, curiosity, and a quest for knowledge.

With no owner's manual or understanding of myself, the only guidelines I had to follow were the 10 commandments and the Golden Rule.

> *"Do unto others as you would have
> them do unto you."*

I spent a big part of my life focusing outwardly and judging myself based on what I didn't have. I focused more on other people's expectations of me, like my employer, parents, and society's so-called "normal." I focused on being nice and kind to others. I apologized for things I did unintentionally, like allowing the door to slam behind me instead of consciously holding it and allowing it to close gently. I apologized over and over for being me.

I didn't know to look at what made me do the things I do. I didn't know how to look inward at my own desires, dreams, and expectations of me and this life of mine. I didn't know how to love myself. I spent more time judging and criticizing myself, my feelings, my behaviors, and all that I wasn't.

Can you relate to any of this? I speak for someone growing up in the United States. I hear it is completely different depending on your country of origin, culture, history, beliefs, and traditions.

Knowing yourself is the first step in growing yourself. Knowing yourself requires self-awareness. Knowing yourself is required if you:
- Want to change
- Wish to be happy
- Are to be successful
- Seek to understand yourself

Psychologist and author Tasha Eurich divides self-awareness into two types: **internal self-awareness**, or understanding why we behave the way we do, and **external awareness**, or accurately judging how others see us. She estimates that 95 percent of people consider themselves self-aware, when in actuality, only 10 to 15 percent of people are self-aware. It's through both internal and external self-awareness that you'll be able to know yourself more clearly and see the identity you are maintaining.

In my own journey to knowing myself, I was introduced to the children's book, *The Little Me and the Great Me*, written by Lou Austin. It's a story of exploring both aspects of the self, from the little me who wants everything for myself—like the toys I want to play with, needing to be first, and being stingy with my belongings, saying, "That's mine"—to exploring the great me, who is more concerned about others, sharing, including all, and having fun together. This little children's book reminded me that we all have a lot to learn about ourselves. There are two voices within: the ego (our human personality) and the higher self (our soul or spiritual aspect). How I respond depends on the voice I am listening to. The little me is egocentric and thinks primarily of myself. The great me is ethnocentric, thinking about and including others.

There are many paths to knowing yourself. It's my intention that this book be a guide to greater knowledge of yourself, that you will embrace a path to knowing yourself, your value, and your contribution to the world and others. And while on this path, you notice the subtle pull to advancing yourself and realizing more of who you've come to be. *Bringing Spirituality into Business* is for *you* if you are ready and willing to:

- Explore the root of your thoughts and habits
- Examine and question limiting beliefs
- Observe socially conditioned ideas
- Face and overcome fears and traumas
- Examine the range of emotions you allow yourself to feel
- Develop faith in your intelligence systems
- Acknowledge and nurture your talents and strengths
- Have those courageous conversations, despite the difficulty and pain
- Establish and maintain daily practices that support health and well-being
- Unite and integrate your humanness with your infinite nature
- Allow your gifts and talents to flourish and your greatness to come forth

To know yourself is to go beyond the identity you currently hold. It requires you to look within to your beliefs, to the limitations and stories that might be limiting your greatness, and to bring forth the necessary and required thinking and actions to allow you to create the identity of who you are here to become.

INVITATION

Reflect on how well you know yourself.

_____

_____

Why are you reading this book? What do you hope to get from it?

_____

_____

What has this chapter brought up for you?

_____

_____

What are you ready to explore, examine, and understand about yourself?

_____

_____

Are there parts of you that you are avoiding, resisting, and pushing away?

_____

_____

Can you be open to looking at a part of you that you've been avoiding?

_____

_____

CHAPTER 4:

GROW YOURSELF

Grow yourself means to seek out a better you, to want to change because you know there is more you are capable of, not because you feel obligated to meet others' standards of excellence. Life is a journey of advancing yourself, learning and up-leveling along the way. You know there is a better version of you ahead. It's just a matter of the steps to get there.

> **As we advance in life it becomes more and more difficult, but in fighting the difficulties the inmost strength of the heart is developed. ~ Vincent van Gogh**

In this fast-paced, ever-changing world, you may be focused on all of your responsibilities, obligations, and commitments. You may think you don't have time to grow yourself. You might avoid growing yourself because you don't know how to start, where to begin, or what to work on. You may feel comfort in where you are. You may feel resistance to growth if you are doing it for someone or something else.

Sure, you can find comfort in taking a pause after a big growth spurt. It is during that pause when you are actually integrating the new you into all areas of your life. Science confirms the value in celebrating your success. Abiding in the gratitude of your accomplishments is just as important as the growth. And there is great value in knowing when you are ready to expand your awareness, evaluate your progress, assess what's next, and begin the cycle again.

A new confidence develops when you invest in your own growth—not just confidence, but a sense of purpose, a satisfaction, and a sense of fulfillment. People who regularly reflect and examine where they are and where they want to be develop a habit of continual growth and development.

Confidence is not "They will like me";
it's "I'll be fine if they don't."

Carol Dweck, professor of psychology at Stanford University, identified two mindsets. A **mindset** is a series of self-perceptions or beliefs people hold about themselves. These determine behavior, outlook, and mental attitude, for example, believing you are either "intelligent" or "unintelligent." In her book *Mindset: The New Psychology of Success*, Dweck shares two mindsets: **fixed mindset** and **growth mindset**. In her research, Dweck built on the **theory of neuroplasticity**, which is the brain's ability to continue to form new connections into adulthood after it has been damaged or when it is stimulated by new experiences. This supports the idea that you can adopt a growth mindset at any time of life.

In my mind, the most important thing you must be aware of is this:

Never get caught up thinking you are
growing yourself for someone else.

It's easy to get stuck thinking your boss is making you learn new skills, or your spouse is mandating you get counseling to be a better communicator, or your kids want you to go to anger management classes, so they aren't afraid to be around you. When you approach change and growth from the belief you have to—someone is making you—the underlying bitterness and resentment get in the way of your growth.

Have you heard the saying, "What you resist persists"? This is a powerful reality. When you resist change, it is often because you are in a rut of sorts. Scientists at the Massachusetts Institute of Technology (MIT) have proven that we repeat certain behaviors because our brain is in a rut. Because of this, it is often difficult for us to change our behavior. This is the reason why having a plan and a coach, mentor, or group to support you will be so valuable.

Leadership is said to be the act of leading others. I think **leadership starts within**; it's your ability to lead yourself to greater, better versions of yourself. Great leaders are people who have endured, found resilience and determination, and picked themselves up again and again to pursue their dreams. It's from their own personal leadership that they are then able to lead others. Leadership isn't always easy, but it is always rewarding. It isn't about the title or award you attain, but more about who you become in the process.

I recommend that organizations bring personal growth and professional development sessions to their weekly roundtable discussions. This will make growth a common and useful component within the framework of the organization as well as develop this framework within each individual. When employees feel supported and recognized in their growth, they feel valued, a warm sense of belonging, and encouraged to keep up the great work. Engagement, interaction, and teamwork are improved as well as individual self-esteem, confidence, and productivity.

In this fast-paced world, personal growth is no longer an option, it is a necessity. It's required to keep up with the evolving world we live in. To grow yourself, you've got to know your:

- Strengths
- Weaknesses
- Interests
- Opportunities

Knowing these four areas of your life tells you where you are now and becomes the building blocks that lay the foundation for your future growth. Change requires that you know where you are and where you want to be.

INVITATION

Look at your attitude and beliefs about your growth and development. How do you feel about change?

_____

_____

Can you recognize your comfort zone? Do you push yourself to do things outside your comfort zone? What's one thing you will do this week that is outside your comfort zone?

_____

_____

Change requires both new thinking and behavior. List your strengths, weaknesses, interests, and opportunities.

_____

_____

Where are you, and where do you want to be?

_____

_____

CHAPTER 5:

LIVING LIFE EMPOWERED

Living an empowered life should be the aim of every human being. Pause a moment and ask yourself, Am I living life empowered? What would it feel like to feel empowered?

PERSONAL EMPOWERMENT

Do you feel like a victim in your life? The victim feels powerless, helpless, as if life is happening to them. The victim suffers and sacrifices their happiness at the mercy of the outer world (circumstances, weather, other people). I have yet to meet a person who doesn't have some area of life where they feel weak or small. In general, the person with a victim complex believes that bad things are inevitable and will keep happening to them; outside factors and circumstances are to be blamed; nothing they do will bring about a change or make any difference to anybody's life, so there is no point trying. Ask yourself, Do I allow the weather to determine my joy? Do I let the driver who cut me off control my happiness?

OR: Do you radiate the victor, the champion in your life? Do you see your abilities, your strengths, and your infinite nature? Do you see the world through an unbiased lens? Do you take full responsibility for yourself, for what you think, for how you feel, and for your words and actions? There is massive power in taking ownership and responsibility for yourself. This is what the following chapters will be exploring, expanding, and integrating.

Living an **empowered life** means living life for you and being true to yourself no matter how difficult the situation. It means fully and completely loving yourself. You radiate confidence, authenticity, and compassion. It's not about comparison, competition, or control.

Empowerment is the act of investing yourself with more authority, integrity, and control over your path in life, health, well-being, career, relationships, and adventures. No, you don't have complete control over what happens in your life, but you do have complete control over how you respond to what is happening in your life.

Between stimulus and response there is a space. In that space is our power to choose our response. ~ Viktor Frankl

This quote emphasizes your ability to live life empowered. It says that in that space is your power to choose and thus your freedom and growth. Frankl was a Holocaust survivor, author, philosopher, and psychiatrist. He founded logotherapy, a school of psychotherapy that describes a search for life's meaning as the central human motivational force.

Even after having been lowered into the pits of humanity, Frankl emerged an optimist. His reasoning was that even in the most terrible of circumstances, a person still has the freedom to choose how they handle their circumstances and create meaning out of them. As Frankl describes it in his well-known book *Man's Search for Meaning*, this meaning is found by realizing the intrinsic dignity that he and others possess simply as human beings. Pause a moment and think about your intrinsic dignity.

In other words, Frankl states that we cannot avoid suffering, but we can choose how to cope with it, find meaning in it, and move forward with renewed purpose. By choosing to exercise his ability to control his reactions and the way he treated others, Frankl discovered the ultimate meaning of freedom. This kind of freedom enabled him to defy his oppressors because, no matter what they said or did, they could not make him believe that any human life—including his own—was worthless. In the book, he exposes how the pursuit of this resistance gave him meaning and allowed him and so many others to endure one of the most difficult burdens in human history—a Nazi concentration camp.

As Frankl describes it, this meaning is found by realizing the intrinsic dignity that he and others possess simply as human beings.

This ultimate human freedom is the freedom to control your attitude toward the situations you encounter. One remarkable aspect of the book is how Frankl is able to write about his experiences entirely without bitterness or vengefulness. Additionally, he does not lose his faith in humanity and is able to discover the goodness even among his enemies. Victor Frankl's story is one of living life empowered.

Can you feel into your own human dignity? Pause a moment, close your eyes, and feel into your value; feel into your worthiness; and feel into your power to choose your response in every moment.

Living an empowered life doesn't mean you discount others. It doesn't mean you blame others. It's quite the opposite. Living an empowered life embraces the interconnectedness of the universe and understands that all you experience will have meaning and purpose when you are able to see it integrated with your natural, intrinsic dignity.

An empowered life requires you to live meaningfully and purposefully and to align your work and your activities in life with who you really are. Empowerment means accessing and gathering all your passion, purpose, and the intrinsic power you have inside you to live and work in ways that are correct for you.

So how does one operate in a world that is unsupportive of personal empowerment? How does one live and function in an environment of control, mandates, and governances that limit and hinder one's personal sense of self?

EMPLOYEE EMPOWERMENT IN THE WORKPLACE

What happens when employees feel empowered? According to the *Harvard Business Review*, "when employees feel empowered at work, it's associated with **stronger job performance, job satisfaction, and commitment to the organization**." Broadly speaking, when employees feel empowered at work, they are more willing to go the extra mile to reach the company's goals.

Employee empowerment is defined as the ways in which organizations provide their employees with a certain degree of autonomy and control in their day-to-day activities. A key principle of employee empowerment is providing employees the means for making important decisions and helping ensure those decisions are correct.

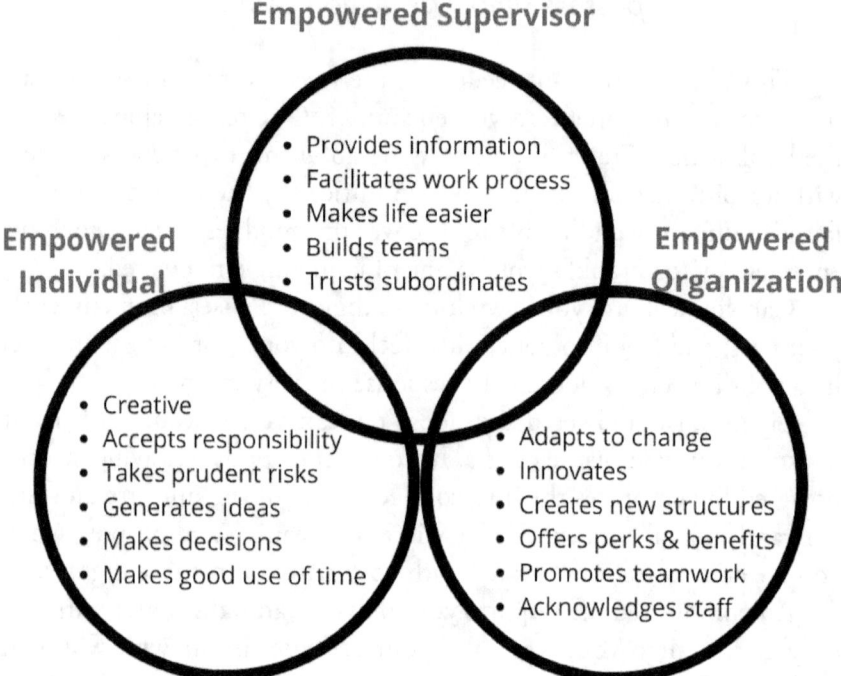

Empowered Supervisor

- Provides information
- Facilitates work process
- Makes life easier
- Builds teams
- Trusts subordinates

Empowered Individual

- Creative
- Accepts responsibility
- Takes prudent risks
- Generates ideas
- Makes decisions
- Makes good use of time

Empowered Organization

- Adapts to change
- Innovates
- Creates new structures
- Offers perks & benefits
- Promotes teamwork
- Acknowledges staff

Company culture either encourages employee empowerment or hinders it. There is no in-between. In 2021, all organizations, for profit and nonprofit, began experiencing what has been labeled as "The Great Resignation," a time when people were leaving their jobs in large numbers, across all demographics and all industries. In my opinion, the Great Resignation is a combination of workers quitting their jobs, many of whom went off to look for higher pay, better conditions, and a healthier work-life balance, the retiring baby boomer population, and those choosing to be their own boss. This is causing organizations to take a hard look at their culture, their mission and vision, and their practices, structure, and organization. It is causing businesses to question what employees need and want. It's allowing businesses to evolve, grow, and meet the needs of the people by innovating.

This is where *Bringing Spirituality into Business* can make all the difference in the world. In the chapters that follow, you will learn some specific ways on how you can begin *Bringing Spirituality into Business*.

INVITATION

Take time to reflect on whether you are living your life empowered.
Look at the areas in your life where you don't feel empowered and why.

_____

_____

What might it look like if you were empowered?

_____

_____

What might you change to take 100 percent responsibility?

_____

_____

CHAPTER 6:

AWARENESS

Awareness is the #1 skill to master. It's also the A in the ABCs to master you and your results in life. According to organizational psychologist and *New York Times* best-selling author Tasha Eurich, only 10 to 15 percent of the population is self-aware. In her bestseller *Insight: Why We're Not as Self-Aware as We Think, and How Seeing Ourselves Clearly Helps Us Succeed at Work and in Life*, she takes readers on a journey exploring this and more with her bold and exhilarating take on self-improvement.

Most people feel like they know themselves pretty well. But what if you could know yourself a bit better and, with this small improvement, get a big payoff...not just in your career, but in your life?

Three types of awareness greatly impact your life and the success of business. Yet everything begins with self-awareness. Each of the three types will be covered; however, the greatest emphasis will be on your personal use of awareness as it relates to every aspect of your life, experiences, and relationships.

The three types of awareness are:

- **Self-awareness** – Self-awareness, the ability to know yourself, is the most known type of awareness.
- **Social awareness** – Social awareness is the ability to understand others, the relationships you have with them, and the relationships they have with others.
- **Organizational awareness** – Organizational awareness is the ability to read a group's emotional currents and power rela-

tionships, and identify influencers, networks, and dynamics within the organization.

Within you is a greatness that is about to be activated and brought fully online. You'll never know the power of your potential until you expand your **A**wareness, understand and monitor who you are **B**eing by aligning all of your intelligence systems, and get **C**urious about what's possible. I call these the ABCs to self-mastery. Self-awareness is the tool that begins this process.

Awareness brings you to this present moment, meaning you aren't focused on the past or the future. There is an openness, a sense of allowing, and maybe an inquisitiveness to what shows up. It requires you live in the "now." In the *New York Times* bestseller *The Power of Now*, the enlightened author Eckhart Tolle guides the reader to awareness of this present moment and to find that deep inner peace that lies within each of us. When you are intensely present in the now, you respond from deep consciousness and flow with ease and joy in life. It allows you to be fully engaged in your experience with all of your senses, all of your energy bodies, and leaves you with an awareness of *being,* not doing.

Allow yourself to become fully present in this now moment. As you do, allow your awareness to expand and notice the sounds around you. Notice the closest sound you hear. What is it? Is it your breath, your heartbeat? Notice the sounds you hear from afar. Can you hear what's going on outside the four walls of your room, outside the containment of the building or dwelling you are in? Notice without being attached to what you notice. Notice all that you hear without an opinion, without judgment or a need to know more.

Next, we'll explore what you feel. Notice how the air feels on your exposed skin. Notice how your clothes feel on your skin. Notice what you notice. Is the fabric soft or rough, cool or warm? Notice how comfortable or uncomfortable you are in your clothes. Notice the soles of feet, your toes. Are they warm or cold? Are they open to movement or limited? Notice the support of the seat beneath you.

If you are in an area with other people, with action going on around you, notice what you can notice to your left, to your right, and behind you. This is particularly expansive if you can sit in the center of a marketplace or park or playground and begin to expand your awareness to what's going on around you without turning your head to see. This is an advance step in awareness, so don't fret if you currently have no clue to what is going on. As your awareness expands, and it will, you will develop your other senses. You are a multidimensional being. You have five senses, and once you are fully and powerfully using these five senses, you will unlock and ignite new awarenesses—your inner knowing, intuition, and clair senses.

Next, we'll take what we notice to inside the physical body. Notice if you feel any pain or discomfort. Notice any tension. Notice any tightness. Notice if you have a need to move, to stretch, or to simply become aware. Notice if you are slouching or slumping. Notice any and all signals that your physical body is communicating to you.

Notice how your head feels. The face has over 40 individual muscles. Notice how relaxed your face feels. See if you can relax your muscles even more as you bring your awareness to the different areas of the face. Notice your forehead, the area around your eyes, and behind your eyes. See if you can relax your forehead and the area around your eyes. Notice your cheeks, ears, and jaw. Notice your lips, mouth, and tongue. See if you can relax your shoulders more than they are.

Notice your breath: the in breath, the pause, the out breath. Notice if it expands your chest or if it expands all the way down into your belly. The breath is a powerhouse. Through your breathing, you have the power to regulate blood pressure, circulation, and heart rate. Your breath has the power to relax you or energize you. Your breathing affects more than most know, and since your health and well-being affect all areas of life, it's important to give your attention and awareness to your breathing.

Did you know shallow breathing can trigger stress and anxiety in the body? Did you know that deep breathing oxygenates your blood, helps center your body, and clears your mind? It's true; every system in the body relies on oxygen. From cognition to digestion, effective breathing will not only provide you with a greater sense of mental clarity, but it can also help you sleep better, digest food more efficiently, improve your body's immune response, and reduce stress levels.

Awareness allows you the shift in perception necessary to see that everything and everyone that you have thought you were are only part of all that you are.

Awareness shows us the physical body is always sending you signals as to its well-being. The question is, Are you listening? In the next chapter, you'll get to assess where you are currently in your awareness to use as a gauge with which to measure and denote your progress as you work through knowing yourself, growing yourself, and living your life empowered. Remember, knowledge is power when you use it, apply it, and integrate change to support you in your growth and development.

> *Self-awareness is your ability to observe and accurately identify your thoughts, feelings, and impulses and determine whether they are grounded in reality or not.*

Self-awareness is one of the most important psychological traits you can develop. Its benefits extend to everything—whether managing emotions or understanding your weaknesses at work or being realistic on what you can accomplish. Every step of the way, self-awareness is necessary to make it happen.

You'll find self-awareness is always in the top 10 list of traits that great leaders cultivate. Personally, I believe it's the #1 trait or skill to cultivate. Without self-awareness, leaders can appear arrogant and clueless to their unskillful behaviors. Self-awareness in leadership is an understanding of how your personality traits, habits, and abilities affect your interactions with the people around you, particularly in the workplace. Leaders who are self-aware actively reflect on how their words and actions are perceived by others and work to change any of their own shortcomings so they can lead their peers more effectively. Self-awareness leads to personal control and growth that help leaders use their strengths to guide teams to the best possible outcomes.

Self-awareness keeps you grounded, attuned, and focused. When leaders are grounded, they are able to be efficient and deliberate in staying on task and being aware of those around them. Leaders who have the ability to control their minds and emotions help to guide those around them to develop their own self-awareness skills and thus have greater success.

Here are some important self-awareness skills:

- **Empathy** – When you fine-tune your self-awareness abilities, you will become more empathetic thanks to your heightened emotional intelligence.
- **Adaptability** – If you know how you will react, you can avoid a challenging situation by taking a walk or engaging in a few deep breaths. Think about how crucial self-awareness is in giv-

ing a sales pitch or handling feedback, for instance; if you are not aware of how you will react or do not have a way to prevent a negative reaction, you might find yourself in an uncomfortable situation.

- **Confidence** – By accepting and even embracing your flaws, needs, and strengths, you will increase your ability to be vulnerable, which allows for stronger relationships in the workplace. Maintaining confidence is key to success.
- **Mindfulness** – When you're self-aware, you become mindful of the present moment, allowing yourself to take situations as they happen rather than dwelling on the past or projecting into the future.
- **Patience** – While your immediate reaction might be to scold an employee for a mistake or let your frustrations out on your team, self-awareness will help you practice patience, even in the face of conflict.
- **Kindness** – This is achievable when you put aside your own feelings to support another person. Even if you're having a bad day, being self-aware and realizing your workers are also human beings with similar struggles can help you be more sympathetic.

Self-awareness will be broken down into four key areas of focus, bringing your awareness to Body, Mind, Emotions, and Spirit. I call these the four intelligence systems within your **being**, and the **B** in the ABCs to master you and your results. The four intelligence systems are:
- **IQ** – mental intelligence
- **EQ** – emotional intelligence
- **PQ** – physical intelligence
- **SQ** – spiritual intelligence

I'll invite you to explore, investigate, and uncover your level of awareness in the next chapter with an assessment to help you measure your progress and results.

One of the most important points I can make here is not to judge or criticize yourself. You see, it matters not where you are in your level of awareness because wherever you are is exactly where you are supposed to be. How do I know this? Because it IS where you ARE. One thing awareness teaches us is to stop trying to dis what is, to stop trying to find fault with what is, and to stop thinking you have to change what is. Awareness shows us instead to change our perception.

*If you learn one thing from this book, I hope it
is to stop finding fault with or in yourself, this
present moment, and others.*

Awareness will show you data. How you perceive this data affects the results you get. Think in terms of quantum physics and the double-slit experiment. If you are not aware of this experiment, I invite you to search "quantum physics, double-slit experiment" in a search engine and watch a short video to expand your awareness to how we can taint our results and thus our reality by our expectations.

If in the beginning of looking at what your awareness shows you, you become critical and judgmental, you will limit your ability to shift your perceptions. You will cause internal suffering and initiate a need to fix yourself to prevent this in the future. You will leave the present moment—the field of awareness—and you will take yourself down a deep and dark rabbit hole that will keep you living in the past, in your problems, and in the stories you have created around them.

It's said you cannot change what you are not aware of, so let's begin by expanding your awareness to where you are right now.

INVITATION

Look at and question how present you are in your day: 50% or more? 20%?

_____

_____

Look at and notice when you are on autopilot, like after getting up in the morning, showering, eating, driving to work. Make a conscious decision to be more present and aware in all you do.

_____

_____

Engage in your activities fully and completely. Example: Be present in the shower to feel the water on your body, the soap on your skin, the touch that activates cells in your body; turn on all your senses to smell the fragrance of the soap, hear the water, feel the wetness, see the water falling, and taste the pleasure of your nice warm shower as it cleanses and awakens the physical body, your mind, your emotions, and the gift of being in this human experience and having a body to cleanse.

_____

_____

Make a conscious decision to stop multitasking, planning the future, or critiquing the past or present.

_____

_____

SECTION II: ENGAGE

ENGAGING TO ACTIVATE AND IGNITE YOUR GREATNESS

In this section, you'll connect your knowledge and wisdom with application and integration. You are invited to be fully present and allow the material, the words on the pages, to be lived as you read them. Try to feel, sense, and know what you are reading. At a deep level, you already know all that is shared. Most of what you'll read will be connecting you with what you already knew but have veiled or forgotten temporarily.

This section is intended to reconnect you with your inner wisdom and awaken things you have known for a very long time. It requires you to engage in the material. Your level of engagement with this wisdom greatly determines what you'll get out of this book. This section is also where you'll be invited to be the Observer. You may have heard it called the Witness, Passenger, Viewer, or Spectator.

Bringing Spirituality into Business will allow you to harness your inner power, step into your authentic presence, and fully activate your connection to higher knowing. It will allow you to create your best version of you.

It's no secret that humans learn through repetition. You learn to walk by trying again and again. Sure, you stumble, you fall, but you get back up and go at it again. Over time, you master the ability to walk. Then once you have practiced it long enough, you set forth an internal program, which is running in your subconscious. It now operates for you without a thought, without trying. It's like a freshly installed program or a software update and works seamlessly on your behalf.

Just like learning to walk, everything in the human experience can be practiced, lived, experienced, and programmed internally to show up for us again and again. Think of the human body as a supercomputer with a direct connection to Source, to the Universe, to the power that gives you life.

The idea that the brain and its functions are not fixed throughout adulthood was proposed in 1890 by William James in *The Principles of Psychology*, though the idea was largely neglected by neuroscientists until around the 1970s. Pause a moment and ask yourself what you believe.

Many are still unaware of the advancements in this area of neuroscience, leaving many humans to think, believe, and function as if they are doomed to live in pain with disease, poverty, and so many other limitations and constraints.

Brain plasticity, also known as **neuroplasticity**, is a term that refers to the brain's ability to change and adapt as a result of experience. When people say that the brain possesses plasticity, they are not suggesting that the brain is similar to plastic. *Neuro* refers to neurons, the nerve cells that are the building blocks of the brain and nervous system, and *plasticity* refers to the brain's malleability. Therefore, neuroplasticity is your brain's ability to create new connections—new neuro-pathways—modify current ones, and thus rewire itself.

Your brain is capable of being partially or completely rewired, upgraded, and advanced. I don't want you to believe me; I want you to question me and experiment with it yourself. I want you to learn through your own experiences and see firsthand just how powerful you are. This section of the book is about your engagement in the experience. So, get ready to engage.

KNOWLEDGE AND WISDOM

In my years of motherhood, I often found myself in uncharted waters. Maybe you're a parent and can relate. Trusting in having the knowledge and wisdom to get through some days was all I could do. And the wisdom seemed to always come right when I needed it. Let me share with you what happened on one particular day. My oldest was three years old and having a very bad day. I'll admit, I wasn't skilled at not letting another's behavior affect me. With my husband out of town with work, my three boys and I were about to drive across town to have dinner at my parents' house. As we were leaving the house, my oldest son was irritable and acting out, and things escalated in the car when he chose to have a full-on fit, crying and wailing. I was not that mother who could allow this to go on and not be affected myself. The hair on my arms stood straight up. I knew I couldn't get into traffic on the highway in this state of mind. Having no idea what I was about to say or do, I pulled off onto a side road and then onto the shoulder. I got out and opened the back door near him, squatted down to an eye-to-eye level and told him I had something very important to share, but he had to quiet the tears to hear me.

I waited patiently as he calmed himself down. Then the words just came through me; it wasn't as if I knew what I wanted to say. I told him God made him as powerful as the president of the United States of America. We had been talking about the president the previous day. I told him he was as powerful as Grandma and Grandpa and Mommy and Daddy. I told him he had all the power in the world to be happy or to be sad, that no one but him could control that. I told him this power he had allowed him to not only feel good inside, but to also help others feel good. I also told him that when we got to Grandma and Grandpa's house, they were going to want to give him a great big hug and some loving, but that his crying might be too loud for Grandma's ears. I told him that whatever he chose was okay but to know that it will have consequences. I told that him that *he* had all the power. He was still mildly upset, with a few tears, sniffles, and those occasional gasps for breath as I closed his door and got back in the driver's seat.

As I was getting onto the highway, I heard from the back seat, "Mommy, Mommy, I chose to be happy." From not knowing what I would say or do when pulling the car over, to trusting, even when I had no plan or idea, to seeing it all work out better than I could have ever imagined, this is every mother's wish. This is trusting, being present in the moment and allowing knowledge and wisdom to come forth in just the right ways and in perfect timing.

Maybe you can imagine how I felt in this moment. I was filled with gratitude. I was beyond elated. But this wasn't even the best of it. Every night at bedtime, our ritual was to read a book. That night and for about a month following, my son would ask if I could tell him the story about how powerful God made him instead of reading a book.

When you are engaging in the experience, you have to trust that the knowledge, wisdom, or words will come. As you begin to trust the knowledge will come, you must apply it and act on it.

APPLICATION AND INTEGRATION

You are always being called to see, do, or be something in life. You are internally guided to more; this is the very nature of life. All this inner pulling and guidance needs to be applied, acted upon, and integrated into your reality. I could have observed the hairs on my arm standing straight up and talked myself into a calmer state. I could have ignored the nudge to pull over, to stop the car, to get out, to have a conversation—a conversation in which I had no idea of what I would say. You have to listen and act. The action is the application and integration of the knowledge and wisdom that serves you.

SUMMARY

You have the power and potential to change and alter so many things. It's amazing to see what can be changed when we know we have the power. Every chapter in this section aims to expand your awareness, invites you to be the Observer, and allows you to reestablish your connection with your infinite and unbound self where possibility and potential are found.

The chapters in this section will invite you to engage fully with your life and all aspects of it. They will encourage you to take 100 percent responsibility for yourself and where you are in all areas of your life. They will focus on the B in the ABCs to master you and your results on who you are Being. The chapters that follow will bring you home to yourself, to reclaim your narrative and live with purpose and intention.

CHAPTER 7:

ASSESSING WHERE YOU ARE

The only thing constant in life is change. You live in an ever-changing world. Advancements in technology, science, and medicine are happening daily. You are being conditioned and affected by your environment daily. Oftentimes, these changes are not noticed or even detected. You may be unaware of the effects of other people or how the effects of changes in the workplace affect you personally.

In 2020, the entire planet experienced the most unexpected, unimaginable, and unprecedented circumstances. Yet many still claim they've been unaffected by the disruptions we all experienced. They still work at the same job, go to work every day, and do the same details and procedures they did prior to 2020.

Fact is, whether you were personally challenged, affected, or influenced, you *have* been conditioned. Many are unaware of the subtle changes going on in themselves. Maybe you are more aware of other people's fear. Or maybe you are more compassionate and understanding of others. The entire planet was changed by the happenings in 2020.

We are often unaware of what makes us think a certain way—what makes us behave a particular way and why we feel alone or introverted. The following assessment will help you become more in tune to your current level of awareness.

To start this section of *Brining Spirituality into Business,* it is important to gauge where you are. This is not a graded test, nor is it meant to be seen as good or bad. It is simply a tool to aid you in noticing your progress along the way.

You may be a person who has gone through life unaware. You may have experienced much pain, many struggles, and feel more deeply than others. Your life—your journey through life—is for you, for your growth and awareness. It's your soul's journey, and wherever you are is perfect for *you*. There is no competition. There is no measuring your results with another. There is no shame or guilt.

This assessment is to provide you with feedback. You want change, right? You want to be able to measure and see real growth, yes? This tool is being offered to aid you in measuring your current level of awareness. That is all—nothing more, nothing less.

Let's begin. You'll find 20 questions with options a, b, or c. Circle your response or write down a, b, or c on a separate sheet of paper. At the end, you will tally the number of a's, b's, and c's. Take a deep breath and make sure you won't be distracted while working through the questions. Your first answer that comes to mind is all that is required. Do not ponder and analyze the questions.

QUESTIONS

1. Can you name the behaviors that you are doing at all times?
   a.   Yes, I'm always intentional with my behaviors and can name what I'm taking part in at all times.
   b.   Sometimes. I'm usually aware of what I'm doing, although at times, I get caught up in something or don't realize what I'm doing.
   c.   No, I rarely am aware of what my body or mind is doing.

While it might seem obvious, it can be challenging to recognize our own behaviors. Every day, we have to make over 2,000 decisions. Because this number is so high, our brain usually takes over and acts without us being conscious of it. All of these unconscious decisions decrease our self-awareness.

2. Can you name the emotions that you are feeling at all times?
   a.   Yes, I can always identify and name the emotion I'm feeling at any given moment.
   b.   Sometimes. I'm usually aware of what emotion I'm feeling. However, it takes me a few moments to recognize it, and strong emotions sometimes catch me off guard.
   c.   No, I rarely think about what emotion I'm feeling. I just feel something and act accordingly.

Emotional intelligence is perhaps the foundation of all self-awareness, but it's not easy. Humans are wired to seek pleasure and avoid pain. Our amygdala sparks emotions deep within us. These driving emotions get in the way of our rational thinking. The more self-aware you are of your emotions, the better you can control them.

3. Can you identify what causes a shift to negative emotions?
 a. Yes, I can always identify what causes me to shift to negative emotions, whether it be an event, person, or recurring trigger.
 b. Sometimes. I can usually identify what caused a shift in emotions, although it takes a little while for me to catch on.
 c. No, I rarely know what specifically causes me to shift to negative emotions. All of a sudden, I'm no longer happy and I don't know why.

I know it's difficult to believe, but we don't just "switch" to negative emotions for no apparent reason. There's almost always something that causes this shift. The problem is that we don't always know what this "something" is (generally because it's hard enough to name our negative emotion in the first place). After taking this free self-awareness test, try to consciously recognize when you shift into a bad mood and what might have caused it.

4. Can you name the emotional patterns you experience the most?
 a. Yes, I can list my standard emotional patterns right now, including what they are, what causes them, and what effect they have on my life.
 b. Somewhat. I generally know what I tend to do, but it's not always consistent or recognizable.
 c. No, I have no idea what emotional patterns I repeat. I have emotions, but I can't name any trends with when or why they happen.

If emotions are difficult to identify, emotional patterns can be even trickier. We all fall into emotional patterns, both negative and positive, that repeat themselves in our lives. Once you're self-aware of these patterns, you can improve your negative patterns and construct your positive ones.

5. Can you name your deepest fear triggers?

a. Yes, I'm self-aware of my deepest fears and what triggers these fears in my everyday life. I understand how pervasive these fears are in my thoughts and actions.

b. Somewhat. I can tell you what I'm most scared of, but I don't fully know how it affects my life and daily actions.

c. No, I have no idea what a fear trigger even is or if I have one.

One of the strongest human motivators is the emotion of fear. Starting in our evolutionary history, fear helped us survive from potential threats. In today's age, this fear still drives us, even when we're not in imminent danger. Additionally, we've all developed our own deep-rooted fears. By increasing your self-awareness of what causes your fear, you can better manage your emotional reactions when it gets triggered.

6. Can you name your deepest shame triggers?

a. Yes, I know the things that give me the most shame and what triggers this shame in my everyday life. I understand how pervasive this shame is in my thoughts and actions.

b. Somewhat. I can tell you what I'm most ashamed of, but I don't fully know how it affects my life and daily actions.

c. No, I have no idea what a shame trigger even is or if I have one.

The other powerful motivating emotion is shame. We're not self-aware of how shame, and the avoidance of shame, drives our thinking and behaviors. To limit the effect that shame has, we need to develop greater self-awareness of what triggers our shame the most.

7. Can you name the principles and values you believe in the most?

a. Yes, I can list my guiding principles and core values right now. I know how to distinguish between what I care about and the outside influence of others.

b. Somewhat. I can name a few principles and qualities that are most important to me, but I haven't given this list a lot of thought.

c. No, I have no idea what values I personally believe in the most.

Self-awareness extends beyond identifying our emotions (although being self-aware of our emotions is the foundation). Understanding our principles and core values is a crucial component of self-awareness. To be happy, you must discover what core values you want to guide your life.

8. How much do you consider these principles when making decisions?

    a.   A lot. Not only do I know what these principles are, but I design my life and decision-making around them. They give clarity to my decisions.

    b.   Somewhat. I know what my principles are but don't really know when they come into effect in my life.

    c.   Not at all. I live my life without ever giving a thought to any principles.

Naming your core values is the first step. The second step includes using these principles to guide your life and decision-making. To be self-aware, you must understand how to orient your decision-making around your core values. Only with this self-awareness can you give your life the direction you want.

9. Can you name your passions, those activities in which you lose track of time while doing them?

    a.   Yes, I know what I'm passionate about and why they give me joy.

    b.   Somewhat. I can list things that I enjoy doing, although I wouldn't necessarily call them passions.

    c.   No, I don't have any clear passions.

Many of us have a false idea of what passion and purpose should look like. Passions do not need to consume your life. Instead, passions are the things that you do that give you joy and energy. We all have passions; it merely takes some self-awareness to identify them and prioritize them in your life.

10. Can you state a list of goals and ambitions you have for yourself?

    a.   Yes, I can state a list of goals right now that include both short-term and long-term goals. I understand what I want out of life and can express these ambitions.

    b.   Somewhat. I have a few goals and ambitions, although they might not be the most defined.

    c.   No, I don't really have any driving goals or ambitions in my life.

Humans are wired for self-growth. This growth is difficult to achieve if you're not self-aware of what you should be growing toward. Self-improvement needs to start with clear goals, and it takes a level of self-awareness to be able to state these goals and pursue them.

11. Can you describe the environment you thrive in the most?
   a.   Yes, I can describe the ideal environment that I need to be happy and be successful, including the pace, energy, and structure that I thrive in.
   b.   Somewhat. I know certain things that I would want, but I can't fully describe the exact environment that I thrive in.
   c.   No, I don't know what environment works best for me. I just try to make it work wherever I am.

It's easy to only look inward when we think of self-awareness. However, real self-awareness also requires us to look outward. The more self-aware you are about your environment and how it affects you, the more you can design your life in a way that brings purpose to your life.

12. Can you identify a list of personal strengths and how they manifest themselves in your life?
   a.   Yes, I can list all of my strengths right now, as well as where they fit into my life and how I use them to find success.
   b.   Somewhat. I mostly know what I'm good at, although I couldn't tell you exactly how I incorporate these strengths into my life.
   c.   No, I don't know what my strengths are. I just try to do my best.

There's a reason there are a lot of strength-finding tests. Being self-aware of your strengths, and how they manifest themselves in your life, is crucial to being successful in life.

13. Can you identify a list of shortcomings and how they manifest themselves in your life?
   a.   Yes, I can list all of my shortcomings right now, as well as how they affect my life and what I need to do to overcome them.
   b.   Somewhat. I mostly know what my weaknesses are, although I don't have an exact list. I try to avoid them, but I don't really know how they hold me back.
   c.   No, I don't know what my shortcomings are.

As fun as it might be to discover our strengths, it might be unpleasant to look for our shortcomings. However, understanding our limitations is 100 percent necessary to be successful. Possessing the self-awareness of these limitations can help us design our life in a way that is realistic and effective.

14. Can you describe your typical reaction to new information, whether it be positive or negative?

    a. Yes, I can tell you right now how I usually react to new information. I understand my natural tendencies with both what emotions I feel and what impulses I have.

    b. Somewhat. I can generally describe how I react to positive and negative news, but I'm not fully aware of my emotions and thoughts.

    c. No, I react in the moment and don't know of any patterns.

We don't often think about a "typical" reaction because every new piece of information feels new. However, if you do think about it, you can become self-aware of your reactions and how they repeat themselves. By doing so, you can work to downplay the negative reactions and build on your positive ones.

15. Can you name what you need in your relationships to feel fulfilled?

    a. Yes, I can name exactly what I need in my life in my relationships to create a sense of belonging and feel fulfilled. Additionally, I'm able to express these needs.

    b. Somewhat. I know what I need from others, although I might not know specifically what I need from each person or in different situations.

    c. No, I don't know what I need from my relationships to feel fulfilled.

We often think of relationships in terms of two people, but this narrow perspective is doing more harm than good. You must be self-aware of what you need to build meaningful relationships in your life. Trust me: self-awareness will immediately improve your relationships.

16. Can you list the relationships in your life and which ones meet your needs?

    a. Yes, I can list the relationships I have in my life right now and evaluate what they give me. I know what I need to feel a strong connection.

b. Somewhat. I can list the people that are in my life, as well as my most important relationships, but my connections aren't always perfect.

c. No, I don't give much thought to the people in my life and which relationships meet my needs.

Not only do we need to be self-aware in our relationships, but we also need to be self-aware about the relationships in our life as a whole. Research has proven that we need different types of relationships to be happy and avoid loneliness. Greater self-awareness will help you identify which boxes might be left unchecked in your life.

17. Can you accurately describe the impact you have on others?

a. Yes, I know the impact I have on others, including what they think of me, how my words and actions affect them, and what my role is in their life.

b. Somewhat. I know what impact I have on others in general, although I couldn't get into the specifics.

c. No, I don't know how my words and actions affect others.

Self-awareness has two types: internal and external. Understanding the impact you have on others falls under external self-awareness, and it's just as critical. While it's impossible to get into the minds of others, there are strategies to help you understand the impact you have on others.

18. Can you identify where in your life biases and natural human tendencies play a role in your thinking?

a. Yes, I'm aware of where my thoughts and actions are influenced by biases and natural human tendencies. I can identify and name when these factors are getting in the way of my self-awareness and mindset.

b. Sometimes. I understand that I'm influenced by human nature, but I don't always know what these influences are or how they affect me.

c. No, I have no idea about natural human tendencies or how they get in the way of self-awareness.

Humans are flawed and imperfect. It's not enough to accept this fact for your pursuit of self-awareness. The more you understand how our human nature affects us, the more you can develop your awareness in life. First, you must learn the different biases that affect you. Then, you can begin to identify where they affect your life.

19. Can you name your primary coping mechanisms, and what triggers them?

    a. Yes, I can list my primary coping mechanisms right now and what situations trigger them. I understand how they developed in my past and can evaluate whether they still serve me now.

    b. Sometimes. I know what coping mechanisms I generally use when trying to defend myself, but I can't always recognize what triggers them.

    c. No, I have no idea what coping mechanisms I default to or why.

We're all deeply influenced by our childhood (especially when it comes to our love life). Somewhere along the way, we developed coping mechanisms to deal with negative stressors. Some of us shut down and practice avoidance; others try to be perfectionists. A self-aware person can name their coping mechanisms and identify what triggers them. From there, they can better manage themselves.

20. Can you evaluate how much of an impact cultural narratives have on you, and can you identify where they influence your thinking?

    a. Yes, I'm aware of the cultural narratives that exist and how they influence my thinking and perspective. I can distinguish between what I know to be true and what I feel like I should do, as told by society.

    b. Sometimes. I know that cultural narratives exist and can sometimes recognize where they influence my thinking. That being said, I imagine there are aspects of society that affect me that I don't realize.

    c. No, I don't know what "cultural narrative" means, let alone how it affects me.

One of the elements of human nature that affect us is social comparison. We naturally look to others for answers. As a result, our culture or environment can have a significant impact on us. To improve your self-awareness, you must understand what these cultural narratives are (and, especially, which ones are myths). Then you can identify where they influence your thinking.

SCORING THIS SELF-AWARENESS ASSESSMENT

To score this test, you will give points for the different answers (a = 2 points, b = 1 point, c = 0 points) and add up your total score. Consider the scores below:

- 35–40: Well done, you're very self-aware!
- 25–34: You're mostly self-aware, with a few areas you can develop.
- 15–24: You have some self-awareness, but there's definitely room for improvement.
- 0–14: You're lacking self-awareness...but you can learn!

Bringing Spirituality into Business improves the awareness of each and every individual and the organization. With greater awareness, you learn so much about yourself. With greater awareness, you can be the best version of yourself.

INVITATION

Complete this assessment. The full assessment is found in the Companion Workbook.

Other awareness assessments can be found on the internet. For a much deeper assessment, you might take the Insight Quiz. The author of the book *Insight* and expert in the field of self-awareness, Tasha Eurich offers a self-awareness assessment on her website at *www.Insight-book. com/Quiz.*

CHAPTER 8:

CHOICES—DESIGN OR DEFAULT

It's estimated that the average adult makes more than 35,000 decisions per day. Are you aware of the decisions you are making? Are you consciously choosing or are you leaving things to default? Every choice you make has consequences.

Do you live your life by design or default? **Living by design** means living according to your plan in order to achieve your goals, dreams, and purpose in life. It's having a plan for your life, your growth, your goals. Living life by design means you're purposefully designing each element of your life. It doesn't mean that your life is perfect, but it does mean that you're living intentionally and that you know where you want to go, who you wish to become, and what you wish to experience.

This book reminds you that you are
programmable by design.

Living by default means you are choosing to follow the crowd. It's letting things happen as you go. It's easy in that you don't make conscious choices, but often harder in that the consequences of the default choices are not of your liking. People I know who have been living by default usually ask themselves at some point, "How did I get here?" I know—I've been there.

One place design or default can be identified with clarity is in how you protect your privacy—by design or by default. The General Data

Protection Regulation is Europe's framework for data protection laws. It replaces the previous 1995 data protection directive. The new regulation started May 25, 2018, and was quickly adapted in the United Sates as well. It's enforced by the Information Commissioner's Office. You have choices. When you visit a website, you can click to allow and accept all cookies, tracking, and collection of your data that the website chooses to practice. This is probably what most people do. You could also choose to look at what is mandatory and what is optional. This requires you to make more choices. What is your standard approach to the choices you make when visiting websites? And why?

It's said that how you do one thing is how you do everything. It's hard to be upset with spam emails and soliciting phone calls when you've given permission to these companies to use your data as they see fit. Banks, credit card companies, insurance companies, and more also have opt-out options that many people are unaware of. I bring this up not to tell you what to do, but to raise awareness to where you may be choosing to live by default. When accepting default choices, you also accept the consequences. If this is you, you might start with asking yourself, where can I start making choices according to what I want, according to what I need, and according to the outcomes I desire to experience?

Believe it or not, by simply reading this book, you are subtly and gently expanding your awareness. You are learning and growing this inner ability to provide yourself with a bigger picture of your reality and your choices. You are slowly and surely increasing your awareness.

Bringing Spirituality into Business is strengthened when every individual chooses to live their life empowered—empowered to make choices of their own choosing. When personal growth and development are key components to your choices, you will notice this empowerment. To know yourself and see yourself more clearly allows you to make better choices.

A fine line of understanding exists around the topic of choices. Choices shouldn't feel like force. They shouldn't feel like control. (More on this to follow.) Your choices should align with your life vision, goals, and growth. Your choices affect yourself and others, so your choices should also create good for others.

In your awareness of choices, you'll see two direct outcomes: if your choices are in service to self or service to others. Service to self often includes service to others. Sometimes service to self is only serving oneself. It's not to say that service to self is wrong or selfish or manipulative, but it can be. Service to self can also be self-sabotaging. This is why awareness is the key to seeing beyond your choices to the effects they have upon yourself and others.

In and out of the workplace, it's important to understand the impact of your choices made in service to self. You might be having a bad day and choose to be quiet, reserved, and keeping to yourself. Others may think that they did something that upset you to cause this separation between you and them. Oftentimes when you make a choice in service to self, it's not really even serving you, meaning it's not the best choice you could make. Often these are not even conscious choices, meaning that they are default choices. This may be a pattern or habit that keeps you from dealing with what's going on inside. It could be your way to avoid dealing with what's right before you. This is an example of living on default.

You may have a difficult time getting along with your boss and make a choice to avoid any interaction with them. This is service to self. It's a choice you are making to avoid dealing with your negative feelings and emotions that are present when working with your boss. The avoidance is no good for the team, for your boss, or even for your own growth and development. We are not here to look for fault in others but to heal these strong emotions within and create greater unity and harmony in ourselves and thus in our environment.

Let's look at how this behavior affects the workplace. Your boss and coworkers may view you as arrogant, avoidant, and incapable of interaction, communication, and working together. This may be the farthest from the truth. Deep in your heart, you may thrive on interaction, communication, and working together. Your coworkers may be distant and reserved around you, or you may find a coworker who shares your feelings, and you bash the boss together at lunchtime. Either way, this is an example of how service to self is not the best choice. You are not helping yourself deal with your emotions nor are you benefiting the dynamics around you.

Next, let's look at an example of where service to self is also working toward service to others. Depending on the culture in the workplace, allowing every individual to share their voice may or may not be practiced. Speaking up to share your thoughts, ideas, and awareness can be challenging for many, even when it's encouraged and asked for. When you are part of a bigger whole, your part matters no matter what.

In a workplace of mandates, directives, and top-down control, it's difficult to feel comfortable sharing your thoughts and ideas. A bad boss can cause the best employees to leave and those who stay to lose all motivation, drive, and initiative. Speaking up and speaking out to your boss about how you feel and what you need is both in service to self and in service to others. When nothing changes, sharing this with management is both in service to yourself and in service to others.

We've become a society incapable of corrective criticism—both giving it in ways that are supportive and kind as well as receiving it as an opportunity for growth and empowerment. This is changing, and workplaces around the globe are thriving in the new cultures they have created to support and serve everyone as equals with a people-centric focus.

If you are happy living on default, you won't be serious about anything in this book. You won't reach your potential. You won't fulfill your dreams and your purpose here. Living in default mode is often painful and uninspiring. Life can lack meaning and purpose. Living in default often leaves you feeling disconnected to life. Sometimes, people living in default mode are depressed and lack the friendships, fun, and adventure that give life that zest and pizazz.

INVITATION

Look at your life in four domains:

    a. Health and well-being
    b. Relationships
    c. Career or vocation
    d. Time and financial freedom

In each area, rate yourself on a scale from 1 to 10, with 1 being not happy at all and 10 being extremely satisfied.

_____

_____

Default is doing nothing to change the results. Design is creating a vision for each of these four domains in your life.

Write out what your life would look like to be a 10 in each of these areas.

_____

_____

CHAPTER 9:

AWARENESS IS YOUR SUPERPOWER

What is awareness? Choose to practice it and you'll soon find a power within to seeing, knowing, and sensing why, what, and how. You'll be blessed with an ability to see the bigger picture as well as the operating system from which you are living.

Awareness will reveal your opinions, judgments, point of view, beliefs, and even the unconscious bias from which you live and operate. The human experience is a journey of learning and understanding oneself, and awareness is the key to unlocking yourself.

Noticing your point of view will give you the awareness to notice other people's points of view. This is where awareness begins to expand in you—revealing more when you are open and willing to see it. The greatest thing that your point of view can show you is if you are fully committed to it and onboard with that line of thinking. Do you still believe your point of view is true? Or was this some thinking you have picked up along the way, having been conditioned to think a certain way by your family, culture, ancestors, or environment?

Maybe you'll discover that you aren't required to have an opinion about everything you seem to have an opinion about. You'll learn that, oftentimes, you have an opinion about something you truly know very little about, and if you knew more, you would most likely have a different opinion. You don't know what you don't know until you explore what you don't know.

Awareness allows you to be curious when someone else has a differing viewpoint and then to listen and understand from their perspective.

Awareness is a gift you give yourself that turns around and gives to others.

By now, you are probably reflecting on your beliefs, your core values, and those truths you hold as true for you. Yes, it's true: your beliefs create a reality for you that continues to validate them as true for you. To add clarity to this statement, reflect on the following quote:

Whether you think you can or you think you can't—you're right. ~ Henry Ford

Based on your inner thoughts, feelings, and beliefs, life will bring into your awareness things that will validate what you think. If you stick with this thing called *awareness*, it will gently and lovingly show you where you hold beliefs or truths that simply are not true.

An **unconscious bias** is an automatic preference or stereotype that controls the way we think, feel, and act. You see, everything can be explained as:

What you think affects how you feel.
How you feel affects your behavior.
Your behavior affects the actions you take.

If you grew up fearing people who look or sound different from you, you'll experience yourself withdrawing around them, closing yourself off, or, worse, trying to feel empowered around them by using force to feel superior or by bullying, dismissing, and discounting them. Consider for a moment: What are your thoughts about yourself and others?

Awareness allows you to see how your thoughts and thinking affect how you feel.

We all know people who allow their day to control how they feel. Take a rainy day, for example. You can let the rain cause you to complain—wishing it were sunny, hoping it stops soon—or you can choose to go play in the rain or do a great indoor project, call a friend, or read a book. Notice how you handle inclement weather. Environment will rule when you are not aware to consciously choose how you want to feel.

Successful people are not changed by their environment. Summer, winter, spring, and fall all bring something of value, something to appreciate. Question yourself: Do you look for the joys in life? Do you look to find fault in your life? You live in a world that is changing and changing quickly.

The only thing constant IS change!

Awareness is the key to making real and lasting change that will literally empower you.

Awareness is your SUPERPOWER.

CURRENT REALITIES

Awareness lets you see your current reality. Just like a thermostat keeps the temperature in the building at a constant level, your current operating system keeps you at a constant level of reality...until you choose differently. There are as many realities as there are people. Each individual will experience a unique reality based on their own perceptions. Allow me to explain realities from a low level, a midpoint, and a high level with the three realities explained here. Every individual lives in their own reality based on their past, their conditioning, and their life experiences. Simply knowing this allows us more compassion toward others.

In the first example, this reality shows up when life gets tough—like when you struggle with your health, a loss, or feel as though nothing is going right. It's easy to get stuck in a negative reality. This is where you might feel like life is happening *to* you. I call this the Doom and Gloom reality in which you feel like you're at the mercy of what happens. You don't recognize your underlying program. You are unaware of your thoughts having any bearing or relationship to what you experience.

Most people think they live in the second example, which I call the Current reality—maybe they do. But the way I describe the Current reality is you take the good with the bad as if life is a roller-coaster ride. Some days you are feeling up and positive, and other days seem challenging and cause you to think, "Ugh, life sucks." In this reality, it's easy to let the weather or stubbing your toe affect your attitude and even ruin your day. In this reality, you struggle to let go of negativity, you take things personally, and you allow disruptive moments to be carried with you for far too long, affecting your happiness.

Then the third example of reality is of Future Possibility and Potential. In this reality, you have a vision for your life and live in the land of pure potential. In this reality, nothing is ever seen as bad but as useful for growth and learning. You live as the highest expression of self—the best version of yourself. You live into your greatness. In this reality, you realize your operating system is always advancing, increasing, and evolving, and you see the greatness in others and in the world. Awareness is now a field of higher potential.

In your awareness of these three realities that summarize your current state, you get a clear picture of how different they are. Not only are they different, but they demand a different level of awareness for each reality. Let me explain this in the four levels of awareness.

Life is happening **to me** is the first level of awareness. This is a Doom and Gloom reality. The belief system you hold says that life is doing this to me and I have no control over it. You feel like a victim in the world you live in with little to no self-awareness of yourself, your thoughts, feelings, or beliefs.

Life is happening **for me** is the second level of awareness. In this level, you take 100 percent responsibility for everything in your life and make changes that align with you being the best version of yourself because you know everything is for your best behalf. Your belief system is that with right thinking and action, you can guide the outcome of your life. You believe that circumstances and events are basically for you to learn and grow from, not to be a victim to.

Life is happening **through me** is the third level of awareness. In this level, you've become aware of the nature of life, the synchronistic alignment and flow that guides you and informs you. Your belief system shifts to knowing, trusting, and having faith that everything and everyone has value—that the universe is friendly and conspiring on your best behalf. In this stage of awareness, you know there is a purpose to your life, that you have something to give, and you surrender control and force over things needing to look a certain way, allowing life to flow through you.

84

The fourth level of awareness is **as me**, and this level is mostly often recognized in the Buddha, shaman, and spiritual gurus. From this state, nothing is impossible. Storms will still occur in your life, but from this level of awareness, the storm has *no* power over you. You don't ignore or deny it; here you have peace of mind even in the midst of the storm. All the water in the world will not drown you unless it gets inside of you. *You* decide what gets inside of you, what controls your mind and emotions, and what can dominate your day. This level of awareness holds the belief and realization that unity and oneness are found in all things. It's the awareness that every thought and every action have an effect on all things—on the collective, the earth, and all of nature on the earth. It embraces that we are part of a bigger whole.

All four of these levels of awareness are fluid, meaning you can move through each of them over the course of your day. Over time and with practice, you don't have to stay stuck in a lower level. Once you notice your level of awareness, you can choose, deciding where you want to live your life from.

This book will expand your awareness to new levels, show you the four intelligence systems within, and help you reflect on aspects of your personality to strengthen and align any aspect that is out of balance. But even more important, this book is about waking up the Observer in you, so you can experience the beauty and fullness of who you are without judgment and criticism.

THE OBSERVER

The Observer is your centering device. It guides the work you do on yourself. Once you understand that there is a place in you that is not attached, you can free yourself from attachments. Pretty much everything we notice in the universe is a reflection of our attachments.

The Observer will allow you to see and feel your pain, hurt, and rejection, and perhaps prevent you from projecting it out onto others. The Observer allows you to see your many **shadows**—those qualities, impulses, and emotions that you cannot bear for others to see and thus cast into the hidden domain of yourself.

You deserve to fall in love with yourself, to become so completely accepting of who you are at your most natural state. This love and acceptance of all that you are allows you to have compassion for other people and understand why someone is too talkative, so sensitive, shy and reserved, or so outgoing. Becoming the Observer inspires compassion and brings forth your wisdom for all of humanity. When you aren't judging yourself and others, you are more loving. And when you are more loving, you take better care of yourself, other people, and the planet.

Humanity longs to be loved and understood. It all begins in you, with you loving and understanding yourself.

INVITATION

Pay attention to what you are paying attention to. Create a page where you can log your results. Divide the page into three columns with headings as follows:

Negative Neutral Positive

_____

_____

During your day, notice your thoughts and log a single word or phrase to describe what you were thinking. You may wish to do this for a few days to get a real clear picture of your current reality.

_____

_____

In general, if most of your thoughts are negative, complaining, and finding fault with yourself, others, and the world, then you may be in a Doom and Gloom reality.

If your thoughts are balanced in all three columns or if they are mostly neutral, you may be in the Current reality. If, however, your thoughts are mostly positive, chances are you live the reality of Future Possibility and Potential. Determine the reality of your awareness.

What is your current reality?

_____

_____

What level of awareness do you mostly see yourself in: to me, for me, through me, or as me?

_____

_____

CHAPTER 10:

WHO ARE YOU BEING?

W ho are you?

Who are you being?

Are you present in your life?

Is your focus more on doing and what you need to do, or more on who you are being?

Who are you becoming?

Are you fully empowering yourself in all areas of life?

These questions call you to reflect on the masks that you wear, the roles that you play, the stories you tell, the beliefs you hold, and the version of you that others see. They cause you to observe who you are being. Who you are Being is the B in the ABCs to master you and your results. The human experience is so complex and multidimensional; *Bringing Spirituality into Business* will focus on who you are Being in relation to your four intelligence systems.

There was no training, teaching, or learning in our homes, schools, or society that directly taught you how to be the best version of YOU. Instead, society, schools, and, often, your own parents strived to teach you to be normal, to be accepted, and to fit in.

Nowhere are you taught to be yourself; nowhere are you taught to be authentically you; nowhere are you taught to be empowered; nowhere are you taught to be resourced; nowhere are you taught to be happy; nowhere are you taught to be well; nowhere are you taught to love yourself, to be kind and compassionate with yourself, or to heal the wounded or hurt aspects of yourself; nowhere in our education system are you taught that happiness, peace, and love come from within.

We have become a society that seeks joy, peace, and love outside of ourselves, that is, unless you've had conscious and awake parents or caregivers. No school teaches children or adults how to have peace, happiness, and love within. No schooling or education teaches self-awareness, reflection, knowing yourself, and understanding what you see, feel, and bring to your awareness, nor how to use what you see, feel, and observe.

But…you were taught to follow the rules.
- You were taught to fit in.
- You were taught to conform.
- You were taught to do what you are told and, by doing this, to please others.

While I am certainly not dissing "following rules," I am wanting to raise awareness to who you are being and to the many conditionings that may be affecting and influencing who you are being.
- Where are you out of alignment with your higher self?
- Where are you out of integrity?

Integrity is the quality of being honest and having strong moral principles, or moral uprightness. Integrity is the state of being whole and undivided. I live by and teach five types of integrity: Physical Integrity, Resource Integrity, Identity Integrity, Mental Integrity, and Energy Integrity.

A great evolution is underway. Planet Earth is evolving, and all people on Earth are evolving with her. We have pushed so far out of the natural and organic aspects that fuel us and are out of integrity. We have lost our inner guidance and begun to listen to and follow the beliefs of others without discerning our own truth. We've become intoxicated in this surrendering of power, intelligence, integrity, and authority. We've become like puppets on a string, hypnotized into society's norms. We've become so programmed and controlled that, from our current level of consciousness, we can't even see what's going on.

We have become the actors on the screen
in a story that is not ours.

As you mature and grow in your human experience, you'll become aware of the patterns, the cycles, and the consistency of support you have when you lean into the Observer.

The Observer honors and respects all aspects of you. The Observer lets you recognize the ego, that chatty, quirky, and sometime critical voice of your personality. The ego wants to be center stage. It knows what you want and steers you to the things that will make you happy and away from the things that cause upset and pain. The ego can be bold and bossy, loud and obnoxious, or quiet and shy. Both the ego and the Observer want what's best for you. They both come at it in completely different ways.

Some people on a spiritual path think their aim should be to destroy and demolish the ego, but this is not so. As you take the Observer role, you will slowly and gently begin to notice a quieting of the ego's voice, or at least a weakening of its constant and continuous need for drama.

The voice of ego tells you how to look, how other people judge you, what you need to do to be loved, and what you need to do to not get hurt. It's often the voice of the inner critic, complainer, and judge and jury. Furthermore, the judging and criticizing that goes on inside you is what you bring to the world. It's what you will inevitably project out onto others, often unconsciously. You don't have to speak the words for another to know how you feel about them.

The Observer, on the other hand, is unbiased. The Observer does not resist what is or judge what is observed. It simply observes through an unfiltered lens, without a motive or agenda.

The ego sounds awful in comparison, doesn't it? It's loud, demanding, and critical. Not to mention, it takes everything personally: poor me; they don't like me; I'm sad; I'm overweight; I'm depressed, unloved, and unworthy. The ego is like the needy new puppy—cuddle me, feed me, train me, walk me, sleep with me, play with me. It's all about ME, me, me, me.

> *How you do one thing is*
> *how you do everything.*

CONDITIONING

In order for you to guide your evolution and live your life by design and not by default, it is important to understand the conditioning that has been put upon you. Every human experience is layered in conditioning. Think of this conditioning as a program in your operating system. This programming can range in scope from trauma your family endured during wartime or poverty to the potential of your skills and talents you are here to uncover and develop. You came into this life experience, this incarnation, with conditions from the past—think history and generations and conditioning that support who you are to become.

You might be a person who is greatly affected by your conditioning and, up until now, unable to move beyond the suffering and constraints. You might be a person who is totally unaware of your conditioning. You might be a person who has been doing a lot of deconditioning and becoming aware of the conditioning that doesn't serve you and limits your growth and potential.

Here are five ways conditioning happens:

1. Your unique Human Design – Every human has a unique blueprint called Human Design that makes them who they are. Your Human Design is unique to you. It includes your gifts, talents, and the treasures you are here to share with the world. Think of it as your contribution, your life purpose, which fills you with all you need to live your life with ease.

2. Imprinting – Imprinting is the conditioning that happens when we are exposed to others on a regular basis. You pick up the habits and beliefs of your caregivers, teachers, friends, etc., society, and the environment.

3. Generational patterns – You came into a family with a history, a past. This history is the generational patterns that add to your conditioning, like cultural habits, beliefs, and traditions.

4. Epigenetics – This is your unique gene expression. Genetic changes alter which protein is made; epigenetic changes affect gene expression to turn genes "on" and "off." Lifestyle, environment, and behaviors, like diet and exercise, all result in epigenetic changes.

5. Trauma – This can be mental or emotional distress, abuse, or harm; physical harm or abuse; and any unprocessed experience that leaves you with a highly charged energetic response.

All of your conditioning is either aiding you in being the authentic version of you or hindering you. How will you know what's aiding you? By its effect on you, by how you feel, and the results in your life. You see, you have all you need within you. Your greatness is recognized once you understand how to use all that you have.

It's important to point out that of all five ways you've been conditioned, only *one* is everlasting and *always* acting on behalf of your best self—it's your Human Design. The other four types of conditioning are often intended for your best self, *and* they are malleable, changeable, and not always of benefit to you being YOU.

Of course, all conditioning aids in forming the life you have. It all has some value in shaping the *you* that you are here to be. All conditioning will aid you in seeing a bigger perspective of how, why, and what is going on within yourself. It's easy to dis what *is*—your perception of what's happening—when you are seeing it from a narrowed lens of vision. So don't be judgmental or critical; be open and receptive to engage in understanding yourself.

Take the example of an introverted child growing up with two extroverted parents. The parents may work hard to make their child sociable and friendly to others and may even force the child to try new things. This is conditioning. The well-meaning parents are intending to expose their child to what worked for them. These parents may attribute their career success and finding one another to their being socially confidant. Therefore, their goal is to raise a socially confident child. However, the child may do best to explore the world at their pace and comfort. The forcing of new people, places, and things upon the child could cause stimulation overload and, thus, cause the child to shut down or act out.

This one example could have a multitude of outcomes. In the worst-case scenario, the child grows up feeling inadequate, never measuring up to the expectations of their parents and others and feeling uncomfortable in their own skin. This is an example of how conditioning can affect a person.

On the other hand, the child could see their parents' good intentions as their attempt to do the best they could with what they had. Realizing this could cause the now adult child to look at their differences; explore their own interests, likes, and comforts; and finally give and allow themselves what they have really wanted their whole life. This may allow them to see how much they love communication and connection with others once they feel comfortable and secure in a relationship. This allows them the opportunity to come back to their power and build their confidence in feeling safe and secure before connecting with others. The real aim for every parent should be to raise a self-confident child.

The real work we do is on ourselves as adults when we become aware of what doesn't feel good and look to fulfill our needs with what does. When not addressed properly, the discomfort can lead to addictions as a way to numb the discomfort and to avoid dealing with it.

Self-awareness is the greatest gift of all.

Don't get caught up in blaming, as this will send you down a spiral that is difficult to get out of. Blaming is a big problem among humans. Blaming is like giving your power over to another. It's saying you are this way because someone else made you like this, or *they* did this to you. Blaming is assigning someone or something else as the cause of why you are this way. Once you do this, you begin believing it at a deep level, and this belief then becomes the limitation that holds you back from becoming all that you are. Blaming keeps you from ownership. As long you don't take ownership, you can't do anything about it. So, take 100 percent responsibility; this is taking your power back.

Accepting what is IS where your power lies.

Once you can accept what is, you stop fighting. You stop making excuses. You stop resisting. You've maybe heard the old adage, "What you resist persists." It's true. Pause and think about it. Once you accept what *is*, you can then ask the really powerful questions: Now what? What do I really want? What's next for me?

Where are you resisting something or someone? Remember, no one is making you resist or do anything; we are all conditioned and affected by others. Seeing this, knowing this, herein lies your power. Once you are aware, it's like a victory, a time to celebrate, because now you can choose. Now you can take back your power. It's time to be 100 percent responsible for yourself, and this means you choose who you are being. You are powerful beyond measure. Let's engage this power.

As you reflect on your conditioning and the beliefs, stories, and values that affect who you are being, it's also important to see all that your conditioning has brought you. Generally, you accept conditioning because it serves you in some way at that time. The safety, security, and protection you felt from your parents and caregivers were one way conditioning could serve you. As children, we accept all that is before us because we are children. As an adult, part of your role is to parent yourself or to re-parent yourself.

Until you fully embrace all of you, you won't be able to see, understand, and step into being the beautiful and authentic version of yourself. Knowing yourself requires knowing which parts of you are yours—your beliefs—and which ones come from others, and, from both, determining your core values.

If you haven't heard it yet, know with certainty that you matter. What you bring to the world is of value. You are a multidimensional being. You perceive the world through your five senses—your eyes, ears, skin, nose, and mouth are all receptors. You may think that everything that comes into the brain enters through one of these doors. Because most of us take the world in through our senses effortlessly, we don't give much thought or attention to how we do this. Amazingly, your senses have the ability to convert real-world information into electrical data that is processed by the brain and body.

You also have multiple intelligence systems that all work in harmony to serve you in being your best self. What do you think of when you hear "intelligence systems"? Is it your IQ?

We'll be addressing Body, Mind, Emotions, and Spirit and the intelligent systems that they bring us in the chapters that follow. For now, allow yourself to reflect on your awareness of these four intelligence systems and how much you understand them and utilize them. They are:
- PQ – Physical Body Intelligence
- IQ – Mental Intelligence
- EQ – Emotional Intelligence
- SQ – Spiritual intelligence

In summary, who you are being is governed by your four intelligence systems and the unique conditioning that creates your personality, talents, and quirks. Who you are being may be ruled by the ego or Observer or a combination.

It's important to point out that at your core, there is peace, a calm and pleasing sense of being in everlasting peace. At your core is love, an all-consuming love that fills and penetrates every part of you. At your core is joy, a joy so encompassing, so enveloping, that it radiates out for others to enjoy. When your four intelligence systems are working together in harmony, you are able to abide in your center, at your core, where abundant peace, love, and joy flow freely.

INVITATION

Reflect and contemplate who you are being. Are you being the best version of you?

_____

_____

If you don't have a regular practice of meditation, now is the perfect time to begin. Still your mind and free yourself from the control and demands of the mind, even if for a few minutes. Contemplation is a form of meditation.

Allow some contemplation time on the following questions and take note of where you will make changes:

1. Who are you?

_____

2. Who are you being?

_____

3. Are you present in your life?

_____

4. Is your focus more on doing and what you need to do, or more on being and who you are being?

_____

5. Who are you becoming?

_____

6. Are you fully empowering yourself in all areas of life?

_____

7. Are you happy?

_____

8. Do you feel love?

_____

9. Are you at peace?

_____

CHAPTER 11:

BRINGING ALL OF YOU TO THE PARTY

In the early 1980s, I had a really big desire to go into sales. This was one of those desires I had to pursue. The company I worked for didn't believe sales was a place for females, so I needed to look elsewhere. I wanted this so bad, I was ready to find another job. Others mocked me and thought I was hoping to attain this by means of my pleasing personality. It was a known fact that you needed a bachelor's degree to go into sales, and I had no degree. Nor did I have support; no one could see what I could see. When I shared my desire with friends or family, they reminded me of all the reasons why I wouldn't be able to make it happen. But guess what? I did succeed. I found a job in sales and got hired, and it was the best decision I could have made. I loved the variety of each day—different people, places, topics, and sales. I had trusted in something so big; others told me I would fail, and no one believed I could do it except for me. This trusting in something bigger than myself came easily when I brought all of myself to the party. It came easily when the desire was from my heart and something I knew I was meant to do.

Every human being has an inner compass. You are designed to trust yourself. You have an internal compass that helps direct your life and your life choices so that you know what to do and when to do it. This is true whether or not you are attuned to it.

What is it that comes to us when we know with certainty what we want? What's going on when you get a nudge to move, explore a new position at work, write a book, or run a marathon? I call it your life force energy or spiritual intelligence; some call it spirit, God, or the divine. What is for certain is this energy is guiding you to more—guiding you to all you came here to be, see, and explore. Trusting this energy does *not* come easy for all. Some people get stuck in their heads and banter back and forth with reason, common sense, and playing it safe. Others are struck with fear, worry, and doubts so powerful they never get beyond the strong emotions held in place by stories of disbelief. And then there are those so elated in the magic of it, their heads are in the clouds, waiting for miracles to land upon them and alter everything without a single action step forward.

Which one are you?

My years in sales brought me many rewards, including self-confidence and financial success. They also taught me things about myself. In looking back, I noticed how I only brought half of me to the office every day. You see, as a woman in a field of mostly men and those with college degrees, I had some tough competition. I knew I did not want to appear weak among my peers. So as to not shed a tear or become emotional, I intentionally left my emotions at the door. I wanted to appear as a strong rock of confidence in the office.

I also noticed I never brought my inner guidance, my spiritual intelligence, into the office. I always connected with it and conversed with it when I got in my car to go on a sales call. In fact, I never listened to the radio during my workday. Drive time was my time to listen, humble myself, and center myself. I knew I didn't get this position on my own; I had help from a power greater than myself, and if I was to succeed, I would do so through my relationship with this power. But it was sort of like my secret, and as with all secrets, there were times it was left aside and omitted, like inside the office with my peers.

So, ask yourself, where are you selectively not bringing all of yourself to the party?

Have you ever tried to talk with someone who was unable to hear your point of view? Someone so rooted in their way of thinking that they will argue, dismiss, and discount everything you say? When this happens, the conversation is pretty much over. Any attempt to continue to express yourself begins to feel like control and manipulation.

Have you ever experienced or been close to someone who has experienced a deep loss? Be it a pet, loved one, or even an unexpected and unwanted divorce, the hurt, sadness, and pain experienced is insurmountable. In this deep pain, nothing can penetrate the energy of the emotions that the person suffering is going through. No matter what you say, they cannot hear beyond their pain; they are deeply rooted in their strong emotions.

Have you ever spoken with someone so firmly rooted in their religious beliefs that they will not associate with you if your beliefs do not match theirs? A Christian who argues so firmly that Jesus is the ONLY way home? How do they know? What about the children, the people in third-world countries who don't have access to the Bible or belief in another God, power, or deity? Do you know someone so firm in their beliefs that they are willing to end the friendship if your beliefs differ?

Each of these examples represents what happens when you don't bring all of you to the party. In the first one, someone unable to hear your point of view is all in their head, using only their mental faculty, or IQ, along with their will, in trying to drive home their point of view. In the second example, someone deep in suffering is consumed by their emotions and stuck in operating only from their EQ. The third example demonstrates someone who is only acting from their religious beliefs. They are unable to access logic and reason or even love and compassion as their strong will to hold only one view consumes them and limits their perception.

Any time you willfully express yourself from only one of your four intelligence systems, you are out of balance. This is why the B in the ABCs to master you and your results is so vital to the results you get in all areas of your life. Bringing all of you to the party becomes the reminder to notice who you are Being at any given time.

There is power in bringing all of you to the party. The **"all of you"** being expressed here is all four of your intelligence systems. Before we get there, let's talk about the human body for a moment. Science has shown that the human body has multiple intelligence systems within it: the brain, which we all thought was the smarts, logic, and in charge of decision-making; the heart, which HeartMath Institute has shown us knows before the brain what we are about to experience; and the gut, which has its own intelligence system. All three of these systems work together, allowing you to function without any thinking or doing on your part. Until you've noticed and become aware of the signals and messages these intelligence systems are sending you, you won't fully grasp their power and potential. HeartMath Institute's director of research states:

Coherence is a state when the mind, body and emotions are in energetic alignment and cooperation. From this state you build resiliency— personal energy is accumulated, not wasted— leaving more energy to manifest intentions and harmonious outcomes. ~ Dr. Rollin McCraty

Your four intelligence systems may never be fully understood or comprehended. But you can experience the fullness that each of them has to offer and award you. As you bring all of you to the party with awareness, you'll see and experience how each intelligence system is serving you. One way to expand your understanding is to look at the polarity within each system and to reflect on them. This is not a chapter to rush through. The basis of the information brought to you here is generally presented over full-day and multiday workshops, with interaction and experiences taking place. So, keep this in mind as you are reading. Try to receive the words with all of your being, not only your mind.

Allow me to set the stage with the story of the four quarrelsome sons. The father was looking to end the bickering and quarreling among his four sons. Day in and day out, the boys would argue and fight among themselves, causing separation and division in the home and affecting their work and productivity on the farm. The father asked each son to find a stick about one inch in diameter and about 18 inches long while at work on the farm and bring it with them to the dinner table that evening. Once they were circled around the table, the father asked each of his sons to pass their stick to him. He gathered the sticks together in a bundle and tied them together securely with twine. He then proceeded to pass the bundle to the son on his right, asking each of his four sons to break the bundle of sticks over their knee. One by one, with all their might, each of the sons tried to break the bundle, each of them unsuccessful. As the bundle made its way back to the father, he untied the bundle and passed a single stick to each son and asked them to break it over their knee. One by one, with a mighty force, each of the sons was able to break the single stick. The father then stood tall and told his sons that alone, they were all breakable and subject to failure. But that together, they created a bond, a strength that made them unbreakable, unstoppable, and stronger than they could imagine.

The moral of this story should be expressed in every business and every individual. For you, this story acts as a reminder to your multifaceted being and the various sources of power and potential within you. When you bring all of you to the party, you are balanced, empowered, unstoppable, and unbreakable. When out of balance, when one intelligence system is running stronger than the others, you'll struggle and maybe even suffer, for you are weakened and incomplete.

In business, it shows us the value of diversity, how every voice matters, and how much stronger the organization is when all come together in a common vision and mission of the organization. It emphasizes the value each individual brings and how different perspectives, cultures, and viewpoints actually strengthen an organization. It demonstrates the value in a people-centric culture, rich in personal growth with regard to building individual strengths, skills, and talents, while encouraging and offering a means to share ideas.

> *The real value in diversity is to see it as an asset, not a compliance regulation, because together we are better.*

For you to be balanced, empowered, and unbreakable, you'll need to understand your four intelligence systems. Each one of these systems is naturally orchestrated to work in harmony with the others. As a reminder, they are:

- PQ – Physical Body Intelligence
- IQ – Mental Intelligence
- EQ – Emotional Intelligence
- SQ – Spiritual intelligence

On a scale of 1 to 5, with 5 being always engaged, listening, and acting accordingly and 1 being not able to hear the messages of this intelligence system yet, rate yourself now.

How do your rate your awareness and ability to monitor, manage, and serve in the best interest with your PQ? Do you reach for a pain reliever to numb the signals and messages of the Physical Body intelligence system? Do you inquire and get curious as to the messages and root cause of the symptoms you are experiencing? Let's face it: We have become a society that seeks to numb ourselves and push on. We've lost the connection to this valuable intelligence that serves our best interest and our ability to thrive. We go to a so-called expert and ask them to fix us.

Often, we think we understand our IQ, but do you? You know that you've expanded your knowledge, memory, and learnings through schooling. We've forced a set of rules, procedures, and historic stories expecting a well-informed and educated society. And we've also stifled the imagination, creativity, and the vast potential of this amazing intelligence system. Do you have a monkey mind? A freight train of thoughts flooding your mind at all times with no ability to slow or stop this train? Do you get lost in endless mind loops and struggle to get free of the control they have on you? Admittedly, we multitask; we try to do many things at the same time and are seriously stressing out our mind and losing our ability to focus and concentrate. Is the mind controlling you, keeping you up at night, creating stress, or is your Mental intelligence the dutiful servant it's intended to be? How do you rate your awareness and ability to monitor, manage, and master your IQ?

How do you rate your awareness and ability to monitor, manage, and respond to your EQ? Depression, anxiety, and other mental health conditions are at all-time record high levels. We blame others for how we feel. We reach to our addictions to numb the stress we feel. More often than not, we project our pain outward onto others. Responding from the height of an emotional storm, we are not equipped to deal with our emotions. Do you find yourself triggered and without the proper coping skills to maneuver those emotions with ease? On a scale of 1 to 5, how do you rate your ability to monitor, manage, and master your EQ?

How do you rate your awareness and ability to listen and connect with your SQ? This intelligence is often the least to be recognized and strengthened and yet yields the greatest rewards, in my opinion. Many people only believe what they can see, touch, and experience with their five senses; I was one of these people. Can you hear your intuitive guidance? Are you able to ask your higher self for answers, insight, and clarity? Your Spiritual intelligence speaks to you in a different language, in different ways. Are you able to discern and listen? Do you follow your intuitive nudges? Are you able to trust yourself?

Awareness is the *key* to your growth. Bringing all of you to the party, to every activity and engagement, is the powerful practice you won't want to be without. You are here to tune into the very patterns and wisdom that wrote you into being.

Next, let's expand your awareness of each of these intelligence systems and see why you won't want to be without this practice. You'll be able to look at your current level of awareness and how your operating system is programmed to assist you—or how it does not. You'll also be able to discern where you wish to make changes to your current operating system.

There is GREATNESS in you, and it's about to be ignited, activated, and engaged.

INVITATION

Answer the questions above and record your ratings to your level of awareness of each of the four intelligence systems.

_____

_____

This will be your gauge to monitor your awareness as you begin to know yourself, grow yourself, and strengthen your awareness and abilities in each of these four intelligence systems.

_____

_____

CHAPTER 12:

PHYSICAL BODY INTELLIGENCE SYSTEM (PQ)

PQ awareness is required to maintain your well-being, develop a strong fitness level, and improve and increase longevity and body functions. PQ informs us just how adaptable and resilient the human body is to change, the environment, and self-care. The Physical Body intelligence system is always sending you signals. Most people are aware of the signals like hunger, exhaustion, and pain. Many believe hunger to be a signal, but hunger may also be a habit. Oftentimes, you can mistake the feeling of hunger to be wholly related to food and, therefore, not inquire as to what you are really hungry for. You could be hungry for peace, comfort, or nurturing. I've worked with many overweight people who through monitoring this one simple signal found that they really were not hungry for food, and once this habit was addressed, they naturally lost weight by simply getting curious as to what they were really hungry for.

Another signal is pain or discomfort. When pain or discomfort rears its annoying head, many reach for a pain reliever, like Tylenol or ibuprofen, to numb the sensations instead of inquiring as to the message it brings. This is another habit that might totally surprise you when you stop the automatic response of numbing the pain. The headache could be stress or tension and often alleviated by a few minutes of deep breathing and quieting the mind. Many body pains can be reduced through stretching and releasing tightness.

Keep in mind that nothing shared here is suggestive of replacing your doctor's advice. This is not to say that an anti-inflammatory, muscle relaxer, or pain medicine is not necessary or required. Nothing in this section or this book is intended to replace medical advice or recommendations. All that is being expressed here is to bring your awareness back to you, to your body, and to the intelligence system at work for you.

Your PQ sends signals when it is out of balance; you may interpret these signals as overwhelm, tension, exhaustion, or stress. These signals are all too often misinterpreted or ignored, leading you to respond in ways that are not the most supportive. What do you do when your body says, "It's exhausted"? Often, fatigue is addressed by eating to refuel the body. But this is not usually the best response. Retreating to the couch to watch TV may not be what it needs either. Exhaustion is the body's way of letting you know it needs recharging, regenerating, and to be restored. By eating, you direct the very resources needed to recharge to instead go to work to digest the food you just ate. When we rest on an empty stomach, the body is allowed to use its intelligence and resources to do exactly what is required. This is why it is recommended to sleep on an empty stomach, as your body goes into repair and rejuvenation mode while at rest. Connecting with nature, taking a warm bath, reading a book, meditation, and sleep are some healthy restorative activities.

Often the signals that your body sends are not addressed in ways that support its ability to function in the most beneficial and powerful ways. This causes the body to be out of balance, leading to excess weight and miscommunication within the organs, cells, and internal processes, which can lead to disease, illness, or death. Your body is meant to thrive, to repair and regenerate itself, and provide you with energy and stamina to be proficient. It is equipped to do all this efficiently when you allow it the balance it requires.

You are meant to be deeply rooted and grounded in the human body, listening to your PQ. Think of this system as your strength, your earth, your home for the other intelligence systems to reside in. This guidance system is always speaking to you in soft, subtle, and gentle ways. Maybe this is why most people miss the signs and signals. What happens when you miss the signs? They will keep coming back around a bit louder and more direct until you do listen.

When my sons were small, life always got really busy in October, with planning and prepping for Halloween as a room parent at school parties and a mother of three boys who always wanted a special, home-made costume. I loved this time of year. It was fun to spend time with each of them in the creation process and watching their little dreams and desires come to fruition. But as a single mom with a full-time job and household to maintain, my life got extra hectic.

The month of October was followed by two of my sons' birthdays in November. I was that mom who didn't want her kids to not have a party just because it was a busy time of year. So, yes, we had birthday parties too. Then there was the big family Thanksgiving dinner, usu-ally at our house.

All this was followed up with the month of December, when my work wanted us to wine and dine our clients with appreciation for their year of business. Add to this the holiday parties and, of course, prepar-ing for Christmas at home. Between decorating, shopping—making sure I paid close attention to the wish list each child had made—and enjoying the holiday lights and festivities, we were always on the go. To say that the last three months of the year were hectic was truly an understatement.

After the holidays, I would take a huge sigh of relief, but as I did, without fail, every year I found myself sick and in bed for a few days. All throughout the busyness, I would notice others getting colds and flus—it being the cold and flu season, you know. I could not afford to get sick. But that huge sigh of relief was indeed saying, *Okay, now I'm done, now I can rest*. Little did I know, I didn't know *how* to rest. So, getting sick was how my body forced me to rest.

Your body operates in cycles, rhythms, and patterns. Whether good or bad, it matters not. From the start of each day to the end of each day, your body has a memory and works to restore itself back to that memory. Through changes and challenges, vacations and celebrations, your body strives to come back to balance and harmony, back to what it knows and believes to support your thinking, emotions, and beliefs.

It wasn't until I started taking a family trip between Christmas and New Year's that I was able to notice a pattern playing out in my life. It was our second annual trip, and this one was just me and my three sons in Mexico at an all-inclusive resort for seven nights and eight days. We got there on Christmas night, and I was already feeling something coming on. By the next morning, I knew with certainty that I needed a doctor or some penicillin to rid my body of this infection brewing inside me before it ruined our vacation. I reached out to the concierge, who was able to set up an appointment for the next day. He instructed me to be in my room at 10 in the morning, and the doctor would see me then. I received a shot of penicillin and a prescription and started feeling better within 24 hours.

With the beach before me and my sons active and joyfully playing in the ocean with boogie boards, I had plenty of time to reflect on the stories I was telling myself—the patterns I had created and played out year after year. I recognized the pushing and forcing myself to do more, accomplish more, and often at the expense of my own personal care and nurturing. I was able to see how after all the hustle and bustle was over, it was as if I gave myself permission to be sick, just to get the rest I needed. What was the story I had about taking time to rest? Was it really me being lazy, selfish, and unproductive? Why was I so uncomfortable doing nothing? I didn't know how to listen to my body and what it needed. But even louder than that was my awareness to my own self-worth. I had adopted the stories about what doing nothing meant. Self-worth is a topic discussed more with EQ. But for my physical health, I had to repattern some of my stories and let myself remember that sitting down to do nothing could be the most loving and compassionate thing I could do in the moment. What is the most loving and compassionate thing you could do for yourself?

Where are you pushing yourself to do while ignoring your body's needs to recharge, replenish, and restore itself? Where can you notice a pattern playing out again and again? Generally speaking, your PQ likes to be in control: to set goals and achieve them; to feel safe and secure in your environment; and to have consistency, schedules, and routine. Your PQ will often show you the other operating systems that are out of balance. Remember, balance is your aim.

Choose discipline and health, and you'll learn to balance pleasures and indulgences, your humanness and your divinity.

Where is your PQ out of balance? Think health and well-being because, without your health, life can be a struggle. This is where you may notice yourself telling stories about your health, thus accepting what is and doing nothing to change it. I noticed this because I, too, found myself telling stories, making them part of my life, incorporating them into all that I am. And I have learned that labeling a diagnosis can have many effects. It can cause me to explore the root cause or to mask and hide the symptoms. I noticed that if or when I would mask the symptoms, I was simply accepting it, learning to live with it, and thus allowing stories to be told. At this point, I noticed I was out of balance. It was as if a part of me was saying, *things are not right.*

But when I would explore the root cause, it would often take me down paths I thought had nothing to do with the problem at hand. I often thought I had gotten distracted and went off on a tangent, but I hadn't; instead, I found that the root cause of my ailment was often something I had no clue was connected.

> *Failure to forgive yourself or another can have huge and damaging effects on your health and well-being.*

Remember, your PQ is made up of trillions of cells sending electrical signals and dumping chemical reactions through your physical body all the time in an aim to keep you in harmony and balance. The brain, heart, and gut all work in harmony with your organs, circulatory system, and nervous system. Your PQ is governed by many factors, such as mindset, diet, exercise, rest, and emotions. The stresses and worries of life impact your PQ and act to send mixed signals, thus altering cells and causing a response or reaction within that shows up to you and me as those soft and subtle pains and nagging disturbances that we are not skilled at discerning and often avoid dealing with as we reach to numb them and move on through our day.

In the world of business, arming and equipping your employees with PQ awareness and skills will greatly increase workplace wellness and their readiness for change and increase the odds that your change initiatives will succeed. It seems that helping employees increase their receptivity to change is often skimmed over or skipped entirely.

The McKinsey Global Institute states that workplace changes are occurring at 10 times the pace of the Industrial Revolution and at 300 times the scale. Yet human beings are not evolving as quickly as the rate of change. This leaves many feeling overwhelmed, threatened, stressed, and struggling to meet or exceed expectations.

I read somewhere that in 2018, stress was the number one symptom searched on Google. In 2019, the World Health Organization labeled burnout an official phenomenon, defining it as "chronic workplace stress that has not been successfully managed." We have not been trained to cope with the degree of change happening around us. As a society, we are not as skilled as we need to be with coping skills, resiliency, and the ability to manage the multitude of changes we encounter.

It's time we begin to have these needed and necessary conversations in the workplace to address workplace wellness and employee resistance to change and begin to empower one another in our abilities to adapt and excel.

INVITATION

Reflect. How do you relate to and with your PQ?

_____

_____

What are some of the soft and gentle messages your PQ is sending or communicating to you? List them.

_____

_____

Reflect on your relationship with your physical body. Is your relationship loving and supportive? Is your relationship critical and judging? How can you make a conscious decision to improve your relationship with your PQ?

_____

_____

CHAPTER 13:

MENTAL INTELLIGENCE SYSTEM (IQ)

Your IQ is probably the intelligence system you are most knowledgeable about or the one you think of first when talking about intelligence. It certainly is the one society addresses and focuses on most, starting with education, testing, measuring, and analyzing. It's necessary, yes, but it's not meant to be a standalone system, nor is it the decision maker. This intellectual intelligence involves your mental capacity to reason, plan, solve problems, comprehend complex thoughts, recall memories, and learn quickly from your experience. It's also the foreground of your imagination and where you can hold multiple perceptions and see a bigger picture.

The average person has between 60,000 and 80,000 thoughts a day. You may have more or less. You may also think these thoughts are in your head, when in actuality, they are merely in your field of awareness. For some, this one statement is all you'll need to begin seeing your thoughts differently. You do get to choose which thoughts you give your attention and focus to.

- You may be a person who thinks you are stupid.
- You may be a person who is highly educated with a master's degree or PhD.
- You may be a person who thinks others know more than you.
- You may be a person who thinks you have an average intelligence.

- You may be a person who has a freight train of thoughts in your head.
- You may be a person who engages in thoughts that have nothing to do with you.
- You may be a person who thinks you need to have an opinion about everything.
- You may be a person who observes the activity in the mind with peace.
- You may be a person who feels stressed by the activity of the mind.
- You may be a person who feels you have no control over the activity of the mind.
- You may be a person who doesn't know that you have any power over the mind.
- You may be a person who is learning to monitor, manage, and master the mind.
- You may be a person who has mastered what you give your focus and attention to.

Real smarts is not about information, it's about having an active intelligence that constantly searches and seeks and looks at things in every possible way.

Have you ever had a really powerful question asked of you, one so powerful you really did not have an immediate answer to it? One so powerful it caused you to contemplate it, ponder it, and explore it to find the truth? Maybe you have, but you reacted defensively or in denial, thus brushing it off and never getting to what the question was supposed to bring you.

Years ago, while on a visit to see my sons, one of them asked me, "Mom, are you uncomfortable with the silence in the room that you have a need to always be speaking?" WOW! I was immediately shocked by the question. I'm not quite sure if I was more shocked that he asked the question or that I didn't know if I was or not. This not knowing told me this was one of those powerful questions that had the potential to change me. This was a question that might allow me to know myself and grow myself. But I never knew how much it would empower me.

As I flew home from the visit, I did ponder this question. I looked at it from an unbiased view. From a detached perspective, it allowed me to see myself in those moments of silence, to see how I truly felt in the silence. I sat in the uncomfortableness. In an attempt to ease the uncomfortableness, I could see my mind scanning and seeking for the next topic to bring up, to talk about. I could also see that this need was fulfilling my need to feel valued and important. When I would talk to fill silence, I had been unaware that, behind the scenes, I was seeking approval, agreement, and acknowledgment. Again, wow! This reflection brought more to my awareness than I could have ever imagined. The biggest awareness was just how awkward and uncomfortable I was in the silence and what went on inside me, trying to end the uncomfortableness.

When you are able to detach from the topic to see it as an unbiased Observer, you will always gain a bigger perspective. This is valuable in business, in personal relationships, in problem solving, and in critical thinking—all areas of your life.

Often, we try to look at things from a linear timeline and perspective. This approach keeps us in the story, as the actor in the scene, and can often leave one feeling attacked or judged. These are human feelings that activate your need for safety and survival and thus can obscure your perspective and your ability to see clearly. This perspective can have you feeling like a victim in your own reality.

This concept is powerful and dynamic at the same time. It says that IF you attach yourself to the story line of your drama or trauma, you will bring to your awareness your need for safety and survival. If you are attached to the story, you also bring expectations, as it's human nature to seek to validate our perceptions and beliefs. If you feel you are a victim in your life, you will validate this as true in what shows up for you. The only clear way to look at these big and powerful questions is from a detached view, from the Observer self.

As I pondered the powerful question asked of me, I realized I had a freight train of thoughts, and yes, I thought they were in my head. My first question to myself was, "Does everyone have a freight train of thoughts in their head?" I was also caught up in the comparison, the competition, and proving myself. How did I compare? Was I normal? What if I'm not normal? How did I get here?

Little did I know that I did not have to answer these questions. I thought my pondering it was to get answers that I had to find. I'm sure you've heard it said before, "Ask and you shall receive." Well, I asked, and I received. All the answers I needed began to appear before my awareness. Thankfully, they did not show up immediately and overwhelm me. They showed up slowly, as if orchestrated and planned—divinely orchestrated.

I don't normally follow Oprah, but one day, I was guided to an episode of her *Super Soul Sunday* where she shared the book *A New Earth* by Eckhart Tolle and interviewed him. In their conversation, Eckhart said that we all have the power to slow down and control our thoughts. Yes, Eckhart Tolle said, it was as simple as slowing the words you speak and noticing the space between the words. In the days that followed, I did just that: I slowed the words that created the sentences of my thoughts.

As with all personal growth, once you see and notice changes happening, it's as if a magnet is pulling you to more and more. I wasn't happy just slowing down that freight train anymore. I asked a bigger question: Can I stop it? I was guided to try meditation. At first, I got what appeared to be no results. In fact, I judged myself. I couldn't seem to get out of my head and find that space of no thought. I felt like trying was creating more stress. Time and time again, I'd sit in silence in my own space. I tried it on the floor, on a yoga mat, in a chair, on the couch, and even lying down. I tried it with music, guided, and completely silent. And guess what? With time and with repetition, I began to notice my mind quieting down. This wasn't days or weeks—it was months before I noticed the effects.

With a daily practice and desire to have better control over myself, my mind, and that freight train of thoughts, I got better and better. The more I practiced, the more I actually believed I could do it. It was challenging at first, I'll admit. I had a program running in me that wondered if I really could stop that freight train of thoughts. I had some disbelief. The greatest thing I noticed was that as I committed myself to practice, my belief in myself was strengthened. I did have the power to stop that train of thinking. You, too, have all the power I do. You, too, can slow, stop, and learn to monitor, manage, and master your mind.

Whatever we plant in our subconscious mind and nourish with repetition and emotion will one day become a reality. ~ Earl Nightingale

The mind is your tool. Its purpose is for processing, critical thinking, imagining, future projections, innovating, creativity, and problem solving. It was never meant to be your sole source of decision-making. It was never meant to control you. It was never meant to cause you stress or anxiety.

Allowing the mind to rule leads to pressure, stress, and egoistic or narcissistic behaviors.

> *Once you know and understand the power of*
> *the mind, you'll program it for success.*

Learning to monitor, manage, and master your thoughts and thinking puts you in control. You get to choose what thoughts you give your focus and, thus, your power too.

Henry Ford said it best when he said, "Whether you think you can or you think you can't, you're right."

> *Belief is the ignition switch that gets you*
> *off the launchpad.*

Think of your thoughts as powerful manifesting agents. These manifesting agents dump the appropriate chemical release within the body to engage and empower your central nervous system, producing emotions that also have a connection to your behavior and thus your response and the actions you take.

> *Your thoughts create your feelings.*
> *Your feelings lead to your behaviors.*
> *Your behaviors lead to your actions and thus*
> *your success.*

MIND IS MASCULINE ENERGY

Think of the mind as your masculine energy force. This has nothing to do with gender; both men and women have masculine and feminine energies. From a balanced and empowered state, these masculine energies have been labeled "sacred masculine" and allow you to be assertive and act. The term "sacred masculine" comes from masculine archetypes seen throughout spiritual traditions. Your masculine energies promote clarity, courage, discipline, and focus and project you outward to achieve your goals. This energy is supportive and certain, brings stability and confidence, and gives freely to self and others.

As with all energy, a polarity exists in the masculine energies—the positive and negative aspects. The negative aspects of the masculine energy are often referred to as the "wounded masculine." The wounded masculine shows up as fear, blame, control, and needing to dominate. The wounded masculine represents itself when you are pushing, demanding, and overreacting. The wounded masculine will abuse power, criticize, become confrontational, and act competitive in situations where equality and harmony are needed. It shows up in leadership roles as avoidance and unsupportive and has damaging consequences in relationships and in the workplace.

In my Winner's Circle, you'll gain the impact and reward that this intelligence and energy provides. It's important to note that you cannot and will not take everything mentioned in this section into action all at once. In the human experience, everything is fragmented into what you might understand as bite-size chunks of data. You operate in patterns, cycles, and structures that only you will know what is best for you at this moment in time. You are on a path to knowing yourself and growing yourself to live your life empowered. You can come back to this section, and each time you do, you will attain a greater insight into more of yourself. You are an infinite being, and your growth and capacities are infinite and always unfolding. Allow yourself to show up anew each day. If you feel called to my Winner's Circle, reach out to me via the website in the introduction to this book.

INVITATION

Ask yourself these questions:

Is your Mental intelligence system running you?

Is it controlling you, or are you controlling it?

What can you do to control the thoughts you give your attention to?

What can you do—what are you willing to commit to—to help you find quiet and calm in your day? (Your best decisions and work will come from a place of calm centeredness.)

Play with asking open-ended questions and allowing the answers to come to you.

Meditation is the best practice to train your mind to relax and quiet down. With practice, this will happen naturally, and you'll find yourself calmer and more peaceful. When the mind is calm, creativity flows, solutions come to you, and you are better able to reach natural states of flow. This is the state in which you receive answers to your questions, inner guidance, and creative ideas.

What practice will you apply to allow you better control of your thoughts, thinking, and the activity of your mind?

Slowing your words and putting space between them allows you to start noticing the space and then expanding the space. Starting a meditation or mindfulness practice allows you to begin the process of calming the mind and the body.

Choose a practice, make it your own, and start to take control of your mind, thus bringing your Mental intelligence system into harmony to work for you and not against you.

In the Companion Workbook, you'll have an additional page on the wounded masculine to explore.

CHAPTER 14:

EMOTIONAL INTELLIGENCE SYSTEM (EQ)

The EQ is probably the most ignored and undervalued intelligence system. Think back to your childhood. Were you allowed to express your emotions, or were they discounted and ignored? We've all heard the sayings, "Big boys don't cry" and "Toughen up, don't be a baby." The collective consciousness aims to stuff emotions and discounts their value, importance, and purpose.

In the following story of the angry man seeking the healing guidance of a Zen master, we learn a bit about emotions and EQ.

A young man approached a Zen master pleading for help with his anger problem. "I have a quick temper, and it's damaging my relationships," the young man said.

"I'd love to help," said the Zen master. "Can you demonstrate your quick temper to me?"

"Not right now. It happens suddenly," the young man replied.

"Then what is the problem?" asked the Zen master. "If it were a part of your true nature, it would be present all the time. Something that comes and goes is not a part of you, and you shouldn't concern yourself with it."

The man nodded in understanding and went on his way. Soon afterward, he was able to become aware of his temper, thus controlling it and repairing his damaged relationships.

The moral of the story is that your emotions are not you, and they can gain control over you if you do not reflect on them. The only way to tame an unconscious reaction is to bring the light of consciousness to it. Once you become conscious of a belief, action, or emotion, it no longer wields control over you.

It's ironic that we tend to avoid emotions, but the avoidance actually allows them power over us.

Until the works of best-selling author Daniel Goleman and his book, *Emotional Intelligence*, the world had been mostly unaware of this powerful intelligence system. Since the introduction of *Emotional Intelligence*, businesses around the globe have been bringing Emotional Intelligence trainings and workshops to the workplace. This has had an impact, and yet, the depth of your emotional trauma may not have ever been resolved. All of humanity needs to understand their Emotional intelligence system, so let's get started.

Emotions are energy in motion. When they are not allowed to be fully felt and expressed, your body holds them inside—in an overly heightened and highly charged state. This highly charged emotion held in the body will then later get triggered and be brought to the surface. Often when this happens, its energy is so powerful that it pushes the main personality aside and takes over. Things get said as you project out your pain onto others. Often, you'll think it was that person who did you wrong when it really wasn't even about the other person. Do you ever say, "She makes me so angry"? Or "He makes me feel inadequate"? This is when you must take 100 percent responsibility for what is going on inside you. By taking responsibility, you'll be taking back your power. You'll be able to get to the root of your feelings and emotions and begin the work necessary to look at them from a detached lens that will allow you to see beyond the original story and see the bigger perspective. Then, when you've changed your view of what happened, you'll release the energy you've been holding onto.

Don't shoot the messenger;
look at the message within.

These overly charged emotions will dissolve and integrate with your whole being once you allow them to be seen, heard, and felt. This isn't always easy. So be kind and gentle with yourself. Whether you were never taught or simply forgot, it doesn't matter. You are aware now. So don't allow yourself to get sidetracked with blame or shame. Step up and take responsibility so you can move beyond your pain and problems.

It's helpful to have a bit of hand-holding the first few times through the experience. So, let's go through it together now. First, be the Observer. Believe me, this is most likely the reason most don't succeed in dealing with their emotions. If you don't step into the Observer role first, the emotion is likely to consume you again. From the Observer position, think of a recent time when someone said something that caused a flare-up of emotions in you. It could be your coworker, boss, or loved one—who it is doesn't matter.

Notice the feelings you experience. Notice *where* you feel these emotions in your body. Notice *how* they feel: heavy, sharp, hard, dense. Notice if you are labeling anything and notice the labels you are assigning. Notice the blame that starts to play out through your Mental intelligence system. Notice how you naturally want to blame the other for how you feel. Notice if you are feeling empowered or weak. Notice if you feel attacked or supported. Notice if you feel alone and separate or engaged and connected. Notice all that's going on in yourself. Notice what this emotion is saying to you. Notice if it's attached to an old story.

Between stimulus and response there is a space.
In that space is our power to choose our response.
~ Victor Frankl

As the Observer, your inner wisdom comes forth to serve you. All your intelligence systems work together, enabling you in this process.

As you are noticing, allow the emotion to be seen, heard, and felt. Breathe deeply into the area in your body where you feel the emotion. As you do, just notice. This is how you let the emotion be felt. With your breath, you can begin to get that energy moving. Remember, **e**-motions, are **energy in motion**. Most emotions would come and go with ease if you didn't find fault with them. If you didn't have resistance to them, if you weren't holding on to them or blaming others, those emotions would be moving through you.

With practice, this is all you'll need to do to get those emotions moving. If you are still attached to this first one, don't fret. Remember, you have habits, patterns, and systems in place that you are slowly,

125

gently, and efficiently beginning to dismantle. Repetition will create a new neural pathway to support you. Often these emotions are stored in many places within your energy bodies, and as your subconscious sees the repetition of you doing this work, it will start to release its hold on more of these trapped emotions.

Remember, it's your choice to hold on to something that doesn't serve you. No one is making you do anything or feel anything. No one can control your experience but you. If you feel sad, hurt, or bad, remember that you have options. Looking at the sadness and hurt allows you to peel back the layers of your pain and suffering to get to the root cause. Keep asking yourself how it makes you feel until you get to the root of your pain. It's in getting to the root of the pain that you'll be able to see it differently and can choose to feel differently about it.

Please note that this is not a replacement for therapy nor is this intended to be medical advice. Consult with your health care practitioner with regards to your medical care. This is simply an overview of some best practices in working with your emotional intelligence system so that it's not controlling you.

Ask yourself, Is this true?

A client came to me to work on leadership, specifically her ability to lead others without the masculine mandates of her past that now felt controlling and manipulative. She noticed that her peers and her team were hesitant and resistant to following her. In her reflection, she observed that others viewed her as bossy, controlling, and self-centered. In working together, she found that she suffered from emotional traumas that would surface as anxiety. As her anxiety arose, she could observe herself feeling out of control in the chaos that rushed through her system; in a struggle to gain control, she would use authoritative, directive, and forceful conversation with herself and others in an effort to regain control. Bullying doesn't work in a leadership role. Her aim was to observe the emotions and allow them to settle before responding and to then respond from a space of compassion, confidence, clarity, and centeredness. She realized in her reflection that she struggled to love and nurture herself. She was mostly mean, directive, and angry, thus coming across as forceful and controlling. She was able to observe that her team had been experiencing this demanding and forceful nature too. She learned to observe the chaos and wait for the emotional wave to subside before responding. She also learned how quickly her new leadership skills impacted her team as she modeled calm, control, confidence, clarity, courage, and compassion.

As within, so without.

Your emotions are personal, based on your life stories, past experiences, and conditioning. While emotions are personal, they are also shared, meaning we all experience the same emotions. No one is exempt from emotions. While some may have turned off their feelings in an attempt to protect themselves from being hurt, the emotions are still there, lying under the layers of protection they deem as necessary.

Once you begin to feel and release emotions, you'll be able to craft a new story. It will be a new version of the old story from your new, now more mature, perspective, which has the ability to see the bigger picture. This new version of the story helps to release any old fragments of this energy within.

EQ should be taught in schools. Many states are now bringing social-emotional learning (SEL) into the PreK–12 levels. It should be taught in homes, and it should be reinforced in businesses. We are far from being an emotionally intelligent society. It will take hundreds of years for future generations to learn to address their emotions naturally. You can do your part by being aware of your emotions and not stuffing them down, pushing them away, avoiding, or fearing them. The human experience is rich with a wide scope of emotions.

Sadness, anger, and bitterness are signals that your emotions are out of alignment with your higher self, and that your perspective, the lens with which you are viewing things, is limited and incomplete. This doesn't make your emotions wrong, unreal, or invalid. They are real and certainly valid. They are part of your life's journey. Don't let anyone tell you your emotions are wrong or that they don't matter. They do and *you* do. You matter.

Take loss as an example. Whether the loss of a pet or a person, through death or divorce, you've bonded with that person/pet for years. You've established habits, routines, and patterns that connected you, fulfilled you, brought joy, and made memories. The abrupt end to all of this is a shock to the human system. It's a massive disruption, and disruption can come in other ways too, like any big change or external circumstances like the pandemic of 2020.

Taking a loss personally, as if it's happening *to* you, is the ego's point of view. Seeing things from this viewpoint is part of being human. Don't disregard it. But don't limit your perception to only this view. Learn to see a bigger picture. We learn from nature, mother earth, our solar system, and our life that this human experience is one of going through cycles. We come into life with our birth and proceed through massive cycles of change, growth, and evolution until the final cycle as we transition out of this human experience.

Learning to view things with a 360-degree lens of awareness can help you look at all the ways you could see the situation. Emotions are a gift when you stop labeling them as good or bad. When you stop avoiding them, they allow you to experience all they came to bring you. A richness and beauty emerge when you can see the negative, the neutral, and the positive in every experience. You'll be filled with the real value and true gifts that the human experience offers. There really is a silver lining if you look for it.

Every cloud has a silver lining.

In my childhood, my dad had a favorite joke. His joke was that I didn't come from mommy's tummy; he got me in a crap game, and he was the loser. My family laughed at the joke, which I took as them laughing at me. I grew up feeling unloved and unwanted. I recall wanting to run away to escape the pain of feeling unwanted. I actually tried to run away many times. At one point, I remember my mother saying, "Let me know next time, and I'll help you pack your bags." This wound followed me into adulthood. It showed up later in my life as rejection, feeling not important and unheard.

The suffering followed me everywhere until I was able to notice the patterns. It's not easy to own that the suffering I felt, I was self-perpetuating. Feeling that the rejection was happening to me kept me from seeing my role in it and from seeing what I needed to heal. Unable to see what I wasn't able to give myself, what I most wanted and needed, kept me in the suffering. What I kept seeking from others, from the world, was love and acceptance. Eventually, you, too, will come to the awareness that you need to be the parent you always wanted. You need to give yourself the love and acceptance you seek. All adults will eventually find that they need to parent themselves with what they deemed missing in their childhood.

You see, most of your emotions are showing you what you need to give yourself. Often it comes back to love—self-love. It comes back to acceptance and forgiveness. As an adult, you get to be your own parent. You get to notice what you need and give it to yourself. You get to be whole, complete, and fulfilled.

Do you want to be right or happy?

Compassion is powerful. If you could be compassionate with yourself, how might your life be different? If you fully and completely loved yourself, all aspects of you, how might your life be different?

EMOTIONS ARE FEMININE ENERGY

Think of your emotions as your feminine energy force. This has nothing to do with gender; both men and women have feminine and masculine energies. Spiritual traditions have labeled them as "sacred feminine" and, from a balanced and empowered state, these energies will cause you to be open, receptive, and inward-focused. Your feminine energies promote ease, understanding, sensitivity, nurturing, and creativity. This energy is calm, intuitive, tender, and allowing. It acknowledges desire, produces a natural energetic flow, and practices surrender to feel and experience all emotions.

As with all energy, feminine energy has a polarity, both positive and negative aspects. The negative aspects of the feminine energy are often described as the "wounded feminine." The wounded feminine shows up as powerless, needy, weak, and withholding. The wounded feminine represents herself as oversensitive, codependent, and overemotional. The wounded feminine is often filled with shame, guilt, doubt, and scarcity while hiding and feeling like a victim. It shows up in leadership roles as manipulation and overexplaining and has damaging consequences in the workplace.

In my Winner's Circle, you'll embody both the sacred feminine and masculine energies. If you notice any of the wounded aspects in you, remember that you cannot and will not change everything all at once. In the human experience, everything is understood and worked with as bite-size chunks of data. Pick one area to be more aware of and reflect on the feelings, stories, and history that lie within that part of you. You are on a path to knowing yourself and growing yourself to live your life empowered. EQ opens the pathway to a culture of high performance, understanding, and creativity.

INVITATION

Reread this chapter and give yourself the gift of loving yourself. Give yourself the gift of healing yourself, listening, feeling, and experiencing all of you. Give yourself the gift of compassion.

_____

_____

Write out your story of suffering, sadness, or discontent. Reread it and notice what it is you've always been seeking. Notice the emotional needs that you have that may have gone unfulfilled. Write it out clearly. And make a promise to give this to yourself always.

_____

_____

Feel the release as you right now give to yourself these longings and desires—be it love, acceptance, forgiveness, nurturing, or compassion. Whatever your needs and wants have always been, give them to yourself.

_____

_____

In the Companion Workbook are a few more exercises: one that will allow you to spot and acknowledge an emotion that repeats itself often and to process and release it, and another that allows you deeper insight through meditation and contemplation. Plus, you'll find an additional page on the wounded feminine to explore.

CHAPTER 15:

SPIRITUAL INTELLIGENCE SYSTEM (SQ)

You may think that spirituality is a separate part of your life, something that is intangible and reserved for retreats or quiet moments spent in meditation, prayer, or deep contemplation. If this is your thought, I wish to challenge it. I wish to invite you to see that the entirety of your life, all the rich, complex, and juicy parts of your life as well as the boring and mundane aspects, is spiritual.

You are a soul experiencing consciousness expressed through a human story. Every part of your human story is vital and spiritual. Doing laundry is no less spiritual than meditating and watching the sunrise. Your contribution to the world is spiritual. This is why *Bringing Spirituality into Business* is so important. You are here to tune into the same wisdom and intelligence that wrote you into being.

Spiritual growth is simply connecting with your inner being and consciousness. SQ has three pillars that often intertwine and overlap: relationships, values, and life purpose. Spiritual growth is not a destination or accomplishment, but a way of life. The path of spiritual growth is a path of lifelong learning, growth from the inside out. It's based on faith and trusting, healing, letting go, and learning.

The spiritual journey is the unlearning of fear...and the acceptance of love. ~ Marianne Williamson

During my spiritual growth and healing journey, I found myself stepping outside my comfort zone to try new things. I joined Meetup groups in my area and signed up to experience new things, people, and places. One Meetup was to hike at the Garden of the Gods in the Shawnee National Forest, about three hours from my home. It was a weekend trip with camping overnight and two hikes. I had the option of bringing a tent or renting a cabin. Something about this Meetup was calling me. I thought about it often, as if knowing this would be a powerful and impactful trip. Days before the event, it was canceled due to low participation. I wasn't going to let this stop me. I packed up my car with food, a sleeping bag, and overnight things, and I went alone. It was a nice, easy drive. About 15 miles from the destination, police officers were stopping traffic to inform drivers to be aware of runners on the narrow road ahead. I chatted for nearly ten minutes with Deputy Dennison. We seemed to have a connection. We giggled and shared a bit, and I told him I was headed to the Garden of the Gods for an experience of my lifetime.

I arrived and began to explore the history of the area, including the rock formations that were over 10,000 years old. I took it all in and meditated on top of the largest, highest rock formation overlooking the forest and seeing for what felt like miles in all directions. After a few hours exploring and enjoying the Garden of the Gods, I journeyed back to my car to grab a bite to eat before I wandered onto one of the many trails. I decided to go on the shortest trail that looped around the Garden of the Gods, mostly because those coming off the trail were commenting on how difficult it was to see the trail. It was late October in the Midwest, and everything was blanketed by a layer of leaves. I grabbed my backpack, with my cell phone, toilet paper, and an extra bottle of water, and off I went. Quickly, I, too, noticed how hard it was to follow the path. I overheard a group nearby, who were part of the Sierra Club out of SIUE. I quickly jumped trails and decided to follow them, as they had become my safe bet for following a trail. As they stopped for lunch, I went on ahead.

It wasn't long before I could not see the trail nor hear their voices. I was literally lost in the forest. I tried to find my way back to them but to no avail. After what felt like an hour without a plan or any sense of direction, I paused to weigh my options. I knew I needed to meditate and seek inner guidance, but I didn't want to sit on the forest floor and get chiggers. The memory of the chiggers I had gotten earlier that year was fresh in my mind. The thought of meditating while standing up was not something I had done before. I noticed all sorts of stories in my head; I was having a battle with my psyche, and I really needed to focus. As I meditated, I realized I had three options: Plan A, follow my inner guidance and allow it to direct my steps out of here; Plan B, GPS my way out via Google Maps and walk myself back to my car; or Plan C, call 911. I elected for the first one. I walked up a huge ravine, truly feeling guided and on my way back to my car. I walked for almost an hour when, all of sudden, I came across a barbed wire fence. I'll admit, I freaked for a bit, thinking that beyond the fence might be a bobcat, snakes, or even bears. You see, I had not seen nor even heard a bird or bug. I heard nothing at all except the leaves crunching beneath my feet and the small twigs breaking as I stepped on them. Never before had I experienced such silence. This barbed wire fence was the first sense of fear I had experienced thus far.

The fear caused me to pause. I used this moment to relieve my full bladder and tied some toilet paper to the fencing, in case I found my-self back here later, then I would know I'd been here before. Crossing over that barbed wire fence was met with such uncertainty, so I quickly moved on to Plan B. I had never used Google Maps for walking, but my kids had shown it to me while visiting just months before. I got to a high point in the terrain to connect with Goggle Maps, found the parking area where my car was, and proceeded to walk in the that direction, up and down the mountain terrain. I paused at the bottom before the next upward climb as it looked like a steep climb. In that pause, I realized my grip on the phone had been hiding an important message: "no signal." Not only had I lost the GPS signal, but I now only had 22 percent battery life. This left me feeling like Plan C was my only option. By now, the angle of the sun made it feel like darkness was settling in on the forest floor. Daylight was waning, and if I did not find a way out, I would need to spend the night here alone, unprotect-ed with no water, food, or warmth.

I wasn't dying, so calling 911 felt wrong and yet my only option. Again climbing to the highest point I could see, I called 911. I spoke, they talked, I answered while they continued talking over me and ask-ing me questions. I quickly realized they were not hearing my replies. How could this be? I could hear them loud and clear. They asked if I needed help, if this was an emergency, who I was, where I was...all of which I was answering. Then, after a few minutes, the call ended. They had hung up on me. NO! I felt a pit in my stomach. But a minute or so later, a text message came through from a 911 dispatcher. They said they got my location from the GPS signal but were unable to hear me. I now answered all those questions via text. They said they were able to get my GPS location, and I appeared to be deep in the Shawnee National Forest just east of Derby Road, and they would send an officer to coax or guide me out. I still heard nothing—no road traffic or anything. I asked for clarity what direction I should start walking. Luckily, I had downloaded a compass app on my phone; I calibrated the compass and began walking in the direction I was told when, lo and behold, after about 40 minutes, I ended up right back at the barbed wire fence. Looking down the fence line about 30 feet from me, I could see the toilet paper I had tied there hours ago.

The same fear came over me. I texted 911 dispatch and told them of the barbed wire fence. He asked me to call back again to allow them to get my GPS location. Well, on the other side of that fence is what they called Derby Road; it was a rescue path, filled with ruts, overgrown weeds, and like nothing I would call a road. It wasn't but another 30 minutes when an officer showed up. It was a 45-minute drive back to my car. I had been traveling further and further away from where I needed to be. I knew I needed a lot of reflection time and that many lessons would be learned from this experience. In my immediate reflection, I could see how quickly I let uncertainty and fear demolish my faith and trust, taking me off the path from listening to my inner guidance. Why didn't I get quiet and go within for more guidance when I reached the barbed wire fencing? Why was I so quick to jump to Plan B? This was showing me my level of spiritual trust and how quickly I had lost my faith.

Well, I didn't spend the night. I couldn't wait to get back home. So, I headed out of town only to get pulled over before I could get onto a major highway. I was super clear that I had to take back my power and not be a victim here. I was certain and firm in knowing I was not getting a ticket. In fact, I wasn't even going to reach for my purse to get out my driver's license, as that felt like ownership of guilt. I pulled over and waited for the officer to approach my car. Guess who it was? Deputy Dennison. He said, "Please tell me you weren't that lost lady in the forest today." I timidly raised my hand and proclaimed, "That was me." He laughed and asked me if I remembered what I had told him that morning. I replied, "No, what did I tell you?" With a smile on his face that went from ear to ear, he said, "You told me you were headed to the Garden of the Gods for an experience of your lifetime, and I think you got it." He did not write me a ticket; instead, he gave me a map and told me to save the 70 mph for the four-lane interstate ahead. I tried my best to enjoy the drive home and save the processing for the next day, as I knew I had learned many lessons this day, all of it for my spiritual growth.

I win or I learn, but I never lose.

Remember, you are not a human being having a spiritual experience; you are a spiritual being here having a human experience. Science, philosophy, medicine, physics—nearly all branches of research—have attempted to explain consciousness, spirituality, and this One Power and Presence we experience but to no avail. Consciousness is still the biggest puzzle to all realms of research.

Thanks to the research and contributions of philosophers and scientists David Chalmers and Thomas Nagel, who reject the idea that consciousness is produced by the brain but who share an alternative view, that consciousness is a fundamental quality of the universe. The brain is a receiver and transmitter of consciousness, not the producer of it.

William James, the father of Western psychology, in 1902 defined spiritual experiences as states of higher consciousness, which are induced by efforts to understand the general principles or structure of the world through one's inner experience. At the core of his view of spirituality is what we might call "connectedness," which refers to the fact that individual goals can be truly realized only in the context of the whole—one's relationship to the world and to others.

Expert meditators demonstrate more harmonious brain waves, which could be indicative of greater synchrony or connectivity within and across different neural areas. In short, spirituality, similar to love, has physiological effects in the brain and body, and EEG provides a window on these changes. Wow, right?

What's more, research suggests that you can do more than just measure this kind of activity. You can train your brain to behave in a more aware way by engaging in activities that facilitate greater connection or neural synchronization. Higher synchronization is found in following the practices of meditation, prayer, yoga, qigong, and tai chi.

One way of interpreting this is that neuronal synchronization enhances your brain's harmony or integrity, achieving a state in which the brain works in a more congruent way, adopting a more global perspective. I experience this as a greater knowing—a connecting of the dots, so to speak. Other findings point to the psychological consequences of this state; greater neuronal synchronization tends to enable a greater ability to make moral judgments and problem solve creatively. It's as if answers to problems simply come to you; an inner knowing of sorts and the answer to your problems are shown to you, like your logic and reason unite in harmony to give you answers.

There is no passion to be found playing small—in settling for a life that is less than the one you are capable of living. ~ Nelson Mandela

Another perspective is that more scientific exploration of such experiences could reveal the mechanisms enabling us all to achieve these states even in the most mundane moments, such as waiting in traffic. This has been my experience and that of those I work with.

*The experience is far greater than
one can imagine.*

Spiritual intelligence is your ability to access higher meanings, values, abiding purposes, and subconscious aspects of the self and to embed these meanings, values, and purposes in living richer and more creative lives. Imagine *Bringing Spirituality into Business* into your workplace and actually loving your work, finding meaning and value in what you do and who you connect with. Take this a step further and imagine full brain activity and functioning to promote higher states of creativity, productivity, and higher levels of decision-making and problem solving.

Through years of meditation, we all come to the truth: the same truth, the same awareness, the same knowing. You are pure consciousness. You are the awareness that knows of your experience. You are the awareness that senses, feels, and views the experience and the beauty and richness within all experiences. You are all things, everything, and you are nothing. Yes, this is mind-blowing from our usual three-dimensional reality.

Planet Earth is evolving at the quickest pace ever recorded. You, too, are evolving faster than ever before. This is why it is important to take control and guide your evolution by your design and not leave it to happen by default. But know, with certainty, that **this is your choice**. Nothing and no one can force your evolution. You are the master of you. You have been given free will. This is what *Bringing Spirituality into Business* will show you. You master and control all aspects of yourself and all aspects of your life. You have dominion over the earth, and this means you and your intelligence systems.

Your SQ reminds you that you are here to thrive and increase. Your actions and behaviors are either showing you how beautifully you are living or how you are slowly dying. It's in this intelligence that possibility and future potential arise to take you on a journey of showing you more of life, more of your talents, gifts, and abilities. This intelligence takes you into wonder, curiosity, and so much more.

So often, humans get comfortable and settle into a routine. This can be good or not so good. Don't become unconscious in your routines. Be present, whether you're doing laundry, cooking, or hiking in nature. Don't lose the wonder and curiosity in your routines. Routines can be pleasurable, powerful, and promote your growth and well-being. Routines can also be limiting and destructive to your well-being. Routines are just habits you've practiced often.

> *Remember, good habits are as addictive as bad habits but much more rewarding.*

Most of the dissatisfaction and depression that humans experience is due to a loss of meaning and purpose in their life. You have access to higher meaning and purpose. Just knowing this prompts you to wonder and curiosity—**wonder**, as in, what if there was another way to see this? Wonder opens the door to your Spiritual intelligence. This wonder prompts **curiosity** and acts to engage it and bring it fully on board. In the wonder, your curiosity begins to explore better-feeling thoughts and emotions. Trust me—it will aid you in your awareness and understanding of the other three intelligence systems.

**When emotional intelligence merges with spiritual intelligence, human nature is transformed.
~ Deepak Chopra**

You are a multifaceted, multidimensional being. Simply being aware of this will allow you to begin living into greater possibility and potential. It will allow you to spot new opportunities, see more synchronicities lining up, and recognize answers to your questions coming into your reality without any effort or research on your part.

Unlocking your SQ brings far more than can be shared here. So, don't limit yourself. Unlocking your SQ opens the doorway to your inner genius, your higher self, your soul/spirit, and taps into infinite intelligence.

In my experience at the Garden of the Gods, where I went to have an experience of my lifetime, I was given that experience. I had an experience I will never forget. One that taught me to trust. One that changed me forever. One that taught me that tuning in to this higher wisdom and guidance needs to be done and practiced over and over, especially when fear shows itself, especially when doubt and our humanness come forth and question our trust and believing, and especially in those uncharted, unexplored areas of life when we don't know and we truly know we don't know. This is when our Spiritual intelligence will serve us best.

Your Spiritual intelligence feeds you. **It fuels you with wonder, knowing, guidance, and pauses.** Let's look at each of the ways your SQ feeds you.

WONDER

A power is found in wonder. It's my hope that you find this power. Wonder is having the ability to marvel about the world you live in—in amazement, admiration, and curiosity.

Wonder helps to put your place in the world into perspective. It not only allows you to see beauty in a bird, but it reminds you that the human experience is finite but that you are also part of something much greater and infinite in nature.

It's a powerful thing that can inspire a deeper sense of connection, belonging, and purpose. A sense of wonder allows you to sit back at the end of the day and marvel at the magic of what may seem like a mundane slice of your weekly routine. It also allows you to look ahead and feel hopeful and optimistic about the future. And it allows you to take delight in the small, simple experiences in daily life, like witnessing the changing autumn leaves or noticing how much you can get done in the one minute your coffee is reheating in the microwave, the knock on the door of an unexpected guest, discovering a love for gardening, or breathing in the fresh air on the first warm day of spring.

It's all too easy to cling to known outcomes. It's all too easy to cling to stories of doom and gloom. You can cling to the diagnosis of your medical condition. You can cling to the pain of your suffering and your struggles, or you can cling to hope and possibility, letting wonder lead the way.

Let wisdom and wonder lead your way.

KNOWING

Knowing shows up in many ways. Your intuition is probably one way you are already aware of but may not have yet cultivated and strengthened. To strengthen your intuition, you will need to work with it, just like strengthening a muscle or a new habit. I recommend you build an intimate relationship with your intuition. You'll reap the rewards as you do and thank yourself later.

However, knowing is not limited to your intuition. Clair senses are seen as spiritual gifts that only come fully onboard and are activated when one is ready, willing, and able to use them. Until then, they lie dormant in the background of all that you are. Many people never develop these gifts, and that is okay too. So don't push or force them; this type of energy actually works against you.

Spiritual energies work without effort; they work with surrender, acceptance, and a natural flow.

Like radio waves, spiritual information is constantly being broadcast around us, so it's really a matter of learning how to tune in to it. To interpret what spirit is broadcasting, you use your five senses just like you do in your day-to-day life. And just as you may feel that some of your senses are more reliable than others for making everyday judgments, you have senses, or clair senses, that are stronger for connecting with spirit energies.

The six clair senses are:
- Clairvoyance is clear seeing.
- Clairaudience is clear hearing.
- Clairsentience is clear feeling.

141

- Clairalience is clear smelling.
- Clairgustance is clear tasting.
- Claircognizance is clear knowing.

We can't talk about knowing without discussing the **inner knowings** of the Universal Laws so often overlooked by our man-made laws and expectations. Universal means every particle feels, or is affected by it, and the gauge of the effect is dependent on the particle's mass or energy. There are twelve Universal Laws, and as they are mentioned, you may notice a resonance within you to a distant memory. They are the law of oneness, vibration, attraction, compensation, polarity, correspondence, inspired action, cause and effect, relativity, gender, perpetual transmutation of energy, and rhythm. These twelve Universal Laws are rewarding when implemented in business because they ignite your own inner knowing and truth, but also because they take the place of some of the more traditional approaches to today's business trainings.

One example is to teach the law of oneness in place of all the diversity, equity, inclusion, and belonging (DEIB) training going on in the business world today. This would activate the inner memory of truth within each and every individual and possibly make DEIB trainings obsolete and unnecessary. The law of oneness states that everyone and everything are interconnected. This law states that we are all connected through creation. Every single atom inside of you is connected in some way, shape, or form to the rest of the universe you move through. You and I are part of a collective consciousness. Others carry strengths and talents you don't, and you actually need others to be fully resourced and empowered.

This fundamental law helps you understand your connectedness on a different level. When you help someone else out, you feel good. On some spiritual level, you are that person. When you hurt someone else, you are hurting yourself. I am you and you are me. Not only are you connected to others and they to you, when you know this, you'll be shown the qualities they bring forth and be filled with gratitude and appreciation.

When this knowing becomes fully activated and brought online, you naturally look to engage and connect with others. You see your own value and worth. You see the value in others and look to connect to engage with what they came to bring. Through your connection with others, it can activate gifts in you that you were previously unaware of.

In business, this matters. Knowing that each and every individual brings a valuable contribution to the organization produces the greatest reward for all. It's a game changer. It brings harmony, teamwork, respect, and greater innovation when it resides in the awareness of all. It brings out individual greatness. Individual talent, expertise, and creative gifts are allowed to be expressed, shared, and utilized. It brings purposeful engagement and builds character, confidence, and the courage to be authentically who you are.

GUIDANCE

Have you ever gotten a nudge to call someone only to find out that when you did, they were thinking of you too or they really needed to talk with you at this particular moment? It's like divine timing.

Have you ever lost your keys or something of value and asked for guidance in finding them? I have. I even put it to the test. I hope you will too. I misplaced my extra key fob and wanted to sell the car but didn't want to sell it without giving the new owner both fobs. I asked for guidance but never really felt I received the answer. Every once in a while, I would go on a mission looking in all the obvious places in my home, only to come up empty again. Finally, I decided to meditate and *wait for the guidance*. I stayed in meditation until I had a clear knowing of where to go to find my fob. I was prepared to stay in meditation for hours if necessary. I was there for over 30 minutes before I felt the urge to move. I got up and found myself using my hands to move mulch around in my flower beds around my patio. My mind wanted to tell a story about it… Yes, I must have set my fob down when planting the flowers in the spring. But before I could even finish the story in my mind, I was guided to go inside. I walked in through the sliding door in the kitchen and opened the pantry door. As I did, I could see the fob and green key holder as clear as day in my mind's eye. Eerie. It was as if I saw nothing in the pantry, but my mind's eye saw the fob I was seeking. From there, I followed this guidance to open a draw in my kitchen, and there it was, plain as day. Right on top. In a drawer I had looked in many times before. In fact, it was in a drawer I get into every week—the drawer where I keep scissors, tape, pens, paper, baggies, aluminum foil, and plastic wrap. *How* did this happen?

Usually when I intend to be guided to resolve an issue, argument, or challenge, I find the guidance comes. Sometimes I find myself in actions to resolve it without the mental knowing or awareness. Other times it comes as a clear mental knowing. Still other times, the energetic charge of the struggle just falls away and dissolves.

When you are open to receive guidance, it will come. Whether you sit in meditation to receive it or go about your day, intending to hold space for the insight and guidance is all that's required. When it shows up, you know it. It's clear and it feels like you just got a free download.

One thing is for sure: when you ask for guidance, you have to expand your awareness to be receptive to receiving it. It may feel like expanding your capacity to receive or holding space for the information to come in and land. Many ask and then get back to being busy. Most ask but aren't receptive to receiving. This is why awareness is a prerequisite to all learning, growth, and development.

PAUSES

Pauses are probably more helpful, meaningful, and impactful than all the doing. The fact is, you probably are not super comfortable in the pauses—the quiet moments of life. Our humanness likes to be busy. Our egos have us filling every little void with something. When bored, that empty little pause gets consumed with scrolling through social media, indulging in Netflix, or gaming online with others. How do you fill those empty moments of your day?

Unless you plan, schedule, and create pauses, they probably aren't going to happen for you. The power of taking a pause is well researched. Not only does **pausing promote relaxation**, a break from the noise and *doing* also refreshes and reenergizes you for hours. The power of a pause gives your nervous system a chance to regain balance. It promotes well-being, focus, clarity, and productivity.

I used to be awkwardly uncomfortable with the silence and had a need to fill it with conversation, action, or doing something. Maybe you do too. The first step to shift this uncomfortable feeling is to *observe* it: Explore why it makes you uncomfortable. Sit in the stillness. Be with the silence. Feel it. Notice what you are afraid of. Notice how it makes you feel. Notice the sensations in your body. As you do, you will learn more about yourself.

Once you are comfortable and regularly take pauses, you'll be able to hear your inner guidance talk to you, to tell you when to pause and when to stop forcing and struggling, allowing your inner knowing to serve you. You will need to experience this for yourself. And, wow, what an experience it is.

Remember, SQ is your ability to access higher meanings, values, purposes, and subconscious aspects of the self and to embed these meanings, values, and purposes in living richer and more creative lives. It's in these powerful pauses that all this happens.

Here are seven common benefits of the pause:

- Improved self-restraint
- Improved emotional intelligence
- Prompts you to remember to mindfully breathe deeply
- Balances the emotional and rational parts of your brain to reduce stress
- Redirection of intrusive, negative, and anxious thoughts
- Improved ability to discern and make optimal decisions
- Empowerment so you focus on what's best in you and for you

Will you intentionally plan and schedule regular and frequent pauses in your day? I bet you will now.

INVITATION

Adopt some practical ways to develop and strengthen your SQ.

Practices to get in touch with your inner voice of knowing and guidance through a pause include:

1. Create intentional pauses in your life and schedule.
2. Practice deep listening.
3. Don't neglect self-care.
4. Try journaling.
5. Experience the benefits of meditation time.
6. Develop an intimate relationship with intuition.
7. Get curious about fleeting moments of insight.
8. Mind your physical and mental health.

Commit to at least one practice and record your awareness during the week to share with your circle of support.

_____

_____

_____

CHAPTER 16:

WISDOM

You've now been introduced to your four powerful intelligence systems. These intelligence systems work together to empower you in your human experience. They work together to guide you, direct you, and inform you. Allow them to work together in harmony, and you will experience all you need and more easily and effortlessly. When understood, applied, and integrated, these systems will bring you clarity of your purpose, your gifts and talents, and your dreams and desires. They'll also equip you with greater compassion, acceptance, and positive regard for yourself and others. They allow you to hold multiple awarenesses and to meet others at a soul level, without an attachment to the roles we are playing. When you are in harmony with your intelligence systems, they bring you wisdom.

The door to wisdom is knowing yourself.

Wisdom is the ability to know what is true or right, your common sense, and your good judgment. Both satisfying and expansive, wisdom comes through the learning and lessons in your experiences. I read an anonymous quote that said, "Wisdom is the reward of experience and should be shared." Wisdom feels like all of you—all your energy and intelligences lined up with a channel or portal to the infinite. When you feel this connection, life flows with ease. It can feel like an insight fills and permeates every cell of your being. You are designed to use and trust wisdom like an internal compass that helps you direct your life and your life choices so that you know what to do and when.

147

Your power and strength will be found in the quiet spaces and pauses that you allow. Allowing pauses bring you back to this "now" moment and your center. See if you can use the pauses to connect back with all of you—all four intelligence systems—and allow wisdom to show itself. It's in these pauses when you can surrender to letting go of thinking you know everything—to allow the answers to come to you. There is wisdom in not knowing. Allow your ego to sit down and shut up. When I began a practice of "knowing I didn't know," even when I did know, everything changed. You'll just have to try this one for yourself. Remind yourself that *you don't know* and allow yourself to be shown.

To better understand this *letting go* of thinking you know everything, let me share this powerful story.

Nan-in, a Japanese master during the Meiji era (1868–1912), spoke with a university professor who came to inquire about Zen. The professor demanded that the Zen master, "Open my mind to enlightenment." The man's tone was one of getting his own way.

Nan-in asked that they have this conversation over tea. He poured his visitor's cup full and then kept on pouring.

The professor watched the cup overflow until he no longer could restrain himself. "It is overfull. No more will go in!"

"Like this cup," Nan-in said, "you are full of your own opinions and speculations. How can I show you Zen unless you first empty your cup?"

The tea story is a great reminder that we must humble ourselves to empty our mind and make room for the new.

When any real progress is made, we unlearn and learn anew what we thought we knew before.
~ Henry David Thoreau

In this busy world of hustle and bustle, with demands screaming at you from all directions, you might wonder how you'll find time for a pause and how to clear your mind. Maybe you feel you have a constant stream of interruptions as well as notifications and expectations. This may be true. So, pause for a moment right now. Realize now that you *can* choose to make excuses for all this. You *can* choose to see yourself as too busy to pause. You *can* keep focusing on the stream of notifications and expectations. And maybe this is the small habit and pattern you need to see in order to alter it, to create something different. You get to focus on your busyness *or* the pause you wish to create—one or the other—and you are always choosing. But you can't have both at the same time. It's one or the other. *You* choose.

What if, just this once, you chose to create a pause for yourself? What if you chose to stop speaking? To stop with the excuses and stories? What if you chose to close your laptop, turn off your notifications, silence your phone, close this book, push away from all distractions? What if you chose differently? Here in lies the pause.

It's funny how hard we make everything seem. We allow excuses. We call them *facts*. As facts, they are more believable and truer. It's easier to say we can't change facts. It's funny how many stories we tell. But the real humor lies in how many of these stories we believe as true and factual.

The ability to observe without evaluating is the highest form of intelligence. ~ Jiddu Krishnamurti

If you are making excuses, trust me, you probably won't be able to catch yourself in all the excuses you make. In addition, all your excuses are limiting you. They are blocking you from seeing, perceiving, and noticing more of what's available for you. They block you from your wisdom too. What if you could catch yourself? What if you could see the excuses you are making? What if you could hear yourself telling those stories that block you from seeing clearly?

Don't measure and focus on your mess-ups. Don't measure and focus on your doubts, fears, and mistakes. Sure, it's important to notice and observe them. It's shown that those who focus on their faults or worries often never get beyond their problems. If they do, they generally take twice as long or longer to achieve the results they seek. Think about this for a moment. To focus on what you are doing wrong makes you think there is something to fix. This can send you down a deep, dark rabbit hole of trying to fix yourself instead of focusing on what you wish to achieve. This one problem could solve everything for some. Observe, yes, then ask yourself, What would I love? What can I do now?

*The longer you focus on a setback, loss,
or problem, the longer it will negatively
impact you.*

Instead of measuring your mistakes, measure your successes. Successful people learn to monitor, manage, and measure their progress. Coaching is all about helping you notice your habits and patterns. You have both patterns and habits that serve your growth and those that don't serve you. This is probably one of the first things I point out in coaching, as these roots travel deep into all areas of life and one's happiness. Said another way, when you observe, practice, and notice your progress, you'll achieve the results you want much faster. This is how you will *master you and your results.*

Measuring your progress builds confidence. Noticing what you are aware of is progress. Think of everything as data. It's what you do with the data that really matters. How you use it and apply it has the greatest impact. If you need to find fault with the data, you may be wasting valuable time and energy. Observe it. Notice if it's helping you or hindering you…then act accordingly.

Wisdom is not a process; it's a collection of knowledge, experience, and inner guidance that comes from within you. It happens naturally when you allow your intelligence systems to operate in harmony. Wisdom will come as a natural response to surrendering control. It comes organically when you stop forcing only one aspect of yourself. Shift to the Observer to see all of you. You may at first doubt this as you won't be able to discern how you know or where the knowing came from, and therefore, the very questioning keeps you from leaning into it.

Your inner knowing is your only true compass.
~ Joy Page

Maybe you can recall a time you knew something with a certainty. I recall when this shift happened for me. I came to my Sunday night mastermind call and shared with the group my new awareness. "How I am learning is changing," I said. "I have an inner knowing. A knowing so bold and true, and yet no research, reading, or studying was done. It's requiring me to trust myself." Trusting myself was something I wasn't as skilled at as I thought I was. Maybe you can relate. Someone else on the call said, "You've unlocked your wisdom."

Wisdom isn't always as it seems. Allow me to share a bit of humorous wisdom.

A lady gets on a public bus. Without saying a word, she gestures to the bus driver by sticking her thumb on her nose and waving her fingers at the driver.

The driver acknowledges the lady, turns to her, and uses both hands in the same type of gesture and waves all his fingers at her.

The woman holds her right arm out at the driver and chops at it a few times with her left hand.

Then the driver puts his left hand on his right bicep and jerks his right arm up in a fist at her.

The woman then cups both of her hands under her breasts and lifts gently. So, the driver places both of his hands at his crotch and gently lifts up.

Then the woman frowns, runs a finger up between her derriere and gets off the bus.

Another woman sitting in the front row of the bus witnessed the whole exchange. She speaks up, "That was the most disgusting thing I have ever seen on a public bus! What the hell were you doing?"

"Listen lady," states the gruff bus driver, "the lady that got on the bus before was a deaf-mute. She asked me if the bus went to 5th Street. I said no, we go to 10th Street. She asked if we make many stops. I told her that this was the express. She asked if we go by the dairy, and I told her we go by the ballpark. She said, 'Shit, I'm on the wrong bus!' and got off."

When you intentionally activate and engage all of yourself, all your intelligent energies in your awareness, in this present moment, without force or control, the magic of wisdom will flow through you, like water flows in the stream.

Knowing yourself is the beginning of all wisdom.
~ Aristotle

What does it look like when you integrate all of yourself and your understanding of your four intelligence systems into your life? What does this wisdom look like?

- You don't take things personally.
- You can apologize easily when you've caused harm or hurt someone's feelings.
- You're able to be vulnerable and honest.
- You take full and personal responsibility for your choices, intentions, and energy.
- You can read and understand your emotions as well as the emotions of others.
- You're calm and less reactive.
- You value the long-term outcome and impact of your decisions.
- You can listen to other people's opinions and feelings without becoming defensive.
- Your needs and preferences are balanced with the best interest of others.
- You spend more time and energy invested in creating and supporting.
- You become less interested in commenting upon and critiquing others.
- You're okay with not having all the answers.
- You look forward to leaning into not knowing, figuring it out, and embracing change.

Researchers are still exploring and defining wisdom. Numerous theories are emerging, and what they all seem to agree upon is that wisdom encompasses cognitive components, such as knowledge and experience; reflective components, or the ability to examine situations and oneself; and prosocial components, meaning benevolence and compassion. Wisdom is also connected to abilities such as perspective, open-mindedness, and intellectual humility.

Your maturity and cultivation of bringing all of you to the party has the potential to completely transform your experience of life and all of your relationships. It will give you a foundation of resilience to lean on as you navigate your unfolding human story. And most importantly, it will inform you of the character you need to cultivate personally so you may set an evolved and higher standard for yourself, our culture, our leaders, and future generations.

In summary, wisdom largely emerges from your reflection and awareness. Being open to new ways of thinking, like challenging status quo, can help to cultivate it. Wise people incorporate past opinions and observations into a more nuanced way of thinking or perceiving rather than in black or white, good or bad. Balance and harmony are key components. Wisdom comes from seeking to understand the motives of others rather than merely judging their behaviors. Wise people generally act on behalf of a common good for all, while also ensuring that their own needs are met, striving for overall harmony among competing goals and demands. In addition to promoting understanding and respect for others, wisdom can provide you a fulfilling sense of purpose in your life.

INVITATION

Answer this question: Where am I still focusing on what's wrong?

Look at the bulleted list on page 152 or found in Companion Workbook and pick one that you would like to observe and be more aware of this week. As you observe, do it from a place of holding all your intelligent energies in your awareness. Allow them to serve you, show you, and guide you to bring you wisdom.

Example: You don't take things personally.

Notice every time you do and don't take things personally. Observe. If you are offended by the words of another, you are taking it personally. Look at why you are offended. Look at the story you are telling yourself. Look at how you feel and where you feel it in your body. Look at other examples of this showing up in your life. Observe and explore what's going on in you. This is time to look at the message and not blame the messenger.

CHAPTER 17:

WORKPLACE WELLNESS

Do you believe it's your natural state of being to be well? Do you believe that at your core, at the center of who you are, that you are well? Believe it or not, your beliefs matter.

Wellness is your natural state. Peace is your natural state. Happiness is your natural state. How connected are you to your most natural states? Place your hand on your heart and say to yourself now, "Peace, well-being, and happiness are my natural states. Today I will practice coming back to my natural state to experience peace, well-being, and happiness."

When an overall aim within an organization is that workplace wellness matters, the organization will do everything possible to achieve this. Until then, we will continue to see the effects that are caused by not addressing the root cause. Businesses will see massive turnover, disengaged and unmotivated people, and low levels of performance and productivity. Businesses will struggle and suffer the effects of this dysfunction.

Let's first look at the bigger picture. We don't have a health care system. We have a system that treats your symptoms. It does not get to the root cause of the illness or disease and correct the cause. When I was struggling with my health and well-being after three back surgeries and a grand mal seizure, I went to a half dozen doctors trying to find one who would listen to me and not get out their prescription pad at the beginning of me explaining my current reality. I knew at the core of my being that my wellness would not come from a pill. I am not saying that drugs are never helpful, useful, and sometimes necessary. I am not a doctor. Nor am I knowledgeable on what is required for you. But I did know that for me, my healing from all this would not come in a pill. I needed to detox my body and release all the traces of drugs that had altered my neurons in attempts to help with the pain I was in.

Wellness is measured in many ways, including feeling:

- Rested, recharged, energetic
- Mentally in control of your mind
- Emotionally in tune with your emotions
- Calm and confident
- Safe and secure

Wellness also means being able to achieve:

- Work/life balance
- Meaningful relationships
- The ability to enjoy life's activities

I get it—it's challenging to feel good when you are overweight. It's hard to tune into your natural state of well-being when you are fatigued; when you are stressed; when you are depressed; when you are broke, unemployed, or going through a life challenge, like a job loss, divorce, or loss of loved one or your health.

Wellness is important to your ability to function at your best. When you don't have great health, you are out of balance. Life pales in comparison. All areas of your life seem diminished. It's hard to be happy, to feel energized and empowered. It's hard to feel good. It's difficult to feel connected and part of things. When you don't have good health, it affects you. Things like clarity, productivity, accuracy, and communication aren't functioning at their peak. You are less friendly, engaging, and able to process what's going on around you. Life itself is masked in a gloom of sorts. Think of a time when you were not well; maybe you've experienced pain, fatigue, or stress. While each of these symptoms are so different, their effects on you are so similar. The mask of illness or disease obscures your ability to see the beauty, joy, and love around you. Stress, pain, and discomfort distract you from being present. It's as though they hold you hostage and prevent you from experiencing the richness of life, holding you in a prison of pain and suffering. They keep you in a hypnotic trance that traps you in an illusion of nothing but hardship and misery.

WELLNESS AWARENESS

Workplace wellness matters more than ever. But why? Is it because more people are sick? Is it because we are more aware? Is it because we are waking up to the power and control we have over the human condition? Is it because of the advancement in technology, the digital revolution? Does AI give us a measurement by which to gauge one's level of productivity against the computer? Are we becoming more compassionate and understanding? Is it due to a cultural shift toward a people-centric culture where people matter more than objects or profits? Is it simply evolution and how we as human beings are evolving? Is it to teach future generations the value of good health and well-being?

What if it's all of these reasons and more? We live in the most extraordinary of times, with a health care system that does little to promote health and well-being but does well to address sickness and to prescribe drugs to hide, camouflage, and rid you of the symptoms while leaving you with a host of new ailments. What happened to the days of getting to the root cause to rid the problem? Have we pushed so far away from our natural innate power and potential to heal ourselves? Are we now ready and willing to look at where we are? Are we ready to remind ourselves of this innate ability within?

> *Why do we take our complaints and aliments to a complete stranger and ask them what's wrong?*

Why are psychedelics becoming so popular? Are we returning to ancient wisdom and indigenous cultures to heal, release, and bring to our awareness the root cause of our illness, trauma, and drama? Over the last decade, there has been a big surge in medicinal and recreational use of cannabis and CBD, in various forms of oils, tinctures, edibles, vapes, buds, and more. Now, we have an explosion of resources to educate us on the power of psychedelics and entheogen therapies as tools to expand consciousness/awareness to what's been obscured in our subconscious as blocks to our wellness. More truth tellers are coming forward with their stories of healing PTSD, addictions, mental illness, and so many other medical conditions. These substances are healing conditions that modern medicine has struggled to do a good job of healing.

My adult son asked me if it was heat or cold to put on a pulled muscle in his shoulder. I told him I did not know; why didn't he ask himself what he needed? Hours later, I asked him if it was heat or cold. He said it was neither. He needed to stretch that area to release the tension and tightness. He said he knew that a nerve had gotten pinched or trapped and needed to be released. I asked him how he felt now. He said great because the stretching released the pain he was experiencing.

How often do you ask yourself what you need? Maybe the better question is, How often do you pause and listen for the answer? And then trust and act on it? If this is what you put into action this week, you'll be well on your way to getting the results you want.

A coaching client was having anxiety attacks and went to her doctor for a prescription. In our conversation, I asked her how the medicine was working. She replied, "I'm really not happy with it. I still have anxiety, and now I feel numb to my husband's bad day and my daughter's good day." She said she didn't feel like herself. I asked her what she was doing about it, and she replied "nothing." She said she would bring it up to her doctor in a few weeks when she went back in for a follow-up appointment. She is not alone; this seems to be a common approach.

After a few weeks of hearing about her situation with no change or resolve, I asked her if she was open to looking at her anxiety from another approach. I asked her if she was interested in getting to the root of the anxiety. She said yes, so I asked her to step into the Observer role so that she could gain perspective on her situation, assuring her that in the Observer role, she would be a bit detached from the anxiety and able to see its initial start. She would be able to spot the moment that triggered her anxiety. As the Observer, you step into your power, putting space between you and your experience. It's in that space where all the insight, awareness, and magic come forth.

She agreed. I asked her to share with me the last time she had an anxiety attack and what was going on. It had been that week, in the office, working on a project that was due by end of day. The day started out okay, but after a few interruptions, phone calls, and a longer-than-planned lunch, she started feeling pressure to finish. After returning from lunch, she saw an email from her boss, questioning her report and her progress. My client stopped sharing with a long pause. I asked her how she felt after lunch, first before reading the email and then after reading the email. She said lunch was good. She was ready to get back to work and wrap up this project…then the email. She noticed while reading the email, she shifted. She noticed the pressure coming into her body after reading the email. She started to notice her own thoughts and stories around the pressure. She noticed her blame— blaming her boss for pressuring her and blaming the email. She knew she was doing the best she could. She started to panic, thinking of all the worst-case scenarios: how she doesn't do well under pressure; how she was going to screw it up, make mistakes, and be late getting the project completed.

When my client paused, I let her sit in the silence of what she had just experienced. In her pause, she laughed out loud. She stated boldly, "My own inner critic was having a heyday with me." And worst of all, she said, "I bought it, I believed it. In believing it, I created the anxiety attack." Wow! This was a groundbreaking insight. This was her habit-breaking insight. This was the start of her being able to end this type of anxiety attack once and for all.

This was great awareness. But the work was not done yet. I told her, "You have a habit of listening to this inner critic. You have a habit of believing it is true. So, let's create a plan of action that will prevent this in the future." Together, I helped her see some options, and she was able to form a plan on how she would respond the next time. Pause a moment. Imagine what plan you would have put in place for yourself if this were your experience. There is never only one way to create change. Your best plan will come from *you*, not from doing what others do.

This is also how *people* create stress in the workplace. What one person calls stress in the job, another will effortlessly move through with ease. It's often the stories going on in our head that create the stress. Don't think I'm saying that a boss or organization does not have rules, regulations, and demands on you in the position you hold. They do. **But how you respond or react to these rules and demands is what creates stress…or not.** The demands are not stress. Demands are simply another's request and call to action. They can be expressed as expectations and rules mandating you to comply, but nothing in these mandates force you to feel a certain way.

It is a well-known fact that poor leadership is the greatest cause of resignation these days. When you don't feel heard, valued, and respected, it's difficult to stick around, to do your best, or to have trust and faith in the organization.

*A bad boss can cause all the great employees
to leave and those that stay to lose all
motivation.*

Awareness to the current cultures and practices in business are on the rise. As more organizations are noticing the need for an environment supportive for all to thrive in, individual well-being rises to the top of their list. They are noticing a need for a culture reform—the need for harmony, respect, and everyone feeling valued as an important part of the whole.

This huge shift happening now is bringing education on both sides—the side of management and the side of the employee. Management is realizing the need to work *with* people instead of applying mandates, directives, and pressure along the way. Management must also have the ability to see individuals' strengths and utilize those strengths in the work they perform, using their social awareness and organizational awareness skills. Management can impact and influence others to see other employees' strengths and thus empower them. Management's shifts will empower employees to better monitor, manage, and master themselves, their responses, and thus their feelings and behavior. Great management also allows employees to voice their opinions, concerns, and ideas, and respects and appreciates the value each person brings, which fuels innovation and change.

Wellness is not just physical well-being. Wellness is mental and emotional well-being. Wellness is spiritual well-being. Wellness is when all of your intelligence systems are working and functioning efficiently in harmony together.

When workplace wellness is at the center of everything, it will create a ripple effect of harmony. This ripple will bring growth, innovation, and prosperity to the organization. This ripple will go out even further to the customers they serve and the community they support to bring unity, connection, and so much more.

*The key to wellness is to accept personal
responsibility for your health and well-being.
The power lies in knowing yourself, growing
yourself, to live your life empowered.*

INVITATION

On a scale of 1 to 5, with 5 being perfect health and well-being (you wouldn't change a thing) and 1 being you have a lot of work to do to get healthy and create well-being in your life (you are not healthy and you know it), how do you rate your level of well-being?

Make a commitment. Place your hand on your heart and say to yourself, "Peace, well-being, and happiness are my natural states. Today I will practice coming back to my natural state to experience peace, well-being, and happiness." Decide how often you will practice this: morning, noon, and night; hourly; or every half hour. Decide your ultimate aim. Share with your circle of support the impact this is having.

What are you willing to do to take 100 percent responsibility for your health?

- Maybe you start with believing you can be healthier than you currently are and question what that might look like.
- Maybe you entertain "what if I were healthier?" thoughts.
- Maybe you are ready to create a plan to be healthier.
- Maybe you are healthy and ready for a detox or to try something new like rock climbing, pickleball, or dancing.
- Maybe you are ready to challenge yourself for 30 days or 75 days to push your peak potential and increase your well-being.

No matter where you are comfortable beginning, just begin.

Make a list of your habits and practices that don't support your well-being.

CHAPTER 18:

EMPOWERMENT THROUGH ENGAGEMENT

This chapter will show you how to use your engagement with others to empower and grow yourself. When you are empowered, you give others permission to step into their power. When you are empowered, you are grateful, appreciative, and feel good, and it shows. Pause a moment and reflect: do you feel empowered right now?

It's important to understand first what keeps us from engaging. This is as personal as it gets in answering the *why* for you. So don't just grasp at one example and say that's why. Often the real why is buried deeper than you really want to go. So be bold. Be courageous. And be loving and compassionate in your inner exploration.

You may avoid engaging with others for many reasons. Here are a few:

- You don't like them.
- You think they don't like you.
- You don't find value in interactions.
- You are uncomfortable with interactions.
- You don't feel confident.
- You lack self-esteem.
- You don't know what to expect and the unknown scares you.
- You don't feel safe.
- You don't feel respected.
- You don't have good communication or listening skills.
- You feel you are better than others.

- You think they won't understand you.
- You have memories of past interactions that keep you from creating new ones.
- You don't know the value of interactions.

It's necessary to bust the myths of your beliefs around interacting with others. Everyone—yes, every single human being—is acting out an inner reflection of themselves. What does this mean? It means, *as within, so without.* It means that every feeling and emotion you have inside is what you bring to the world, to others, and to every engagement.

Your engagement is an inner reflection of your stories, beliefs, and comfort within yourself. When you are aware of this, when you bring all of you to the party, and when you get curious as to the inner shifts necessary to have the interactions you would love, you then see the empowerment that engagement brings. Allow me to explain further.

If you don't like someone, you will act and behave accordingly. And guess what? There are no private thoughts. Your energy and actions speak a silent language that others receive. How you feel about the other person is often felt and known. Others can feel your energy.

If you think they don't like you, you will avoid them because no one wants to feel rejected. If you do have to interact, you will look for validation that they don't like you—a word, a gesture, something that you personally give meaning too. This validation goes on unconsciously. I'm not saying that you knowingly look for validation. It's the way we are wired in the human experience. It's all going on behind the scenes in a sneaky and yet supportive way.

If what keeps you from interacting and engaging with others is a story or belief about them…well, maybe it's time for you to take 100 percent responsibility for what's going on inside you. Until you are self-aware to see the stories you have crafted or believed about another, you won't be able to move beyond them.

As I was growing spiritually, I attended an ACIM (A Course in Miracles) conference. This was the first time in my life that I truly *felt* I was surrounded by loving, accepting, and supportive people. I'm a reflector as described by Human Design, or an empath by others' definition. I have always felt the energies of others. I also often feel the judgments of others. I notice the disconnect between the words they say and the energy I feel. At this conference, I truly felt the love and connection with all. It was powerful. One man, Dave Fishman, whom

I will forever cherish and remember, introduced me to a phrase I wish to share with you: **"You spot it, you got it."**

Allow me to explain this phrase because so many get it confused. It's easy for us to say to another who might be expressing how they feel, which could come across as complaining or criticizing us, "you spot it, you got it," meaning that *they* have some inner work to do. If this happens, there is probably some defensiveness or avoidance going on in the one saying it. It's important to listen, to hear another, to validate what they are saying, feeling, and expressing, and to reflect from the Observer self to see the situation from their perspective. You just might see something in yourself you hadn't been able to see before. If you are blaming another or thinking that *they* need to change, I invite you to pause. I invite you to reflect on how you feel. It's in your feelings where the message lies.

> *You may be wanting to blame the messenger*
> *and, in doing so, avoid the message they bring.*

"You spot it, you got it," showed me with clarity that whatever I was seeing, feeling, and experiencing was in me. In this situation, all that love and support I felt was what I, too, brought to the conference. He showed me the beautiful reflection of myself being reflected back to me from each and every being. Keep in mind, this was a conference of some highly conscious individuals. Keep in mind that I, too, was growing in my spirituality and learning to come from my center, from love, peace, joy, and well-being.

"You spot it, you got it," can also show you what you most need to see and shift within yourself. Let's say you think someone doesn't like you. This is when it can be of value to look at how this makes you feel. It's in blaming others that we avoid the real message within. First, address the feeling that this thought brings you. How does it make you feel when you think another doesn't like you? Then, I would invite you to look within and see where you may not like yourself. Reflect on this a moment. If you are able to shift your own self-love first and then release the hold you have on the thought or belief that another person doesn't like you, you will allow this energy to move or to transform. And you will allow a new experience.

If you don't feel confident or have low self-esteem, engagement with others can be challenging for you. You'll want to do your best to avoid reminding yourself of your low self-esteem or lack of confidence. Thus, you'll avoid interactions. Confidence comes from having the experience and seeing you are okay, in noticing that all went well. Confidence comes from experiences. Small steps in interactions with others can build your confidence quickly. Start with what feels natural to you—a hello, a compliment, or a question you know they can answer.

It's through your engagement with others that you will find your own empowerment. Without engagement with others, you won't have the reflection of those parts in you that need healing, release, or alignment.

Your human experience is complex and diverse. Not a single human being gets an owner's manual on how to self-operate the intricacy of their four intelligence systems or how to be in a human experience. *Bringing Spirituality into Business* can be your owner's manual. Let it show you your innate power. Let it show you how to know yourself, grow yourself, and live your life empowered.

> *It's through your engagement and interaction
> with others that you will see more of yourself.*

Have you ever heard that old saying, "You only hurt the ones you love"? It's in those deep, intimate relationships with others that all of your own inner hurt is brought to the surface. Yes, it's brought to the surface and then projected out onto others. We live in a world where we have not done a very good job at healing our hurt, our pain, and our problems. When you understand *as within, so without*, you'll also understand that hurt people hurt people—often unintentionally.

> *Hurt people hurt others.*

It's not because we don't want to heal. It's because we *don't know how* to heal and we lack awareness. Our mental health professionals have been trained in a model that isn't working. It's no fault of the mental health providers; they have stepped forward with their heart in the right place to make a difference and help others. Schooling and training for the mental health field was the first of its time, and as it's called, they are *practicing* medicine. Even the doctors, therapists, and educators in the field are learning as they go. We now have enough data to see that more work needs to be done in the mental health field.

We also know that to truly understand and, thus heal, means to mend at the root cause.

Talk therapy allows one to talk about their problems. This certainly is better than holding it all in. It certainly helps one be clear on the story they are telling. But until one is aware of what they really want, how can the effectiveness of the therapy be measured? Talk therapy is beneficial when there is a goal or aim in all that is discussed, an end result of accomplishment.

I had a meeting with a woman who wanted me to understand her pain and wanted to tell me story after story to allow me to truly understand. When I told her that I didn't need to know any of the stories, she was befuddled. It shocked her. I thought she was about to leave. It really pissed her off that she didn't get to share her pain. You see, she had become so attached to *why* she thought she was where she is.

Where are you holding on to your pain so much that when you aren't allowed to share it, it pisses you off? Or, when others aren't interested in hearing your story, it bothers you?

Once she could allow me to ask her some important questions, she was able to start to release her hold on those stories. I asked her what she wanted. I asked her if we could wave a magic wand over your life right now, what is it that she would love to have? Until she knew what she wanted, what she was truly seeking, she wouldn't be able to see the value that each of her stories was trying to bring her. Without knowing what she really wanted in life, all those stories were simply validating her pain and hurt and thus showing her why she wasn't happy and successful.

It took her nearly an hour to even begin to get close to what she wants. Often when we have spent so much time validating our pain, we can easily get distracted from what we really want. You can focus on your past or you can focus on your future, but you cannot focus on both at the same time. Until you are ready to move forward, until you firmly decide to move forward, you will be pulled by the pain of your past. WHY? Because that is the habit within you that you have become comfortable with.

Engagement is powerful at every stage. You see, we need other people to help guide us in our journey through life. Other people empower us to realign and thus achieve our dreams and goals. Other people also connect us with a different perspective, thus expanding our awareness and allowing us to see a bigger picture. Other people bring talents and skills that we don't have. They fill in where we are weak. And you bring to others your strengths and talents to fill in where they are weak. Other people are mirrors to what we most need to see within.

Ernest Holmes said, "Life is a mirror and will reflect back to the thinker what he thinks into it." Everyone is your mirror. Your own reflection in others shows you not only who you are, but also how to be better.

> ## Everything that irritates us about others can lead to an understanding of ourselves. ~ Carl Jung

Only when you are able to see and use the message that another brings will you be able to understand this mirror. It won't come in their words or actions but in what their words or actions stimulate in you. The mirror is seen when you can look at the feelings and messages within you that their words and actions cause or create.

The Ford Institute website explains this phenomenon brilliantly:

> ## The way you feel about yourself on the inside determines what you will create for yourself on the outside.

It continues, "Your external world is a direct reflection of your internal world. The way you feel about yourself in the privacy of your own thoughts will show up in the quality of your relationships" and your ability to engage and interact with others, proclaiming the key to unlocking this "lies hidden in your shadow."

The work of the Ford Institute goes on to say that your "shadow is made up of all the parts of [your]self that [you] hide, deny, suppress, and don't see in [yourself]—both the positive and the negative. [Your] shadow is all the aspects that [you] reject out of shame, fear, or disapproval. It is made up of any part of [yourself] that [you] believe is unacceptable, will be met with disapproval by others, or that annoys, horrifies, or disgusts [you] about other people or about [yourself]." As Carl Jung said, "Our shadow is the person we would rather not be."

With all this knowledge and understanding about others being mirrors and the need to address our shadows, why is it that it's not being addressed? It's time we have these courageous conversations—the conversations that heal. It's time to stop avoiding the elephant in the room and stand up to do the necessary work to be fully ourselves.

In the workplace, businesses are struggling to create engagement. But they are going about it in all the wrong ways. They are trying to force it from the outside in. It's next to impossible to make people want to engage with others when they have never learned to engage with themselves. Everything starts within. And yet most of these trainings are focused on trying to alter one's outward behavior and expression. As I polled numerous companies on their past trainings, the responses were all the same. Employees felt the engagement trainings were a way to force them to behave differently. Many felt resistance to the training, and thus, the training proved not beneficial.

When we look at healing the disconnect, the disengagement within us, we will correct the outward expression of this in the workplace. It's Universal Law, the law of cause and effect.

There are two main reasons for disengagement in the workplace. The first reason lies in the internally disengaged employee. The second is ineffective management. Some managers may be psychologically absent or lacking awareness and therefore fail to build meaningful connections with their teams. They may lack their own inner engagement. Ineffective management leads to high levels of stress and low employee morale and, eventually, active disengagement.

Bringing Spirituality into Business is meant to correct the inner workings and the leadership structure within the business and bring awareness to the importance for leadership training and development, focusing its aim at individual empowerment. When the leadership and management of the organization are trained and experienced in creating effective teams and teamwork, engagement and better communication follow naturally.

Empowerment through engagement means that as you engage with those parts of you that have become disconnected, judgmental, and feeling separate and alone, you will empower yourself back to being whole and complete. In this process, you will additionally empower yourself to see the value you bring to others and your workplace. This allows engagement to be natural and beneficial. Once you can see your own value, you will be better able to see the value others bring and thus want to engage, as it's in the engagement with one another that your true potential and talents are brought forth.

INVITATION

Look at some of the reasons why you don't engage at the beginning of this chapter. Being totally honest with yourself, how many of those apply to you?

_____

_____

Reflect on one fairly current situation where you have an opinion about someone in your workplace. Observe what you see in them that you don't like or fear.

_____

_____

After reflecting and noticing what you dislike or fear in the other person, turn this around to where you see this in yourself. This may take a bit for it to surface since it lies in your subconscious.

_____

_____

CHAPTER 19:

CRITICAL THINKING AND COMPLEX PROBLEM SOLVING

Each year, research firms like Gallup collect and share data from their surveys. One of the surveys they regularly do is a list of skills that businesses should focus on improving and look for in hiring new talent. Critical thinking and complex problem solving have been on this list for a few years and has now risen to the top of the top ten.

With all the advancements in artificial intelligence (AI), which is programming a computer to do what people do and more, we now realize how important critical thinking and complex problem solving are. Think about it for a moment: The programmer must use critical thinking, have 360-degree awareness, and apply complex problem solving to do a good job at the coding required to get superb operations and results from the program they create. For AI to work well, a range of skills are necessary.

It is now evident that businesses need to work on the skills of critical thinking and complex problem solving. Is this so that all organizations have their own talent to create and use AI proficiently? Or is it to make sure that their people are advancing equal to and greater than the rate of digital technology? It's both and more. Training and professional growth and development have not had a front seat in the advancements in business until now.

Bringing Spirituality into Business is one big step toward advancing the human to new and greater potential. Its focus is on personal growth and development of the unused, untapped knowledge, resources, and inherent talent that lies within you. Its aim is to improve and advance human potential to be greater than the technology we have created to support us. Humans were never meant to be completely replaced by technology.

Sure, automation is great, necessary, and cost effective, and many, many things will shift to being fully automated. One example of these advancements is the push to self-driving cars. Eventually, this will greatly affect an entire field of work for humans. Truck drivers, delivery services, taxicabs, Uber drivers, bus drivers, and more could be replaced by this technology.

Let's begin by looking at where your mind goes when you think about being replaced by a machine or automation. Do you get angry because you or someone you know and love will lose their job? Do you get creative in your thinking about other opportunities for those in that industry? If you have learned anything in reading this book, I hope you have learned to focus on what you can control and not what you can't. What is meant here is that you can't change technology and the creative flow of change, but you can control how you think about it. What if every time you found yourself angry and upset over something greater than you, something you have no power to change, you could **pause** and reflect to observe yourself. Observe the insanity in getting upset over a massive change in technology.

You have an innate ability to solve things. By your very human nature, you are equipped with all you need to **solve** any problem. The fact, and often the problem, is that many people try to solve the problem from the same level of consciousness with which the problem was created. This doesn't work well and causes the individual to think they can't solve it or they aren't good at solving problems. Frustration, aggravation, stress, and anxiety set in.

We cannot solve our problems with the same thinking we used when we created them. ~ Albert Einstein

If you are getting upset at new technology and angry over things you have no control over, you are stuck in the energy from which the problem was created. I know this is hard to see and understand from your anger and upset. Rise to a new level of consciousness and all becomes clearer. Step into being the Observer.

You can fight against war, or you can focus on the peace and harmony you wish to achieve. One focuses on the problem, the other focuses on the solution—the end result you wish to obtain.

Being objective is a fundamental part of critical thinking. This requires analyzing the problem without allowing personal bias, emotions, or assumptions to influence how you think. A strong critical thinker will only analyze a problem based on the context and facts collected after conducting thorough and impartial research. Strengthening your ability to be objective requires self-awareness and discipline.

It cannot be expressed enough the value of being the Observer. Being a good Observer enables you to take a step back and peak into yourself and others. Just looking produces nothing. Observing produces insights when you assess for patterns, styles, and results. In the workplace and in your personal life, in relationships and social gatherings, observing will provide you a full 360-degree perception, control of your emotions, and alertness to what might be out of the ordinary or having an undesired effect.

Critical thinking requires you to walk through a process and to be open to observing what you think the problem is, but not being so rigid in your thinking that you are not open to what may reveal itself. Think flexibility and adaptability. Think open and receptive.

Here are steps you might take when using critical thinking at work to solve a problem:

1. Identify a problem or issue.
2. Collect information and data on the issue through research.
3. Organize and sort data and findings.
4. Form inferences on the problem, analyze, and formulate solutions.
5. Develop and execute solutions.
6. Analyze which solutions worked or didn't work.
7. Identify ways to improve the solution.

Critical thinking and complex problem solving go hand in hand. They are like peanut butter and jelly or bread and butter. **Critical thinking** is defined as the objective analysis and evaluation of an issue in order to form a judgment.

Complex problem solving is a series of observations and informed decisions used to find and implement a solution to a problem. Complex problem solving also involves considering the impact of the solution on the surrounding environment and individuals. It requires definition, validity, and assessment along with thorough and complete thought processes to review and assess the outcome. Even with all the work and observation, analysis, and assessment, you may find your solution did not bring the results you were seeking. It's important to monitor, manage, and assess your results. Focus is on the solution and not the problem.

This is where building the right team is of the utmost value. Team building is both an art and a science. It's a process that, when well-planned and organized, will produce the results you want quickly and easily. Some people work best digging into problems to uncover the root cause, and others work best when focused on the desired outcome. You need both on your team. When solving problems, you must maintain focus on the ultimate aim.

These four tips can foster improvement of your problem-solving skills:

1. **Focus on the solution.** It's easy to become hyper-focused on the conditions that created the problem.
2. **Clearly define the problem.** It's hard to solve a nebulous problem you never took the time to clearly define.
3. **Agree on a process.** Lay out the steps you'll take and the structure of your process.
4. **Implement active listening.** Listening to understand the ideas and views of others will take you out of your own view and narrow mindset and allow you to see a bigger perspective.

One thing is certain: both critical thinking and complex problem solving are best utilized in group settings. When working alone with critical thinking, you might benefit from a quick five-minute sharing of your ideas, awareness, observations, and resolutions to simply hear yourself processing out loud. This can evoke a new insight or spur a question from the listener that greatly helps you. Ask your boss or a coworker to allow you to share your work to better process your ideas and allow you the clarity and think time you need.

You are unique. Your human design is specific to you. Knowing how you function best, your strengths, your weaknesses, and the value you bring can powerfully shift the results you get and how fast you'll be able to progress through your work, specifically the challenging projects. If you experience a block or overwhelm, take a break—step away from the work for a few minutes, take a walk, or close your eyes to clear your thoughts. Before you begin again, bring all of you to the party, set an intention for what you aim to achieve, and regain your focus to begin again.

Two things will aid you in developing your proficiency in both critical thinking and complex problem solving. The first one is "slow down to speed up," and the second one is the power of the "flow state." When I first introduced this concept to business leaders, they thought I was insane. They had formed habits of pressuring themselves to achieve more, to work hard and for long hours. If you are thinking slowing down is crazy, take a PAUSE. Allow the thought to sink in: *Slow down...to speed up.* In the slowing down, you will allow insight and intuition to serve you. You'll be better able to recenter yourself, to bring all of you to the party. In slowing down, you'll allow your brain to pause and clear itself to gain clarity, focus, and better concentration. This is one of the most important lessons you can learn. I can't emphasize enough the need to practice this one. Slowing down releases tension, anxiety, and force, and allows you to increase your capacity to hold many ideas, perceptions, and resources in your awareness to see a bigger picture.

> *Sometimes you have to slow down*
> *in order to speed up.*

If you normally work hard, hustle, and force yourself, this thought might be met with great resistance. If this is you, I invite you to play with the idea of slowing down to speed up. Until you have experimented with not forcing and learning to slow down, you won't know the value it offers you.

One of the greatest benefits of slowing down to speed up is when you drop into the zone, also known as a flow state. Many high-level executives have looked for ways to biohack their way into states of "flow." **Flow is a state of mind in which a person becomes fully immersed in an activity**, in which one can get a day's worth of work done in mere hours. In the flow state, there is a balance between challenge and skill; your tasks feel effortless, you move through time with ease, and it's as if you are supported by something that is guiding you. Insight, intuition, and action meld into a seamless process. Flow is a powerful state of mind where you are extremely productive and you feel great. You don't have to force yourself to work hard. The truth is, getting into flow state is not something that only happens by accident; you can actually put yourself in flow state proactively.

You are more creative and productive when in flow.

The flow state was named by psychologist Mihaly Csikszentmihalyi in 1975, when he first introduced the concept in his book, *Beyond Boredom and Anxiety: Experiencing Flow in Work and Play.* The concept has been widely referred to across a variety of fields (and is particularly well recognized in occupational therapy), though it's been claimed that the concept has existed for thousands of years under other names. He discovered that people find genuine satisfaction being in a state of consciousness called *flow.*

The flow state shares many characteristics with hyperfocus. However, hyperfocus is not always described in a positive light. Some examples include spending too much time playing video games, bingeing on Netflix, or becoming pleasurably absorbed by one aspect of an assignment or task to the detriment of the overall assignment.

The flow state engages concentration, skill, the present moment, the unknown, the challenge, and your ultimate aim. Many athletes know this state well. It's where they seem to surrender into the moment and allow everything to unfold as pure perfection. Runners have called it their second wind. Surfers describe it as being one with the wave. Many athletes describe the flow state as a shift of the mind; they proclaim to experience total calmness and a complete awareness of what is going on and yet an effortlessness in their performance, as if they merely observe and feel one with the activity.

It's in highly focused tasks like critical thinking and complex problem solving that many will benefit from slowing down to speed up and experience states of flow.

This is for sure: there is greatness in you. You have more power, abilities, and potential just waiting to be unleashed.

INVITATION

Practice the seven steps listed earlier to use critical thinking to solve a problem. Chunk it down and only do one step at a time.

Put a break of at least one hour between each of the steps and observe how easily and efficiently you are able to move through each step. If one step challenges you, repeat it, coming at it from a different angle or perspective before moving on to the next step.

Once you can successfully use all seven steps independently, you'll be able to put them together for a more cohesive flow.

Practice slowing down to speed up. Be sure to monitor what you notice in your slowing down. Notice the calmness that comes over you. Notice your clarity come forth. Notice the regrouping of ideas, your energies, and your ability to expand your awareness as you slow down.

SECTION III: EMPOWER

TIPS, TRAININGS, AND TOOLS

In Section I: Educate, you learned the basics, which laid the foundation to discover and implement your soul's mission and journey here. It's through the knowledge and understanding of the basics that you build a blueprint and lay forth a structure for your growth and development.

In Section II: Engage, you learned to connect the knowledge and understanding from Section I with application and integration. In this section, you were invited to be fully present and allow the words to live through you. You awakened your wisdom and connected with all parts of you. You assessed where you are, explored awareness, stepped into the Observer, and learned the value in bringing all of you to every experience. You engaged all aspects of you to be fully present.

In this final section, you'll use all that you've learned and all you have, inside YOU, to live your life empowered. You'll be putting all that the first two sections spoke to in action. You'll learn a few tips to help you along the way, like the power of a question—not just any question, but the right question—how curiosity is a good space to be in, and what it means to see your shadows and the power in your vision.

This section will talk about ongoing and additional trainings to aid in your journey through life, daily practices that you may want to make part of your day, as well as the obstacles that could derail and destroy your dreams. You'll learn both the ways to help yourself along the journey and the blocks, limitations, and aspects of being human that show up to delay and distract you along the journey of your life. You'll be empowered to see where you are putting on the brakes and taking detours that prevent you from reaching the results you seek.

This last section will also explore and discuss tools that may enhance and advance you, both ancient wisdom and modern untapped modalities that heal your human wounds and expand consciousness. You'll be introduced to what our ancestors knew and what many others know as truth, power, and wisdom. You'll learn about free or readily available resources that you may have never considered, from ways of healing and transformation, from altered states to sound and frequency, to plants as medicines and the power of the breath.

This last section is meant to empower you in your unique and beautiful being that you are. It will ground you and aid you in remembering all that you are and all that you came here to be. You are magnificent. Your life has meaning and purpose at a deep level that is often masked by the details of your active and busy life.

Enjoy this last section and allow it to expand you beyond your current reality. Let it sweep you into the ethers of the cosmos, into the quantum field of all possibilities, to explore yourself and who you are at the core.

This section concludes with bringing you home—home to yourself, where you have never left. Oh, the beauty of this human experience! May you find richness and reward in the pages that follow and allow them to empower you to being all that you are.

CHAPTER 20:

SHINING LIGHT ON YOUR SHADOWS

Your shadows have been talked about through all of time. Not "your" shadows specifically, but shadows in general. They are like the elephant in the room—you know, that topic that few wish to discuss. It's big. It's obnoxious. It's in everyone's awareness. And yet, it is often avoided, taboo, rejected as if poison or sinful.

Shadows are those dejected parts of us that lie hidden deep within: hidden in your past memories; hidden in your stories; hidden in your hurt, betrayal, abandonment, or loss. Shadows lie in your subconscious. It's all that you deny in yourself—whatever you perceive as inferior, evil, or unacceptable. But guess what? All that's denied becomes part of your shadow.

Your shadows, these unexamined or disowned parts of your personality, don't really go anywhere. Although you deny them in your attempt to cast them out, you don't get rid of them. They'll hang around but remain in your subconscious; you'll be unaware, which makes it easier to steer clear or ignore the hell out of them. But they don't go away on their own. In fact, your aim is not to make them go away or disappear, but to integrate them, to own them.

Until you make the unconscious conscious, it will direct your life and you will call it fate. ~ Carl Jung

Your shadows show up when you least expect them. They show up again and again, and when they do, they are often projected outward. They can cause you regret, suffering, and often guilt and shame. Ultimately, the more you suppress feelings and negative emotions into the subconscious, the greater the power they have over you. Furthermore, they can assert themselves in different ways. This could be through mental health issues, chronic illness, anxiety, addiction, or low self-esteem.

Here's a fact: you can't live your life empowered without integrating your shadows. You must explore them if you wish to live from your beautiful, whole, and centered being. These shadows taint and camouflage your radiance. They veil your true essence and beauty. It's time for some truth telling. Be honest with yourself. Do you really wish to avoid or suppress parts of you? Sit with this question if you must because no one is making you shine the loving light of awareness on your shadows. No one. Know this. You control YOU.

While we are being honest, let me be honest with you. It will take courage for you to look at your shadows—not maybe, not just a little—it *will* take a boatload of courage. You'll need to muster this courage. Not because these shadow aspects are big and bad and fight back with a double-edged sword of strength and power, but because you have made them bigger than you. You have feared them. You have taught your inner operating system that you can't deal with them. You've sent messages to your central nervous system that these parts of you are bad and you want to hide them—hide them from the world and hide them from yourself. Why are you afraid of your shadow?

Fearing your shadows is both a cultural and societal conditioning passed down from generations. We live in the most powerful of times. We live in times when the human potential is being brought into its fullness. This fullness is showing us that we are in the process of making more, becoming more than we have been in the past. Humans are evolving. You are shown new tools to see your reality and to spot your blocks to the fullness of life and yourself. Your shadows are simply blocks to all that you are.

Fearing your shadow will:
- Keep you playing small
- Prevent you from evolving
- Keep you from becoming all that you are here to become
- Limit your growth and development

- Hold you bound by your fears

The shadow's aspect and role depend greatly on the living experience you have had because much of the shadow develops in your mind rather than simply being inherited in the collective consciousness.

So, if you are fully onboard to look at and integrate these heavy anchors that are literally holding you hostage and preventing you from living an empowered life, *pause*. Take a deep breath. With courage and confidence, put your hand on your heart. Take another deep breath and say with me, "I am fully ready to look at my shadows and release myself from the hold they have on me, preventing me from living my joy and purpose. I wish to fully integrate all aspects of me into my being."

Many amazing people like Byron Katie, Debbie Ford, and Louise Hay have shared their process and procedure for exploring, transmuting, and integrating these shadows within. This work goes back in time to Jung and Freud and before. It's been a part of human history since, well, forever. No more avoiding it. We have all the power and resources we need to create change. YOU have all the power and resources to face your shadows and create and live a life without the restraints and limitation of your shadow aspects. You have the power and potential to integrate all aspects of yourself into your wholeness, so that no one aspect has the power to limit you or hold you back.

Shadow work, in psychology, is a term for
everything we can't see in ourselves.

The shadow is the "dark side" of your personality because it consists primarily of primitive, negative human emotions and impulses like rage, envy, greed, selfishness, desire, and the striving for power. But don't let it fool you—it has both positive and negative aspects.

Everyone carries a shadow... ~ Jung

Your shadow includes everything outside the light of consciousness and may be positive or negative. Because we tend to reject or remain ignorant of the least desirable aspects of our personalities, the shadow is perceived to be largely negative. This is not true. There are positive aspects that may also remain hidden in one's shadow. This can be seen in people with low self-esteem, anxieties, and false beliefs.

...the less it is embodied in the individual's conscious life, the blacker and denser it is. ~ Jung

More importantly, when the shadow self contains a side of the personality that is potentially destructive, then the conscious mind is not able to fully address those traits or recognize that they might be a problem. For example, when we are disengaged from our shadow, it can lead us to practice something that Jung referred to as a **psychological projection**. This is the process whereby we recognize and criticize undesirable qualities in others that we, in fact, hold ourselves. Sound familiar?

If you are noticing undesirable qualities in someone else, you might benefit from "The Work" by Byron Katie. In her mighty process she calls "The Work," she offers a direct and powerful approach to working with projections in general and the shadow in particular. Byron Katie created the "Judge-Your-Neighbor Worksheet." This worksheet is a process where she helps you first project without holding back, then examine this projection, and lastly, find what you see in the other also in yourself. This is powerful work. It has the ability to shift your perception as it allows you to see in yourself all those qualities you despise in someone else.

Each step helps make the process gentler, as together, they make it easier to find in yourself what you see in another, recognize it, own it, and often experience relief from (finally) finding and acknowledging it in you. It requires practice and repetition. After doing this process many times, it also becomes easier to do it spontaneously and naturally in your everyday life. The inquiry lives in you (more on this in Chapter 24).

I want to make sure you understand the term projection. **Psychological projection** is when a perceived personal inferiority is recognized as a perceived moral deficiency in someone else. Stated another way, projection is the mental process by which people attribute to others what is in their own minds. For example, individuals who are in a self-critical state, consciously or unconsciously, may think that other people are critical of them.

Projection refers to a type of defense mechanism, whereby unacceptable feelings and self-attributes within yourself are disavowed and attributed to someone else. An example is a man who has an attraction to a woman in the office but doesn't come to terms with what is going on in himself and denies it, and then accuses his wife of being attracted to another man. Or a woman who's dieting but recently cheated on her diet accuses her partner of intentionally making dieting hard for her by tempting her and eating in front of her the same foods she cannot have.

In business, there has been a push to understand our feminine and masculine energies and to bring more balance to these qualities. A man who has been called a sissy or a baby in his childhood says to a coworker, "Toughen up, man. You're acting like a girl."

The resistance to own the softer, gentler, more compassionate aspects within ourselves is unconsciously projected outward and seen as dislike and judgment of others. It's a real slippery slope; as stated, you could be (and often are) unconscious of your own inner workings (your own inner upset) and projecting onto others what is going on inside you. It's easy to see when someone else is projecting. It's a lot more difficult to notice when you're the one projecting. Why? Because projection is typically unconscious.

Some signs you might be projecting are:
- Feeling overly defensive, hurt, or sensitive about something someone else said or did
- Feeling highly reactive or quick to blame
- Difficulty being objective, gaining perspective, or seeing another's point of view
- Noticing that this situation or your reactivity is a recurring pattern

If you can accept all of your thoughts and feelings and not try to get rid of them, you won't need to project them onto others. In addition, you will become a more tolerant and flexible person.

So, what can you do when you are feeling hurt or defensive? What can you do if you feel quick to blame? If you notice any signs you might be projecting, ask yourself:
- Is the behavior I dislike in this person something I find intolerable in myself?
- In what ways do I act like this person?
- What types of stories am I telling myself about this person or situation?
- Who or what does this person or situation remind me of?

There's a reason why this chapter comes in Section III. You needed to learn awareness and the Observer to aid you in spotting your shadows, these hidden aspects within. You needed to be able to bring all of you (EQ, IQ, SQ, and PQ) in this present moment so not to be overly emotional, all in your head, or resistant to even seeing your role in it. You need an unbiased lens with which to view what's going on to see where you are not dealing with your shadows.

In the book *The Secret of the Shadow*, Debbie Ford shows how your shadow side holds the key to your happiness. She reminds you that you have a shadow that whispers stories of your own self-defeating fears to you. For example: that you aren't enough, that you are unworthy of being loved, that you will be deserted by those whom you care about. Debbie guides you to hear those stories and find the positive message within each of them. She shows how understanding your own shadow side can lead you to lives of tremendous fulfillment and peace. Her book is packed full of case studies and exercises to help you through integrating your shadow aspects.

The Shadow Effect, which is both a book and a movie, combines and shares the groundbreaking work of three *New York Times* best-selling authors—Debbie Ford, Deepak Chopra, and Marianne Williamson—to deliver a comprehensive and practical guide to harnessing the power of your dark side. It's a journey through awareness, acceptance, forgiveness, and being okay with your shadow. It's a powerful message that creates compassion and understanding of oneself and others.

The Shadow Effect, as a movie, can be viewed with a gaia.com subscription or via HayHouse.com for a streaming fee. I highly recommend businesses mix up the way they educate, engage, and empower their people, and this can be a creative and fun way to add value, growth, and development.

As stated earlier, it's easier to see when another is projecting. Here are six signs someone is projecting onto you:
1. They have selective hearing.
2. They don't see you for who you are.
3. They expect history to repeat itself.
4. They overreact.
5. They treat every argument the same way.
6. They put up walls.

You are not here to change another person. In fact, the only thing you can change is you, your thoughts, perceptions, feelings, and actions. Knowing these signs of when another is projecting can aid you in recognizing if this relationship is one you wish to pursue. It aids you in knowing when to stop talking about a particular topic. It helps you understand and see the bigger picture, thus being able to make better choices.

This is of the utmost importance in working together in the workplace. How do you deal with projection in the workplace? Individually and together as a department or team, it's important to have regular conversations where managers model good communication and great listening skills. Next, having a plan in place for personal growth sets the stage for all to be more aware of themselves. Setting team guidelines of every voice being heard, hearing all points of view before reaching conclusions, and creating next steps together as a team are beginning steps to creating the outcomes that work.

Workplace culture and practices are changing. Businesses shifting and adopting a people-centric culture are on the rise. The rewards are many, and both management and employees are experiencing the win/win/win effect it has.

When we bring awareness to these aspects within each of us, we open up space for each and every person to look within. As you heal or learn to accept all aspects of yourself, you give others permission to do the same. What the world needs is more people ready, willing, and able to do the work necessary to learn and accept their shadows and thus themselves.

I can't share with you enough the power and joy you will experience when you are brave enough and bold enough to shine the loving light of awareness on your shadows. You will empower yourself more than you know when you bring your darkness to the light. Everything you've learned in the previous chapters of this book—awareness, the Observer role, and bringing all of you to the party—will aid you in your bold and courageous path to shining light on your dark side and illuminating your shadows.

In summary, everything you see in another is but a mere message for you to look within. It becomes a sign, a signal, to the work you must do, to see where you also hold this energy, subconsciously unaware. I saw the last decade of presidents in the U.S. bring out more shadows and also more people unaware of these aspects within themselves. As more human beings are becoming conscious and aware, it's becoming more obvious the need to foster greater personal and professional growth and development in the workplace. Best of all, the decisions, time, and energy spent will create the most positive win/win/win for all.

INVITATION

Invest the time to watch the movie *The Shadow Effect* if possible.

_____

_____

Take time to invest in your own shadow work via YouTube videos or a good book on healing your shadows.

_____

_____

Download the Judge-Your-Neighbor Worksheet and walk yourself through a few of your stories as you look at your shadows and allow the healing to happen. The "Judge-Your-Neighbor Worksheet" can be found at *www.thework.com* or see a printed version of it in the Companion Workbook.

_____

_____

CHAPTER 21:

VALUE OF A VISION

Throughout time, mankind has been told to "follow your dreams." Your dreams are your heart's desires, those sometimes subtle yet often big and bold desires to be, to accomplish, and to experience more in life. I believe your heart's desires are the way your Spiritual intelligence system communicates with you, letting you know what and where to lean in, to explore, and maybe even experience more than you deemed possible. It's your soul nudging you to be, do, and have all you were born to experience in this lifetime.

Maybe you have experienced those times when you did follow your heart's calling. It comes as a longing, an inner wish, a yearning, a hunger for that desire in your heart. Maybe you don't feel it with or in your heart; maybe you simply know it in your body, your bones, your blood. How and where you hear the longing matters not. Learning to listen to this message is what's of value and doesn't come easy for all.

As you become more present and aware to all of you—all four intelligence systems—you'll notice the longings of your heart, the dreams and desires you are meant to pursue and experience. You will want to allow yourself to become open and receptive to your Spiritual intelligence specifically. This intelligence system was the most challenging for me to grasp. But this was only because I had not learned to trust myself and thus to trust this inner guidance and allow it to guide me. Trust me: You want to learn to trust your Spiritual intelligence, for it knows more than you do.

I worked with a business owner that had programmed himself to *not* allow himself to hear and feel his heart's desires. It came to him as an insight in one of our discussions on creating his vision. An old story came into his mind saying, "You can't have that; don't even go there." This story went on to point out his limitations and validate all the reasons why he wasn't worthy or capable. As he shared the stories that were coming to his mind, he was able to see why he struggles to create a vision. In an effort to protect and avoid hurt and disappointment, he taught himself to avoid his heart's callings.

Together, we explored the original hurt and disappointment. Through his reflection, he was able to see the situation differently. He saw exactly what that event brought him instead of focusing on what it didn't bring him. He shifted his perspective and changed an old story that had been preventing him from listening to his heart.

I asked him how he got to be so successful in life. He shared that he has a passion for others and a natural ability to see beyond what they can see in themselves. He helps his employees see their talent and strengths, thus building their character, courage, and confidence. He is a great supporter for his wife and children, always helping them to believe in themselves and feel more confident in their own abilities.

As he was able to see what he is best at, I asked him how he uses his strengths to support himself. He smirked as he saw my point. You see, he had stopped serving and supporting his own dreams and desires. The gift and strength that he gives to others, he was not giving to himself. Had he become so focused on others—his wife, family, friends, employees—he had forgotten about himself? Or was there a deeper message as to why he had denied himself the right to dream, to allow himself to see his own desires?

We often teach others what we most need to learn ourselves.

As he opened to the desires within, he grew his business. He bought another company and merged their activities into one. He expanded more than his business. He met an amazing new friend who became his new CEO. He expanded his relationships and friendships, so his personal life expanded as well. His whole life changed as a result of leaning into the callings of his heart and his ability to create a vision for his future.

We are pushed by pain until we are pulled by vision. ~ Michael Bernard Beckwith

About a year later, this businessman asked me if I would work with his wife. She, too, struggled to hear the callings of her heart and her desires within, or so they thought. When we spoke, she said she felt jealous and envious of others who followed their dreams. She wanted and desired all that she saw others achieving but felt it all through jealousy, hurt, and disappointment that it wasn't happening for her.

I explained to her how to be the Observer and the viewer of her life. I told her that I was going to ask her some questions, and these questions were an invitation to recall past memories in her life. I explained that as these memories came up, she would be able to notice things coming into her awareness. I told her she would notice feelings, and these feelings were simply the emotions moving through her from the recall of that memory. I told her she would notice thoughts and a dialog in her mind would begin to play as if on auto replay. I asked her to go slow and share with me the feelings, sensations, thoughts, and stories that came forth.

As we talked, I asked her if she could recall a dream of her childhood. I asked her to share with me a time in her life when she allowed herself to dream, to want, and then to believe that her wants and dreams were possible. Immediately she recalled that she had always wanted to be married to her best friend, to find a husband and life companion. She said she found and dated her now husband for a few years and then married this amazing man. She proclaimed that to this day, he is still the most amazing person in her life. He was the best decision she ever made.

Then she started to recall the doubt that she also felt. Her inner stories started to show themselves. She shared how in those years of courting, she often doubted they would marry. She feared she would lose him. She questioned whether she was good enough, pretty enough, and smart enough for him. She wondered why he would love her. She said that these stories followed her into the early years of their marriage, until one day when, her husband said, "STOP. Stop doubting me, us, and our marriage. I'm here for our lifetime, I promise."

I asked her how she was able to just stop. As she recalled, she said it wasn't easy. It was work. She made a promise to herself to honor her husband by not doubting, and every time her fears, worries, and doubts showed up, she stopped and reminded herself of his words, "Stop doubting me and our marriage." She laughed a little and said that she didn't even recall the day or time when the thoughts stopped coming to haunt her. She just started to believe in their marriage and trust it.

We talked about another big dream of hers, being a mother, and the beautiful children she has. She realized she used to dream, and those dreams did come true. But she also noticed a big, nagging voice of doubt, uncertainty, and despair that always showed its ugliness.

She told story after story of how supportive her husband has been to build her confidence as a wife and then as a wonderful mother. As she spoke, I asked her if she was able to see and spot a pattern in her stories. There was a lengthy pause before she answered in tears that she had noticed the pattern. She did have dreams, and often those dreams were destroyed by her doubt, dissuasion, delay, and distraction caused by those aspects of herself that she thought she was ignoring. She wasn't owning her shadows. All those aspects of her that she had been avoiding most of her adult life were ruling her.

The key point—the big insight in her awareness—was that she thought she was avoiding the negative voice within. She thought that by not listening, not dealing with, looking at, or going deeper into these parts, she was succeeding. She had not realized that what she had resisted would persist to come back again and again. She did not know that the fastest way to her dreams and desires is through all the muck and messiness.

What you resist will persist!

You have dreams and desires. We all do. Yours may not come as monumental achievements, at least not through the eyes as you see things now. In both of these stories, they didn't seem to be monumental achievements.

The businessman had a dream to do great things that benefited others, to have a greater impact in his community, and to build deeper relationships along the way. He did not see these as big, bold monumental achievements, and yet he was awarded and honored as businessman of the year, became the community's largest employer, and owned the place everyone wanted to work at. The owner of the business he bought became his new CEO and best friend. Their wives and children had so much in common, they created deep bonds and friendships. His life changed in monumental ways, and he now values having a vision. Every year, he rallies his employees to share his vision and create their own. He has impacted the lives of so many people.

His wife also had a dream that had been in her heart since she was a little girl. In our time together, she realized her dream was to follow her heart, to dream big, and never lose sight of her dreams. This was eye-opening for her. She noticed she could either focus on the longing in her heart or she could focus on the absence of it. Her big insight was the awareness to how often she had been discounting herself, feeling inadequate and incapable, thus making the desire unattainable. Her next big dream didn't come to her that day. And she was okay. Simply knowing that she was back in alignment with following her heart and listening for those dreams was enough. And guess what? It did come a few months later.

She had a vision to bring the dreams of others together. Not fully knowing what this meant, she allowed her dream to unfold within her. She partnered with her city and local residents to create a central park theme, a gathering place and space on a five-acre parcel of land on the outskirts of town. In this space she created was a community garden, fruit trees, nature walks, a playground for the kids, and a big pavilion with tables, benches, and grills for cooking out. Best of all, there was plenty of room for growth and expansion. This space attracted visitors from nearby towns, and a year later, they added baseball diamonds and tennis courts. As they did, all the business owners in their small town noticed more business, greater revenue, and the growth and expansion that this once small and tiny dream was able to bring forth. She truly did bring the dreams of others together.

Allow your heart to show you your soul's desires. It's always bigger and better than you can imagine and envision. So, dream big and bold, and be open to all that your dream brings with joy and gratitude.

THIS or something even greater still.

In the remnants of your Soul lie waiting your felt-most dreams and desires, the longings that you came here with and knew in the depths of your being before your innocence was denied

and abused. The fulfillment of your destiny is not dependent on your past or who you think you are today but solely in your acceptance of the light of God within you and on your willingness to be a channel through which that love is radiated out into the world. ~ Diana Viola

So, claim your innocence and step into the unknown—the innocence of your childhood, the innocence that was yours before the expectations of society, family, culture, and being "normal" were instilled in you.

Your journey through life is exquisitely crafted in ways that allow you to explore the deep and meaningful longings of the soul, the mysterious inner workings of your dreams and desires, and the bittersweet wisdom that comes from the richness and fullness of truly living your life as the co-creator of your journey.

The only thing worse than being blind is having sight but no vision. ~ Helen Keller

Realizing the power in your vision requires you to create a **vision**. Creating a vision requires you to see it first in your mind's eye and feel it inside you. Like your relationship with your Spiritual intelligence, it's totally an inside job. First, you'll need to lean into your longings and discontents and begin to trust your desires. You might want to spend time on this part alone, depending on how easily you are able to notice your longings, desires, and dreams.

I've worked with many clients who struggled to create and craft their vision, so if this is you, know that you are not alone. You may find it helpful to ask the question, What would I love? Don't force yourself to answer it. At first, just ask it and allow things to come into your awareness naturally. You'll be invited to create your vision in the Invitation at the end of this chapter.

Once you are able to know what you would love, you'll be better able to notice your longings and discontent. If you are too focused on the details, you'll spin into a spiral of all your discontent, finding fault with others, yourself, and blaming and shaming instead of following your vision. If this is you, be aware that you may have some patterns in play that are not serving you; in fact, they may be sabotaging your chance at success. This is why I say to take your time here. Always notice without judgment.

Once you are able to align with your longings, desires, and dreams, allow yourself to get in touch with how they make you feel. This is important because it's really the feelings that you want more so than the end result. Your soul is not actually about your acquisition of material things so much as it is about the experience you will have in achieving the goal or desire. If you want a start a nonprofit, think about how you will feel once your dream comes to fruition, the people you will serve, the impact it will have in your community, your contribution to humanity, etc. This realization is sometimes an eye-opener.

You come into and leave your life experience with nothing; everyone leaves this life experience empty-handed. Anything acquired in the human experience stays with the human experience. Consider the thoughts of your vision as the necessary component to mold your vision into form or matter and the feelings as the magnetic energy to bring them into your experience.

You can have a personal vision and also a professional vision, and they can be different and separate. This is pretty common actually. More organizations are realizing the power and value in sharing their vision. Today, organizations are creating visions and rallying their employees to hold that vision with them, as they encourage and empower them to create their own professional vision too.

Your vision is your most important dream or mental picture. It can also be a set of dreams and long-term goals. Your vision defines the optimal desired future state; it tells what you would like to achieve over a longer time. You then use your imagination, creativity, and inner guidance to envision what is possible.

Once you stop focusing on what you don't have and begin to acknowledge the inner workings of your dreams and desires, you'll notice a natural pull, a universal energy that seems to organically, magnetically draw you to what you desire. It's this natural magnetic pulling toward your vision that *is the power*.

Until you can experience this power magnetically drawing you, you won't fully be able to wrap your head around the value and power in your vision. Some things in life must be experienced to fully understand them. Your vision is one of these.

Let go of what you've been told to do and grab hold of what you were born to do. ~ Ed Mylett

I recently listened to *The Ed Mylett Show* podcast, "My Most Powerful Episode Ever," where Ed was interviewed by Jamie Kern Lima. While the entire interview was impactful, the specific moment I wish to share is when they discussed Chapter 7 of his new book, *The Power of One More*. This chapter, "One More Dream," begins with Ed sharing that the happiest people in life operate out of their imagination and dream. He further explained that most people operate out of their history and memory and not their imagination and dreams. If you are living and operating out of your history and memory, you are constantly replaying old stories, patterns, and thoughts that regenerate limiting beliefs about yourself. You won't get to your dreams this way. It's through living from your imagination and living from your dreams and from your vision that you will create and achieve all that you desire and more. Allow yourself the gift of imagining where you are going, what you'll achieve and experience, and who you'll become.

Who do you look up to; who do you admire? Most often, those people you look up to and admire are dreamers. The people who achieve much in life are dreamers and know how to use their imagination. Think about it: Walt Disney, Dr. Martin Luther King Jr., and Albert Einstein all had a dream. Do you think our Founding Fathers had a dream before they become presidents or leaders of the newly formed United States?

Your dreams will make you come alive. Your imagination will connect you with fun, creativity, and new levels of increase and abundance. When you use your imagination and dreams to craft your vision, you'll be on your way living your life empowered.

INVITATION

What would you love? Allow yourself to think about four domains of life:

- Health and well-being
- Relationships
- Career or vocation
- Time and financial freedom

_____

_____

What's your dream? Create a vision for yourself. Make it something you will achieve over the next three years. Why three years? It's far enough away to not trigger your ego's response of the negative, and it's realistic enough to actually create what you want.

_____

_____

As you write out your vision, write it from the place of having already achieved it. Let it begin with: "I am so happy and grateful now that…"

_____

_____

How can you begin to live from your imagination throughout your day? Allow yourself to daydream.

_____

_____

How can you begin to live from your dream during your day?

_____

_____

CHAPTER 22:

TOOLS TO AID YOU

You are learning to work with your mind, your emotions, and your body to be the co-creator of your life. This requires you to let go of old ways and incorporate new ones at every stage of your growth. As you do, new tools may be used to aid you. The tools mentioned here are aids to bring all of your intelligence systems into harmony and balance, to aid you in healing, releasing, or bringing to your awareness anything that may be blocking your growth and progress. All tools work to align you, body, mind, and spirit.

While meditation and journaling are great tools, I call these practices that you *must* incorporate into your life. (More on this in the next chapter.) The big difference between a tool and a practice is that tools are picked up and used to move you forward when needed—sometimes for a specific period or through a stage of development. You may use a tool once or a hundred times. A practice is something you do daily. A practice is something you do 365 times a year and more. A practice becomes part of your routine, a habit, and part of your life.

When you get a promotion in the workplace, you must let go of your old job duties and responsibilities and step into a new role with new habits and responsibilities. You may get a different office, new title, bigger paycheck, and a brand-new process and structure to your workday. Maybe you have a mentor or trainer to get you started. Oftentimes, you'll be incorporating your ways, your tools, and your ideas into this new position to make it your own. Either way, you'll be picking up new tools to help you. From that mentor or coach to a set of reminders and spreadsheets, they all become the tools that help you craft a new way of being to meet the criteria and demands of your new position.

This is the same with the tools shared here. They are meant to aid you in your growth and development. Some will be calling you, others won't. Some you'll explore and use, and others won't resonate with you at all. Take what resonates and leave the rest.

FINO: Feel invited not obligated.

It is important that you do your own research and gain the knowledge and information necessary to know if it is right for you. I don't believe anything that is shared here could be harmful to you when you learn to use it correctly from a trained and experienced professional.

If you are not aware, you may miss the nudge.

You will find your own tools because we all do. Some come to you from your wisdom and intuition. Others come from the ideas, practices, and habits you observe from others. Actually, everything you need will show up. It may show up in a book you read, a website you are drawn to, or that leadership coach your organization brought in. The tools you will be drawn to will be as unique and individual as you are. There is no book of tools that must be followed for you to succeed. I believe the best tools are natural, organic, and come from within you, other people, or from Mother Nature.

Tools can and will:
- Bring you greater insight
- Help you see a bigger picture
- Clear stagnant energy and blocks to your creativity
- Bring your energies into harmony and balance
- Release tension, stress, and a busy mind
- Aid you in higher consciousness
- Help you bring the unconscious conscious
- Move you forward with clarity and purpose
- Help you move forward in quantum leaps

MOTHER NATURE

Mother Nature is one of the best tools to bring you home, to ground you, and to connect you with life. Mother Nature takes you out of the busy, fast-paced material world. Mother Nature could be a hike in the woods, a day at the beach, or a visit to your local park. It could be sitting in your yard under a big maple tree, enjoying the present moment, feeling the earth beneath your feet, the air on your exposed skin, and the warmth of the sun, and observing the ants, the bees, and the birds.

Mother Nature is one tool that many make a practice until the changing of the seasons when they let the cold or wet weather interrupt their habits. If you don't make Mother Nature your practice and habit, at least remember this one tool is always available to you. You might consider finding a way to spend an hour a day outdoors.

COACH OR MENTOR

Working with a coach or mentor can be a game changer and one that you may not want to go without. This one is listed as a tool because most people only use a coach or mentor for short spurts of time. I recommend finding a coach you like and trust and work together with them for a year. It may prove to be one of the best years of your life. Heck, you may even decide to invest in another year or even longer.

SOUND/VIBRATION/LIGHT THERAPY

Sound therapy uses sound, music, and specialist instruments played in therapeutic ways, combined with deep self-reflection techniques to improve health and well-being. Choose from many options in sound therapy: sound baths, drumming circles, tuning forks, binaural beats, and more.

To create your own mini sound experience, take a Tibetan singing bowl and, before creating any sound, hold it and set an intention for your experience. Then, gently strike the edge of the bowl with the mallet. Let your mind focus on the sound and the intention you set as the note gently fades.

Vibrational sound therapy can retune your body, mind, and spirit, encouraging relaxation, healing, and wellness. This may be a one-on-one service that uses therapeutic singing bowls placed on the body to create a combination of tones and vibrations that produce a state of tranquility and act as a massage for the nervous system and can provide balance and harmony at a cellular level.

Harmonic Eggs® are wooden chambers that create the perfect environment for deep relaxation and promoting inner balance. The Harmonic Egg uses sacred geometry, light, color, and sound frequencies (music) to empower the body's own healing energy.

Tuning forks are a wonderful and effective method of applying vibration and sound to the body, including acupoints, trigger and reflex points, bone, muscle, and tendons to help tonify qi or disperse qi to help relieve pain and attune the body on a cellular level.

Recent research indicates that **drumming** accelerates physical healing, boosts the immune system, produces feelings of well-being, and helps release emotional trauma. Drumming also induces deep relaxation, lowers blood pressure, and reduces stress.

FLOAT

Floating, also known as sensory deprivation, is a transformative experience where the floater effortlessly floats in a solution of water and Epsom salt in a sensory-controlled environment to achieve intentional solitude. Frequent floaters have described their escapes into the void as an integrative life hack, an adventure that provides a vast spectrum of benefits and solutions, such as increased creativity and productivity, emotional regulation, pain relief, reduced inflammation, and increased self-awareness.

ENERGY WORK

Energy work helps to facilitate healing and realigns the energies of the body. Some modalities are done working within the client's personal aura and through little body contact, and yet it has a powerful effect on the individual. Sensations may include warmth, tingling, and a lightening up or total relaxation.

Massage is one way to get energy moving in the body. Massage includes full-body massage or on specific areas, like neck, back, shoulders, or feet. The potential with physical manipulation in massage offers two major physical effects:

1. Increase in blood and lymph circulation
2. Relaxation and normalization of the soft tissue (muscle, connective tissue, tendons, ligaments), which releases nerves and deeper connective tissues

Reflexology is based on the idea that different points on the feet (and hands) correspond to specific muscles or organs in the body. A reflexologist will apply pressure on these points in order to improve health in the related area of the body. Let's say you're having back problems—a reflexologist would focus on the big toe to help relieve symptoms.

Reiki is an energy healing technique that promotes relaxation and reduces stress and anxiety through gentle touch or no touch. Reiki practitioners use their hands to deliver energy to your body, improving the flow and balance of your energy to support healing as well as removing or moving trapped energy in your body.

Tapping, also known as emotional freedom technique (EFT), involves touching various acupressure points on the body in a specific pattern in order to ease stress, anxiety, depression, and possibly even chronic pain. The basic tapping technique requires you to focus on a negative emotion you are experiencing. This can be a fear, a worry, or any unresolved issue. While maintaining your mental focus on this issue, use your fingertips to tap five to seven times on nine specific meridian points of the body. Tapping on these meridian points while you think about what is causing you stress helps your mind understand that you are not in any physical danger and it is safe to relax, reducing cortisol levels. It works by calming the amygdala to achieve greater results faster while working with past fears and limiting beliefs.

Acupuncture is part of the ancient practice of traditional Chinese medicine. Acupuncture is the practice of penetrating the skin with thin, solid, metallic needles at strategic points on your body, which are then activated through gentle and specific movements of the practitioner's hands or with electrical stimulation. Most commonly used to treat pain, it's increasingly being used for overall wellness and stress management.

Breath work is a tool that brings many benefits. Breath work refers to any type of breathing exercises or techniques, and there are many different kinds. People often perform them to improve mental, physical, and spiritual well-being. All breath work exercises focus on your conscious awareness of your inhales and exhales. These exercises use deep, focused breathing that lasts a specific amount of time. During breath work, you intentionally change your breathing pattern.

The many forms of breath work therapy involve breathing in a conscious and systematic way and include:

- Shamanic Breathwork (*shamanicbreathwork.org/shamanic-breathwork*)
- Vivation (*vivation.com*)
- Transformational Breath (*transformationalbreath.com*)

- Holotropic Breathwork (*holotropic.com/holotropic-breathwork*)
- Clarity Breathwork (*claritybreathwork.com*)
- Rebirthing Breathwork (*rebirthingbreathwork.com*)
- Wim Hof Method breathing (*wimhofmethod.com*)

FASTING

Fasting is the willing abstinence or reduction from some or all food, drink, or both for a period of time. Although sometimes viewed as unhealthy, depriving, or reserved for religious reasons, short-term fasting can offer excellent health benefits. As research grows in this area of health, fasting is becoming more widely accepted as a legitimate means of managing weight and preventing disease. At the same time, it is important that fasting is done in proper and healthy ways. Fasting is seen as a discipline and provides clarity of mind, emotions, and a clearing and cleansing of the physical body. Everything from a healthy green organic juice fast to intermittent fasting are showing promising and beneficial results in more than just one's weight.

Fasting is a challenge—a challenge to break the habit of eating, chewing, and filling our mind and moments with thinking about what to eat, when to eat, with whom, etc. You may find the first day literally brutal as you continually ward off the mental activities associated with eating, whether it's cooking, preparing, ordering, or joining others. You'll get to notice how much time in your day is spent simply thinking about this one activity. And by day two or three, you'll notice the freedom that comes from not having to think about what, when, where, and how you will be eating.

You will end your fast feeling proud of your accomplishments: your discipline, what you've learned, and what you've overcome. You'll be more aware and in tune with your body, the signs and signals it sends, and how well you are listening to the messages your body is communicating.

Silent retreats encourage participants to take a vow of silence for a given time. Think of it as abstaining from speaking, written or aloud. By removing distractions and communication, participants can reach a deep level of solitary contemplation and personal reflection. The silent retreat is a withdrawal from electronics and all digital technology—consider it a digital detox. It's a deep dive into mindfulness or maintaining a moment-by-moment awareness of your thoughts, feelings, bodily sensations, and the surrounding environment through a gentle, nurturing lens. It's both healing and restorative.

EARTH'S NATURAL HEALERS

Plants are tools that come to you in various forms. The first one introduced is the natural growing of plants outdoors or indoors, in pots, a garden, or a hydroponic tower. Plants can heal the body, stimulate the mind, and calm the nerves.

Did you know that **oil of oregano** is widely recognized for its antimicrobial activity as well as antiviral and antifungal properties? Recent investigations have demonstrated that oil of oregano is also a potent antioxidant, anti-inflammatory, antidiabetic, and cancer-suppressor agent. Do your own research and validate for yourself. It is a must-have in my home.

Aloe vera is commonly known as a topical gel used to treat sunburn. Promisingly, it may also provide other health benefits, largely due to its antioxidant properties. Research has indicated that aloe vera may benefit your skin, dental, oral, and digestive health. It may even improve blood sugar control.

There are way too many specific plants to mention here, so please do your own research. You can grow herbs and plants for their healthy eating, flavors, and, of course, for health and well-being benefits. Every home should have a resource manual at their fingertips. I like the work of Andrew Chevallier. A few good ones are:
- *The Encyclopedia of Medicinal Plants: A Practical Reference Guide to over 550 Key Herbs and Their Medicinal Uses*
- *Encyclopedia of Herbal Medicine*

Essential oils are compounds extracted from plants. The oils capture the plant's scent and flavor, or "essence." Unique aromatic compounds give each essential oil its characteristic essence. Essential oils are obtained through distillation (via steam and/or water) or mechanical methods, such as cold-pressing. Once the aromatic chemicals have been extracted, they are combined with a carrier oil to create a product that's ready for use. The way the oils are made is important, as essential oils obtained through chemical processes are not considered true essential oils. When applied to your skin, some plant chemicals are absorbed. It's thought that certain application methods can improve absorption, such as applying with heat or to different areas of the body. However, research in this area is lacking. Inhaling the aromas from essential oils can stimulate areas of your limbic system, which is a part of your brain that plays a role in emotions, behaviors, sense of smell, and long-term memory. They are not intended to be swallowed.

Unlike essential oils, **flower essences** are odorless, don't contain plant material, and are made to be ingested. The flower essence is extracted with water and believed to contain the energetic imprint of the flowers. The intent is to address emotional symptoms, not physical.

Plants are tools that aid you.

EARTH MEDICINES

It's likely that humans have used plants as medicine for as long as we have existed. With the enactment of the *Comprehensive Drug Abuse Prevention and Control Act of 1970*, which was signed into law by President *Richard Nixon*, many of these earth medicines became illegal and marked as schedule I substances. Since then, mental health issues and suicides have been steadily increasing, and the addiction to prescription pain medicine and synthetic opioids has become a serious national health crisis.

The Johns Hopkins Center for Psychedelic and Consciousness Research has been leading the way in exploring innovative treatments using **psilocybin**. The molecular structure of psilocybin, a naturally occurring psychedelic compound found in "magic mushrooms," allows it to penetrate the central nervous system. Scientific and medical experts are now beginning to understand its effects on the brain and mind and its potential as therapeutic for mental illness and many other conditions.

MAPS, the Multidisciplinary Association for Psychedelic Studies, is a 501(c)(3) nonprofit research and educational organization that develops medical, legal, and cultural contexts for people to benefit from the careful uses of psychedelics and marijuana. Their data validates the potential aid that psilocybin has in the areas of PTSD, depression, and anxiety, as well as eating disorders. Research is now being done on the benefits of psychedelics to combat opioid addiction as well as other addictions and Alzheimer's disease; research on both is showing promising results.

The benefits of psychedelics go far and wide, yet few countries have legalized them to be used to help treat the mental, emotional, and psychological issues they're known and shown to help with. Meanwhile, C-suite executives across the U.S., from Silicon Valley to New York and everywhere in between, are seeking these magical fungi for their powerful impact in raising consciousness. These substances produce an altered state that brings the unconscious conscious. They are mind menders, known to rebuild the brain and expand consciousness.

Psychedelics may work in these ways:

- Mystical or spiritual experiences: Intensely meaningful experiences under the influence of psychedelics may shift a person's mindset or belief system, causing them to think or behave differently.

- Increased suggestibility: People using psychedelics may be more suggestible. This can make them more responsive to positive suggestions from a therapist, coach, or integration expert, or to the benefits of their own hallucinations.

- Neurotransmitter changes: Neurotransmitters are chemical messengers in the brain. Many mental health drugs act directly on neurotransmitters to change mood.

In addition to psilocybin, other psychoactive compounds (following nicotine, alcohol, and caffeine) found in Mother Nature are mescaline, salvia, cannabis, ayahuasca, and dimethyltryptamine (DMT). As of February 2022, 37 states allow the medicinal use of cannabis products. **Cannabis** is a plant that makes a thick substance full of compounds called cannabinoids. CBD (cannabidiol) and THC (tetrahydrocannabinol) are the most common cannabinoids found in cannabis products. THC and CBD are in both marijuana and hemp. Marijuana contains much more THC than hemp, while hemp has a lot more CBD.

The benefits from both cannabis and CBD are too numerous to mention here, and many amazing sources are available to educate you. So, if you are meant to know more, dig in and learn something new. If we work together, I have trusted sources I can connect you with that act as educators, guides, and coaches to allow you to get the most of these earth medicines, especially when prescribed for medical support. I believe we have much more to do in the education aspect to aid in the medicinal use of this plant.

HUMAN DESIGN

Human Design says you are coded at birth with a map, or a manual, that tells you how unique you are and guides you in living in a manner that is in sync with who you are. **Human Design** is a logical system that brings together principles of the *I Ching*, astrology, Kabbalah, Hindu-Brahmin chakra system, and quantum physics.

Your Human Design Chart, also called a Body Graph, is calculated using your birth date, time, and place to reveal your genetic design. It can show you your life purpose, your communication style, and how to align with your Human Design to find joy, peace, and abundance and be in flow with all of life. It will show you your challenges and shadow aspects, strengths and weaknesses, how you make decisions, your role in life, and so much more.

Search the internet and you'll find many Human Design sites to assist you. You'll need your birth date, time, and location for an accurate blueprint of your design. Don't expect to learn everything overnight; this is a system that will continue to grow you as you learn and integrate each new awareness.

STRENGTHSFINDER ASSESSMENT

The StrengthsFinder assessment, now rebranded as the Clifton-Strengths assessment, is a personal development tool developed by Gallup Education, which provides individuals with their Top 5 strengths. Thirty-four different strength themes are divided into four domains of Strategic Thinking, Relationship Building, Influencing, and Executing.

Remember, tools will bring you greater insight. They help you gain a bigger-picture perspective, often guiding you to what you need to know, to next steps, and greater awareness. Tools can clear stagnant energy and blocks to your creativity. Tools can bring your energies into harmony and balance. Tools can release tension, stress, and a busy mind. Tools will aid you in higher consciousness. They help you bring the unconscious into your awareness, allowing you to experience more of who you came here to be.

INVITATION

What new tools are calling you? Explore what you are called to explore. As you are growing, it's common to let go of old tools, even habits, and find new ones that will serve you better at this stage of your growth.

_____

_____

Be open and receptive to the gentle nudges and your inner guidance as you continue to enjoy your human life journey. Be responsible and work with a professional to gain the full benefits that each tool offers.

_____

_____

CHAPTER 23:

PRACTICES TO EMPOWER YOU

A practice is the act of doing something again and again. The aim of a practice is to get really good at something, to master it. What really happens is that as you practice, you are sending signals to your subconscious to permeate this behavior or activity into the operating system within that really runs the show for you when you are not conscious and aware.

These **Practices to Empower You** are the practices you might want to make habits to grow yourself in your journey through life. Hint, hint. They are practices you might choose to adopt as your own. The practices shared here are merely a few of the most powerful and beneficial ones I, along with my mentors and peers, have found beneficial. You may learn of other practices equally as valuable, and I hope you do. Learn to trust what comes to you and go with what you are guided to explore. Remember to take what resonates and leave the rest. This chapter might sound like an instruction guide, and in a way, it should because these are the practices that will expand your awareness, allowing you to bring all of you to the party and to remain curious. Yes, these are the practices that will aid you in knowing yourself and growing yourself to live your life empowered.

OBSERVER

The easiest way to free yourself from the busy, always active mind is to observe the activity of the mind. As one of my mentors, Ram Dass, taught, "One way to get free of attachment is to cultivate the witness consciousness, to become a neutral observer of your own life." The witness place inside you is simple awareness, the part of you that is aware of everything—just noticing, watching, not judging, being present in the here and now.

This witness, or the Observer, is another level of consciousness. The Observer coexists alongside your human consciousness as another layer of awareness, as the part of you that is awakening. Humans have this unique ability to be in two states of consciousness at once. Observing yourself is like directing the beam of a flashlight back at itself. In any experience, there's the experience—the sensory, emotional, or conceptual data—and there's your awareness of it. This awareness is the Observer, and you can cultivate that awareness in the garden of your being.

The Observer can be your centering aid. It will guide the work you do on yourself. Once you understand that there is a place in you that is not attached, you can free yourself from attachments. Pretty much everything you notice in the universe is a reflection of your attachments.

The goal is to be the Observer of your thoughts and not let your thoughts control you.

Along with being the Observer and being self-aware comes the subtle joy of being here, alive, enjoying the present moment. Eventually, you will come into the spiritual self, the spiritual heart, which is pure consciousness, joy, compassion, and love. So, your first job is to work on yourself. The greatest thing you can do for another human being is to get your own house in order and find your true spiritual heart.

LIFESTYLE

They say you can't change much of the environment around you or your genes, but plenty of lifestyle choices are available to improve your health and boost your well-being. It starts with being intentional and informed about a healthy diet, adequate rest, proper physical and mental activity, and adopting manageable lifestyle choices that are in alignment with your human design and vision.

Manage your lifestyle habits and you'll manage your life.

Your choices and your disciplines matter if you want to be in control of your physical body and your happiness. Learning the right foods for you is of utmost importance. Awareness is key in food choices today. No one should be telling you what to eat or when. But deep down, you know what's right for you. You know when to stop. You know what to avoid. And listening is what matters. Avoiding processed foods and overindulging is a great starting point. Figure it out along the way and be easy on yourself. Your body knows what you need, when you need it, and how much, so listen to it.

Exercising, staying active, and enjoying life is where *joy* and *gusto* are found. Do what you love. Explore new adventures and get out of your comfort zone. Explore the beaches, the mountains, and everywhere in between. Walk, run, hop, skip, and jump your way into seeing more of what excites you and makes you come alive.

For some, learning to really rest is a bit more challenging than diet and fitness. If this is you, go easy on yourself, be kind and gentle as you learn self-care and listening to what your body needs. Take a pause, a conscious loving break, when you need it and put yourself to bed before you are tired and exhausted. Why? Because you deserve it.

The way you live your life matters because every cell in your body is listening and responding accordingly. Love yourself. Love your life. Love how you spend your days and who you spend them with. It matters, and life will love you back.

Did you know that most overweight people struggle with self-worth? Did you know that between 30 and 50 percent of all cancers are avoidable with lifestyle changes? Did you know that mindset plays an important role in your well-being?

> *Being sick is hard; being healthy is hard.*
> *Choose your hard.*

In summary, a healthy lifestyle has many benefits. In the short term, it helps you feel good. In the long term, it helps you stay well for longer and maybe live longer too. In contrast, an unhealthy lifestyle has negative effects on your health, making it more likely that you'll develop a serious medical condition that may have been preventable. And the choice is yours.

CONTEMPLATION

Contemplation involves thinking, pondering something, studying and musing over something—usually something worthwhile and important pertaining to life and meaning. As this kind of reflective activity goes deep, it requires you to become still and highly focused as you ponder; the ego dissolves temporarily, and contemplation becomes increasingly like meditation. Solutions to life's problems sometimes appear spontaneously at such times.

The contemplative mind is about receiving and being present to the moment without judgment, analysis, or critique. Contemplative "knowing" is a much more holistic, heart-centered knowing, where mind, heart, soul, and senses are open and receptive to the moment just as it is.

Contemplation is the practice of being fully present—in heart, mind, and body—to what allows you to creatively respond to what could be. Our contemplations and inspirations are not designed to be acted upon, but to be used to keep us in an inspired state, preparing us to explore our outer reality with curiosity and presence.

A man who realizes the potential of his mind by means of introspection and contemplation does not lack self-confidence. He has control over his mind, and he is able to realize its full potential.

NONJUDGMENT

If you have ever been in constant judgment, you would agree that judgment can be a toxic way to live and is detrimental to your emotional and mental well-being. Do you jump to conclusions easily? Is your mind usually made up before you hear all the facts, meaning you aren't even listening to what another is saying?

Judgment robs you of the ability to hear your inner guidance. It can be a way of conforming to what is commonly accepted, making it more likely that you will fit in and be accepted or, in essence, loved. The fear of not being loved and accepted can lead you to shun and reject others in an attempt to ensure that you are not shunned and rejected. Be careful—this is a slippery slope of no return.

When you free yourself from judging, you create a state of being that is freeing. It's open to give and receive love on so many different levels. You feel calm and at peace because you're not assigning labels to everything or creating positives and negatives. Everything is seen for its own inherent beauty.

Judgments are ingrained so deeply in your subconscious, it can be hard to break the habit of immediately labeling people, things, and events. Nonjudgment doesn't mean that you never make judgments. It's human nature to evaluate things and determine whether they are positive, negative, or neutral. It becomes problematic for your well-being when you hold onto those judgments, when you never let them go and allow yourself or another to show up differently. When you bring judgments of the past into the present, you are expecting the same things to happen again.

In order to let go of your judgments, you need to first be aware of what they are. Once you can identify your judgments, you can actively let them go—possibly by imagining them floating away like clouds. Either way, when you learn to stop judging your experiences, you get to just be present. When you are truly present in the moment, you can enjoy your life more fully. You won't take things personally and have problems with what others say or do.

This one's big, so we'll conclude with this: Like all emotional skills, nonjudgment is a skill that can be developed and improved over time. Here are three ways to build your nonjudgment skills:

- **Self-awareness** – Sometimes you can judge yourself and others without realizing it. That's why improving your self-awareness can be instrumental in uncovering judgments.
- **Mindfulness** – A mindfulness practice is often thought to be the combination of awareness and acceptance (nonjudgment). And mindfulness is one practice that will bring you to nonjudgment.
- **Positive thinking** – You are judgmental when you are overly consumed by the negative things in life. By cultivating your ability to pay attention to the positive things, you may be able to improve your ability to be nonjudgmental.

The fastest way to nonjudgment is through contemplation, reflection, and meditation.

MEDITATION

According to the Mayo Clinic, meditation can wipe away the day's stress, bringing with it inner peace. Anyone can practice meditation. It's simple and inexpensive, and it doesn't require any special equipment. Best of all, you can practice meditation wherever you are—whether you're out for a walk, riding the bus, waiting at the doctor's office, or even in the middle of a difficult business meeting.

Meditation has been practiced for thousands of years. Meditation originally was meant to help deepen understanding of the sacred and mystical forces of life. While still practiced for spiritual growth, these days, meditation is commonly used for relaxation and stress reduction.

Quiet the mind and the soul will speak.

Meditation is considered a type of mind-body complementary medicine. Meditation can produce a deep state of relaxation and a tranquil mind.

During meditation, you focus your attention on one thing, say on the breath or a word or a candle flame, and by doing so, eliminate the stream of constant thoughts that may be crowding your mind. Generally, the five constant elements to meditation, no matter what type of meditation you practice, are:
- Attention, focused or nonfocused
- Breathing, relaxed or controlled
- Quiet setting
- Comfortable position, straight back, good posture
- Open attitude

The benefits of meditation don't end when your meditation session ends. Not only can meditation help carry you more calmly through your day, but it may help you manage symptoms of some medical conditions.

Meditation promotes emotional well-being.

When you meditate, you may clear away the information overload that builds up every day and contributes to your stress. The emotional benefits of meditation can include:
- Gaining a new perspective on stressful situations
- Building skills to manage your stress

- Increasing self-awareness
- Focusing on the present
- Reducing negative emotions
- Increasing imagination and creativity
- Increasing patience and tolerance

Meditation dissolves the invisible walls that unawareness has built.

Meditation might also be useful if you have a medical condition, especially one that may be worsened by stress. Sometimes pain and discomfort can be relieved through meditation. When you stop resisting the pain and focus on it, fully present with it, you create space for it, sort of like acceptance of it, and as you do, you might find it dissolve away.

While there is a vast amount of scientific research supporting the health benefits of meditation, some researchers still believe it's not yet possible to draw conclusions about the possible benefits of meditation. Really? Maybe put it to the test for yourself. It shocks me that some researchers are still unable to draw conclusions, but I am not here to judge another. Find your own data, but give it a full six months before you stop to say it did nothing. Often your results are subtle and only detectable with your expanded awareness.

With that in mind, some research suggests that meditation may help people manage symptoms of conditions such as:

- Anxiety
- Asthma
- Cancer
- Chronic pain
- Depression
- Heart disease
- High blood pressure
- Irritable bowel syndrome
- Sleep problems
- Tension headaches

With all this being said, be sure to talk to your health care provider about the pros and cons of using meditation if you have any of these conditions or other health problems. By no means is it suggested that meditation be a replacement for traditional medical treatment. But it may be an addition that proves itself to be a useful practice to better your well-being.

TYPES OF MEDITATION

Meditation is an umbrella term for the many ways to a relaxed state of being, to higher states of consciousness, and even changed brain wave states. All types of meditation share the same goal of achieving inner peace and calm. Here are some of the many types of meditation and relaxation techniques that have meditative components:

- **Guided meditation** – You'll find various guided meditations via apps like Headspace, Insight Timer, Unplug, and more. You can find YouTube channels specifically designed to share guided meditations. In the guided meditation, they often try to use as many senses as possible, such as smells, sights, sounds, and textures as you are led through your meditation.
- **Mantra meditation** – In this type of meditation, you silently repeat a calming word, thought, or phrase to prevent distracting thoughts. It could be a word with meaning and intent for you to understand more deeply, like "I am LOVE." The word or phrase doesn't need to have any meaning; it could be PEACE to simply remind you to be present.
- **Mindfulness meditation** – This type of meditation is based on being mindful or having an increased awareness and acceptance of living in the present moment. In mindfulness meditation, you broaden your conscious awareness. You focus on what you experience during meditation, such as the flow of your breath. You can observe your thoughts and emotions but let them pass without judgment.
- **Qigong** – This practice generally combines meditation, relaxation, physical movement, and breathing exercises to restore and maintain balance.
- **Tai chi** – This is a form of gentle Chinese martial arts. In tai chi, you perform a self-paced series of postures or movements in a slow, graceful manner while practicing deep breathing.
- **Transcendental Meditation®** – Transcendental Meditation is a simple, natural technique. In Transcendental Meditation, you silently repeat a personally assigned mantra, such as a word, sound, or phrase, in a specific way. This form of meditation may allow your body to settle into a state of profound rest

and relaxation and your mind to achieve a state of inner peace, without needing to use concentration or effort.

- **Yoga** – In yoga, you perform a series of postures and controlled breathing exercises to promote a more flexible body and a calm mind. As you move through different poses and flows that require balance and concentration, you're encouraged to focus less on your busy day and more on the moment.

As we evolve to these new practices, many workplaces are adapting to them. I've seen businesses adding wellness rooms, quiet rooms, Zen space, and even fitness rooms, exercise space, and mothering rooms. The quiet rooms are a space where you can go and sit and let go of thoughts and stresses, and recenter energies, recharge, and reestablish yourself for clarity, creativity, and to better align yourself to being productive and focused in your work. Workplaces around the globe are learning how to invest in their employees in new and creative ways. These are just some of the many ways to encourage workplace wellness.

The mind is everything.
What you think, you become.

JOURNALING

From as far back as I can remember, people have kept diaries, daily journaling their thoughts, feelings, and experiences. I had a diary once but never quite grasped the practice to make it my own. Left with nothing but empty pages, I wonder what might have come of me had I been able to express myself on those pages.

Maybe you've kept a diary. Maybe you haven't. Don't let what you read next taint or tarnish your experience, but be open to more ways to use this practice called journaling.

Today, I do journal. I don't write of my worries or upsets, and I don't write about how my day went or didn't go. I discovered this amazing woman, Janet Conner, author of *Writing Down Your Soul, How to Activate and Listen to the Extraordinary Voice Within*. Her book touched my soul and called to me, and this has become my journaling. I write, or shall I say, I hold a pen and allow my soul to talk to me. I began this practice over a year ago. It has been an amazing practice and one I feel will always be with me. It's as if I tap into a higher realm and allow words of wisdom to flow through me, through the pen, and onto the paper. Oftentimes, they are words I knew but never embraced, practiced, or truly acknowledged. As I reread what I have written, it's often exactly what I needed at that time. This practice has brought me to trust and believe in myself and this connection I have to my soul.

I have also journaled when I was overwhelmed and stressed. This practice was introduced to me as a "brain dump," the process of dumping all that you have in your head out onto the paper. When overwhelmed, it's a way to relieve stress. Once I completed the brain dump, I was amazed at how I could look over my over 50 lines of writing and see that there were really only three or four major concerns. It was as if I was blowing everything out of proportion, making it bigger and more stressful than it really was. This is one practice I would definitely recommend if ever you feel stressed and overwhelmed, stuck or challenged.

Keeping a journal can help you create order when your world feels like it's in chaos. Keeping a journal can help you get to know yourself by revealing your most private fears, thoughts, and feelings. Look at your writing time as personal relaxation time. It's a time when you can de-stress and wind down.

However you choose to journal, listen to your heart and allow the words to flow. You can't get it wrong.

GRATITUDE

Okay, this is a big one. Gratitude has been scientifically proven to help and provide benefits. For example, a University of California, Davis study found that grateful teens had higher grade point averages, life satisfaction, and social integration, and lower envy and depression in comparison to materialistic teens.

Another study followed three groups of participants in keeping a journal to record one of three things, depending on their group: what they were grateful for during the week, what aggravated them, or what affected them (without specifying a positive or negative emphasis). After doing this exercise for 10 weeks, those in the gratitude-recording group were more optimistic, had better life satisfaction, exercised more, and had fewer visits to their physician. With all of these benefits, it's no surprise why gratitude is included as a practice to understand.

Statistics show that gratitude has benefits in four areas of life: physical, emotional, mental, and social.

Physical – Your physical well-being is positively impacted by an increase in gratitude practices. A 2013 study in the *Journal for Clinical Psychology* found that grateful people feel fewer aches and pains and feel overall healthier in comparison to others. This is because gratitude gives us a more positive disposition and motivates us to pursue positive pursuits.

Here are a few other physical benefits from practicing gratitude:
- Reduces symptoms of depression
- Lowers blood pressure
- Improves quality of sleep
- Increases prevalence of physical activity

Emotional – Our emotional well-being is directly affected by an increase in gratitude. Many studies from Robert A. Emmons, a scientific expert on gratitude, as well as other researchers say that gratitude reduces feelings of envy, frustration, and other toxic feelings that, in turn, increase our overall happiness and reduce depression. The reduction of negativity clears our minds to allow us to take in positive feelings.

Here are some emotional benefits from practicing gratitude:
- Increases long-term happiness
- Reduces envy
- Increases life satisfaction
- Makes us more optimistic
- Lowers instances of depression

Mental – A person's mental health can be affected by gratitude. For instance, researchers found that athletes with higher levels of gratitude from their coaches had increased self-esteem over time. Another study on gratitude found that people who engaged in gratitude activities were more prone to happiness and positivity than those who did not. People who express and recognize gratitude are more confident and compassionate overall.

Some other gratitude benefits for your mental health include:
- Boosts self-esteem
- Increases selflessness
- Improves decision-making
- Makes us more resilient

Social – We reap a ton of social benefits when we choose to engage in gratitude practices in our social circles. Gratitude in the workplace has shown to increase work performance as well as helps improve employee health and well-being. Feeling and expressing gratitude promotes a positive and happy mood. These brain boosts can have significant positive effects on employees' physical and mental health. In a group tested to see if an expression of gratitude made those on the receiving end more likely to desire friendship, those who expressed gratitude developed more friendships than those who did not. Social benefits make sense since people are usually more attracted to positive people. A greater appreciation for others is also an attractive trait since people inherently love to feel praised and acknowledged.

Here are a few other social benefits you gain for practicing gratitude:

- More well-liked by others
- Improves and strengthens relationships
- Increases social support
- Strengthens feelings of work fulfillment

When working on gratitude in the workplace, here are few ways to start:

1. Be sincere. Authenticity is perhaps the most important aspect of being grateful.
2. Begin by giving thanks. Start your workday or meetings by sharing what you are thankful for with your coworkers and encouraging them to do the same.
3. Be personal and specific.
4. Share the spotlight. Give appreciation to those who have helped you along the way.
5. Compensate accordingly.

Showing appreciation in the workplace can help you to strengthen workplace relationships. If done on a regular basis, expressing your appreciation can impact the morale of the entire office. In early 2021, Indeed.com shared an article, "120 Coworker Appreciation Messages." If gratitude and appreciation don't come easily and naturally for you, look up the article. Reading and reviewing a list of different coworker appreciation messages can help you craft great ones to share with your own colleagues.

*Empowering others is how empowered
people share and give.*

INVITATION

Pick one of the practices in this chapter and write it down here or in your journal. Commit to learning more about it. Commit to integrating it into your day.

- Decide **when** you will allow time for it.
- Decide **how** you will practice it.
- Decide **where** you will practice.
- Know **why** you chose the practice you chose.

_____

_____

Put it on your calendar. Schedule it into your day. Look forward to it. Look forward to the benefits and the positive impact it will bestow on you. Put a smile on your face and let it be felt on the inside. Be glad you are strong, committed, and invested in your self-care.

_____

_____

The real invitation is to come back to this chapter again and again as you pick a new practice to implement, integrate, and make your own. Enjoy!

CHAPTER 24:

EXPANDING THROUGH CURIOSITY

What are your thoughts about *curiosity*? By now, you are becoming more aware of your stories, beliefs, and judgments. There is value when you begin with a clear look at any underlying objections or beliefs that you have about the word itself and the meaning you currently hold and apply to it. Pause a moment and ask yourself: Does curiosity excite me? Do I feel expanded or contracted when I think of curiosity? And WHY? What does curiosity mean to me?

Many myths warn us that curiosity killed the cat. God banishes Adam and Eve from the Garden of Eden because they ate of the fruit from the Tree of Knowledge of Good and Evil. The Faust legend describes a man who sells his soul to the devil in exchange for unlimited knowledge. Do you unconsciously hold a belief that curiosity could get you into trouble?

If you said yes, you are not alone. This is simply an example of how you are conditioned by your environment, culture, and the stories passed down through generations. Awareness is your gift. The real gift is in dismantling the myth and learning anew.

It is in the curiosity about your beliefs that the true power and gifts of curiosity are realized.

I was brought up and conditioned to believe I needed to know everything. Teachers called on me even when I didn't raise my hand, expecting me to know the answer. Whether I knew or had to guess, that teacher wanted a response from me. Right or wrong didn't matter in the initial energy and emotions I was experiencing. I felt pressure because I didn't choose to respond; I didn't raise my hand. I wasn't sure of myself. And I was too focused on the pressure I felt: how I might look or appear to others if I was wrong; the embarrassment and humiliation I would place upon myself if I was wrong. Yes, this was pressure for me. As I reflect, curiosity never even entered my mind. What if I did know the answer? I was too focused on the pressure. What if I had gotten curious? What if the teacher called on me because she thought I had great insight, awareness, and good answers even when I didn't know all the facts? Curiosity could have aided me in so many ways.

Be curious, not judgmental. ~ attributed to Walt Whitman

I began to embrace curiosity in my early 20s. First, in my own abilities, I took up running and watched the progression of my skill, duration, and distance increase as my curiosity took me further and further. The runner's high is real, and to feel the shift of that so-called second wind kick in, to ride the wave of effortless motion and ease as you observe your body and breath work together in the most harmonious unison, is seriously something to be experienced.

Curiosity took me into sales. Sitting behind a desk all day was starting to tell my body, this wasn't for me. I wanted more. I wanted more variety, freedom, and variation to my days. Once I latched onto the idea of sales, there was no turning back. Curiosity was all I needed. Once in the position, I found myself curious every day. Who, when, and where were all different and unique from morning to afternoon—every day.

Years later, motherhood sparked my curiosity in a whole new way. While parenting doesn't come with an owner's manual, I got curious and asked, What if I do know what to do? What if the so-called owner's manual was encoded in my cells and DNA? What if I had access to the knowledge and wisdom I needed to be a great mom? I had to believe that life did not give us children with no knowledge and resources to tend to them. I was always curious, as if leaning into the empty space of not knowing and trusting the answers would come…and they did.

In the 1990s, I got fired from a job. I was shocked or, better said, I was devastated. It rocked my world and took me off course for quite a while. As I reflect back, things could have quickly spiraled into a whole new chapter of life had I just gotten curious once again. It's amazing how long we can stay attached to our pain when our world gets massively disrupted. I carried this devastation for much longer than I would care to admit.

Fast-forward to 2020 and the shutdowns, restrictions, and quickly changing environment, which was a shock for all. Although I also felt this massive disruption, I actually felt okay, as I knew I had the power to step back and take a bigger view of what was going on and how to best use this time. To me, this was an indication of my growth and evolution that had been going on for the last two decades. Asking myself, *What if this is good, not bad?* has always been the most valuable thing I could do. I had learned the value in looking at a situation from multiple perspectives, as if I had the power to create space around the situation and sit in that space without giving judgment to my experience, emotions, and concerns. Please don't think for a moment that I saw the pandemic as a good thing, but knowing I couldn't fight the reality of what *is* was most important to me. Working with my current reality in the best way was my new focus, and getting curious—as you'll soon see—is part of the process.

There is no greater time than when we are pushed out of our comfort zone for curiosity to show us its true value and potential. It's in those moments of unknown, in uncharted waters, that this one process becomes the valuable, irreplaceable tool that it is to our growth.

So, what is **curiosity**? It's the **C** in the ABCs to master you and your results. The one process to apply is **C**uriosity. Curiosity lets you question, What would I love? It allows you to pause before applying meaning to something. It allows wisdom and guidance to come to you, through you, as you refrain from past knowing and remain open to future potential.

> *Curiosity is defined as a need, thirst,*
> *or desire for knowledge, for more.*

The concept of curiosity is central to motivation. The term *curiosity* is used both as a description of a specific behavior as well as a hypothetical construct to explain the same behavior.

Is curiosity a characteristic, a skill, an instinct, a trait? What is it? Maybe it is all these and more. We know for certain, curiosity is a fundamental human trait. In the beginning, every child is curious: What's this? What's that? Their curiosity is endless. As a child, it's a daily process. As I observe a small child, it's as though curiosity is an activity in and of itself. At some point in your life, you ask yourself bigger questions: Who am I? What am I here for? You get curious.

CURIOSITY: THE PROCESS FOR SUCCESS

The fastest path to divine magic is found through curiosity. The Curiosity Quotient, CQ, is as important as intelligence. Curiosity says, I don't know. Curiosity says, Show me. Curiosity is the one process that activates divine knowledge and insight. Curiosity is an invitation to allow higher guidance, intuition, and deeper knowing into your awareness.

Pause a moment. I want you to gain the most you can, the greatest benefit, from what is shared in this chapter. It's important to know that **how** you take in your awareness is a real thing. Notice how you take in your awareness. You might be a person who has a rigid and small window of what you deem acceptable, and that becomes the view in which you see and experience the world. You might be a person who has no agenda as to how things need to be and allows each moment to unfold in awe.

At this time, I invite you to be *curious*. I want to invite you to welcome in some fresh perspectives for your consideration. Pretend that this moment has been created just for you—to grow you, advance you, change you, and connect you. Why? Because you are here and reading this now.

Curiosity is the lust of the mind. ~ Thomas Hobbes

Many things shared you'll already know, and that part of you that knows will wake up and resonate. There will be things stated that may make you question. Here I want to point out two ways to question:
1. To validate your beliefs
2. To learn and possibly expand your beliefs or to see things differently

I invite you to apply a bit of curiosity to what you will learn. I invite you to choose the second way of questioning. I invite you to begin to embrace your curiosity now.

Curiosity means the ability and habit to apply a sense of wonder and a desire to learn more. Curious people try new things, ask questions, search for answers, relish new information, and make connections, all while actively experiencing and making sense of the world.

Curiosity is the fuel for discovery,
inquiry, and learning.

Much like empathy and self-awareness, curiosity is a proven and useful leadership skill. Until recently, curiosity has been a struggle for many leaders to integrate into their leadership approach. Curiosity is being open and asking questions. You use smart, strategic, thoughtful, and targeted questions to get information to see more, understand more fully, and allow yourself greater insight.

Apply curiosity as your #1 process and you'll tend to express more empathy because you'll prefer asking questions instead of reacting with your opinion. Apply curiosity and you'll be held in high regard as one who values another's point of view, shows respect, and makes others feel welcome. Use this process to engage with your team, to allow others to feel valued and included, and to create harmony and respect in the workplace.

Curiosity is an essential leadership process. I say *process* because a process is a series of small steps or actions that are taken in order to achieve an end result. The difference between a skill and a process is that a skill is a capacity to do something well; skills are usually acquired or learned, as opposed to abilities, which are often thought of as innate, while a process is a series of steps or events to produce a result or desired outcome. Curiosity is a process that leads one to greater awareness, understanding, a bigger picture, and often—exactly what is needed—insight.

A curious mind learns about people, connects better with others, and inspires innovative thinking. In preparation for his book *The Corner Office,* Adam Bryant asked over 700 CEOs, "What quality do you see most often in those who succeed?" The number one answer on their lists: **curiosity**.

I have no special talents. I am only passionately curious. ~ Albert Einstein

As children, we are naturally curious, born with the impulse to seek new information and experiences. As we age and gain more experience, we become less reliant on curiosity for answers and more reliant on knowledge. The shift back to curiosity will require practice using the process. You'll need to have a plan. Curiosity gives way to comfort and certainty.

Curiosity throughout adulthood requires approaching experiences with the open-mindedness and the innocence of a child. Buddhists call this "beginner's mind." It's said that the correct approach to Zen requires a lack of preconceptions because:

In the beginner's mind, there are many possibilities; in the expert's mind, there are few.

Why is curiosity so often linked to success? Curiosity pushes people toward uncertainty and allows them to approach this uncertainty with a positive attitude. From this empty space of uncertainty, you actively engage all aspects of yourself (body, mind, emotions, spirit) to steer your curiosity in a kind, loving, compassionate, and empowering way. Empathy, creativity, innovation, and the ability to learn quickly all spring from curiosity.

Curiosity has no agenda or desire to drive a specific outcome, which means it can open you up to experiences you never thought were possible. This is how groundbreaking discoveries are made, markets are disrupted, and barriers are overcome.

While curiosity comes naturally to some, many adults must develop it, and like a skill or habit, it takes practice. In talking about her book, *Big Magic: Creative Living Beyond Fear*, best-selling author Elizabeth Gilbert advises that if you want to live a curiosity-driven life, you must commit to being vigilant about looking for what's piquing your curiosity. Her advice is to follow what is interesting to you, even if that interest is faint at first. She proposes that instead of following your passion, it might be a better idea to follow your creativity. So, let's all get a bit more curious.

Curiosity is not only linked to success because it leads to creativity and discoveries. It also helps you develop meaningful relationships that enrich your personal and professional life. When you interact with others thinking you know what they want or what you want from them, there's a tendency to steer your conversations toward that, limiting the possible experiences with them. When you let curiosity lead your conversations, you open up possibilities. Curiosity allows you to establish deeper, more meaningful relationships because your interactions become about discovering others rather than using them to fulfill your agenda.

Curiosity is the engine of achievement. ~ Ken Robinson

Curiosity is linked so closely with success because it drives you into the unknown, which is where you make discoveries, develop relationships, uncover opportunities, and experience growth. While curiosity alone does not always lead to success, in relationships, in business, and in life, it's a great place to start.

THE NEUROSCIENCE OF CURIOSITY

Curiosity is one of the oldest cognitive pathways, which means:
1. It is well-ingrained in our brains.
2. It works well.

Neuroscience tells us that curiosity and extrinsic motivation activate and recruit the same brain area. They're both influenced by the rewards process—the dopamine response that makes us feel good when we get something we desire, triggering the need to do more and thus get more done.

Curiosity can arise from connecting past experiences to your current knowledge, and when you get a match—which is to understand something—your brain rewards you with dopamine. To lead and motivate teams through trust demands a lot of energy. Leaders can use this information: **The more curiosity you trigger, the more motivation you'll receive**. Quite a strong benefit of curiosity for leaders!

This explains why successful organizations share their corporate vision with their employees, get them onboard, and invite them to get curious about their own vision and how it aligns with the organization. I hope you, too, can see the win/win here for all.

Dopamine is linked to the process of curiosity, as it is responsible for assigning and retaining reward values of information gained.

Research suggests higher amounts of dopamine is released when the reward is unknown and the stimulus is unfamiliar compared to activation of dopamine when the stimulus is familiar.

Curiosity is the process for your success, the process that requires a step-by-step practice of inquiry and questioning to bring you what you seek. It requires not just any kind of questioning, but asking those bigger questions, the questions you don't have the answers to but know they exist within you, which will become the spark of curiosity that quickly advances you.

Curiosity is the driving force behind
everything we know.

The fact is, humans are innately curious. Your curiosity is an important feature of cognition. Although there are many theories about how curiosity works, all theories agree that curiosity's immediate function is to lead people to explore and learn.

Curiosity is a driver for developing
knowledge and competence.

Have you ever gotten curious about why you say what you say? Have you ever gotten curious about your own curiosity?

LET'S GET CURIOUS

What do you believe is the most important thing in your life? Many will answer, "To be happy." In fact, in a 2007 survey of more than 10,000 people from 48 countries published in *Perspectives on Psychological Sciences*, happiness was viewed as more important than intelligence, success, maturity, knowledge, wisdom, relationships, wealth, and even meaning in life.

I agree, happiness matters. Until now, both in my professional research and in my personal experience, I've observed that when you focus solely on what you think will make you happy, you can lose track of what actually does.

You don't really know what you don't know.

From one organization to the next, from one executive and leader to the next, I ask, "How has our social progress, economic prosperity, and technological advancements over the past 50 years changed the quality of your lives? Have these new opportunities allowed you to spend more time doing what you care about most, thus increasing your satisfaction, happiness, and meaning in life?"

As I help you know yourself, grow yourself, and live your life empowered, I invite you to get curious, to inquire, and to ask bigger questions. I invite you to *not know the answer* even when you think you do. I invite you to play in the playground of curiosity.

Curiosity is one of the great secrets of happiness. ~ Bryant McGill

One of the most reliable and overlooked keys to happiness is cultivating and exercising our innate sense of curiosity. It's because curiosity—the process of active interest and genuinely wanting to know more about something—creates an openness to unfamiliar experiences, laying the groundwork for greater opportunities to experience discovery, joy, surprise, and delight.

The best in business have boundless curiosity and open minds. ~ Robin Sharma

In working with a small boutique shop owner who prided herself on her bachelor's in marketing and economics and a minor in Spanish along with her master's in finance, she thought she knew everything about crafting, creating, and operating a successful business. She got lost in her vast knowledge. She left no open space for new awarenesses, curiosity, and growth. I told her that her greatest growth would come from joining my Winner's Circle for Entrepreneurs. She joined, and in her first month, she was introduced to curiosity. In only 30 days, she learned to nurture and develop her curiosity to transform everyday tasks into interesting and enjoyable experiences. She started asking clients what they loved and what they were looking for; she used curiosity to connect her with her boutique and her clients. Six months later, her traffic and her profit had doubled. She admitted it was challenging to shift her mind from knowing to not knowing but so rewarding. Not only has her boutique benefited, but also she is experiencing increased joy and satisfaction in life.

It all starts with wanting to know more.

BENEFITS OF CURIOSITY

Let's investigate empowering you with the benefits of curiosity. Let curiosity be the backbone supporting the process of your learning, becoming, acquiring, and achieving in all aspects of life.

For children and adults alike, curiosity has been linked with psychological, emotional, social, and even health benefits. Here are a few:
- Curiosity helps us survive.
- Curious people are happier.
- Curiosity boosts achievement.
- Curiosity can expand our empathy.
- Curiosity helps strengthen relationships.
- Curiosity improves health and well-being.

Using curiosity in your life and work can bring many valuable benefits.
- It improves your ability to make decisions and solve problems—think complex problem solving and critical thinking.
- It increases your engagement and boosts your performance—think productivity and relationships.
- It supports collaboration and teamwork—think cooperation and results.
- It increases your resilience and improves the way you manage uncertainty and change—think optimism and solutions.
- It increases your ability to manage stress and pressure—think adaptable and confident.
- It heightens your senses, and as a result, you will experience positive emotions more intensely—think joy and happiness.
- It leads to more moments of creativity and to more innovative and new ideas—think evolution and change.

Knowledge is having the right answers.
Intelligence is asking the right questions.

CURIOSITY IN BUSINESS

New research points to three important insights about curiosity as it relates to business, as reported in the September–October 2018 issue of the *Harvard Business Review*.

First, curiosity is much more important to an enterprise's performance than was previously thought. That's because cultivating it at all levels helps leaders and their employees adapt to uncertain market conditions and external pressures. When our curiosity is triggered, we think more deeply and rationally about decisions and come up with more creative solutions. In addition, curiosity allows leaders to gain more respect from their followers and inspires employees to develop more trusting and more collaborative relationships with colleagues.

Second, by making small changes to the design of their organizations and the ways they manage their employees, leaders can encourage curiosity—and improve their companies. This is true in every industry and for creative and routine work alike.

Third, although leaders might say they treasure inquisitive minds, in fact, most stifle curiosity, fearing it will increase risk and inefficiency. In a survey conducted of more than 3,000 employees from a wide range of firms and industries, only about 24 percent reported feeling curious in their jobs on a regular basis, and about 70 percent said they face barriers to asking more questions at work.

In most organizations, leaders and employees alike receive the implicit message that asking questions is an unwanted challenge to authority. Often you are trained to focus on your work without looking closely at the process or your overall goals. But maintaining a sense of wonder is crucial to creativity and innovation.

The most effective leaders will look for ways to nurture their employees' curiosity to fuel learning and discovery.

Implementing and encouraging the process of curiosity is a work in progress as we transition out of old fears and ways of operating in the workplace and cultivate a culture that is rich and rewarding as it makes the best use of human potential, progress, and future innovation.

INVITATION

Tune in to your curiosity. The best ways to truly appreciate the power of curiosity is to start exercising it more consciously in your daily experiences. By doing so, you can transform even your routine tasks and enliven them with new energy.

Allow curiosity to build knowledge. Allow your curiosity to bring knowledge to fill the gaps of what you don't know. In a hobby, around nutrition and your well-being, or in your work, let curiosity begin to expand in your awareness to show you even more. Be open to what you don't know.

Allow yourself to thrive in uncertainty. While many experience stress and tension in uncertainty, this doesn't have to be. Research shows us that people who take part in new and uncertain adventures and activities are happier and more able to adjust and adapt than those who rely on the familiar. Allow curiosity to fill those uncertain moments with wonder, excitement, and joy.

Allow yourself more play. Be curious as to how you might add an element of fun into your everyday tasks. The attitude of play will naturally add interest and curiosity. Allow yourself to be free, curious, and adventurous in your playfulness.

Look for the unknown in the known. This is a great little way to expand curiosity into all you do. As I listen to other people speak, I often hear their presumptions. Maybe you can find where you have a pre-assumption. Where have you labeled, prejudged, or intentionally circumvented expectations about a seemingly familiar activity?

It's human nature to have an opinion, and it's easy to prejudge a situation because we think we have seen it before or avoid a situation entirely because we expect it to be boring or unpleasant. The invitation here is to set a goal of discovering the unfamiliar in the familiar. It is to suspend all judgments and attend to how things are, not how you expect them to be.

Look for the unknown in what you think you know: **get curious**, live in that space of not knowing, and allow yourself to be shown anew.

CHAPTER 25:

HABITS

The human experience is a real puzzle until you choose to slow down, pause, and look at all the minute parts of the process. This chapter will expand on how you create the processes that are programmed into your subconscious to support you in life. This chapter is all about your habits. By the end of this chapter, you'll want to be creating new habits to serve you.

You have a million tiny little habits that are running in the background of all you do in your daily life. You have some really great and supportive habits, like bathing, brushing your teeth, walking, and taking care of your physical body. You have habits that help you be kind, generous, and loving to others, and other habits allow you to focus and perform your job with ease.

You have habits that don't really help you; in fact, you have habits that hurt you. You might allow one event, circumstance, or thought to take you away from peace and bliss and into a dramatic and dark place. Whether it's anger, guilt, betrayal, love, or loss, you fight to hold on and you fight to let go. You get trapped in your own prison, the prison in your mind. You hold onto the pain and hurt. You tell stories about it to make it true for you. You then allow those stories to continually replay and repeat themselves, as you self-perpetuate your own living hell...

Until you are fed up with the suffering. Until you decide you are done. Until you choose to not go there, to not think about this anymore. Getting out of the prison is much harder than getting into it.

Life is crazy and insane. Change is hard.
Whether it's hurt, anger, guilt, betrayal, love, or
loss, we fight to hold on and we fight to let go.

Left unattended, your habits, the thoughts and feelings you can't let go of and fight to hold on to, send signals to the cells in the body and allow illness and disease to present itself. I know; I watched my own stories first unfold into lupus and, years later, a back issue. I also know how easy it is for you to be blind to what is going on and how you live in the stories of your pain, disappointment, depression, and anguish. I've been there too.

You are always creating new habits, patterns, and processes. The process of ending an unsupportive habit is the loop into the new process and thus a new habit.

A change in bad habits leads to a change in life.
~ Jenny Craig

Consistent habits give you power, authority, and all you need to succeed. Willpower is fed through habits. It takes the Observer to see the habits you have in place and at work on your best behalf. It takes awareness to look at the small details that are creating the results for you in your life, in your health and well-being, in your relationships, in your career, and in your time and money freedom.

You are in this human experience to have dominion over the physical body, mind, and earth. You are here to craft order, habits, and rhythms that support you. You are here to master staying in tune with consistent habits—habits that keep you in alignment that support your growth and evolution, no matter what is going on around you or in your environment.

REQUIREMENTS FOR MANAGING YOUR HABITS

Managing your habits is taking control over them. It requires the dismantling of old habits and the construction of new habits. If you have ever tried to break an unhelpful habit without a new one to replace it, you know the struggle. It's not that it can't be done because, with enough desire, determination, willpower, and resilience, you can achieve just about anything you want. So, let's see what will help you do this with ease.

Managing your habits requires:

- **Growth mindset** – A growth mindset says you want to grow, change, and evolve. You are open to seeing what's necessary to cultivate new habits and eliminate your unhelpful ones.
- **Observation** – The ability to observe and discover through your available senses and to move past the familiar is required to access a fresh perspective. It's through observing your discomfort that you will also notice your longings.
- **Development** – Create and identify skills, methods, and practices that are needed to accomplish your desired outcome. Develop trust in knowing what skills and practices are right for you. Just because everyone else did it one way doesn't mean that way is correct for you. Develop an inner trust in knowing you know what methods to apply.
- **Stretching, expanding, and exploring** – It's vital that you move out of your comfort zone with courage and playful discovery. To embrace and feel comfortable being uncomfortable sounds like an oxymoron, but it's vital to your growth.

In summary, you'll need to craft the right rhythm, order, and habits in your life. You'll need to have a growth mindset, one ready to support your evolution. You'll use awareness, the four intelligence systems, and your Observer self to spot and discover the habits you are ready to move beyond. You'll craft the right methods and practices to aid you. And you will need to get comfortable in the unknown as you stretch and expand into greater aspects of yourself as you craft new habits that will support your vision, life, and well-being. If this seems overwhelming, don't fret—this is where a coach or mentor could support you. In fact, some coaches, like myself, are truly expert at spotting the blocks and repeating habits that keep you stuck.

> *You'll need to focus on what you want,
> not what you don't want.*

HABITS OF HEALTH

*A healthy lifestyle requires you
develop healthy habits.*

Believe it or not, you already know what you need to do. This is the point in which many people will feel the rub, the resistance, and want to deny, deject, and shut their ears to what is said. Many don't want to hear the truth. And so many don't want to take responsibility for where they are. Maybe this is you. Maybe this is someone you know, someone you love and care about.

*A healthy lifestyle is a choice. Being sick is
hard; being healthy is hard. Choose your hard.*

Your health is vital to having an amazing life. Without good health, your focus will be on your lack of health. You'll be focused on the pills you need to take, the limitations you have, and all the things you can't do instead of what you can do. Your health is not predisposed. You are not a victim to your life. You have more control over your well-being than you know. The old narrative was that you have the genes and are predisposed to cancer, lung disease, heart disease, dementia, and so many other diseases because your ancestors died of them. We all have the genes. Yes, we all have the components that trigger and create illness in the body. Scientific advances in the field of epigenetic and quantum physics expand on this knowledge and show us how powerful you really are. So, let's look at habits of health, behavior, and mind to get a better picture of these habits in you.

I have a friend who has high blood pressure and does all the wrong stuff. He knows what causes his high blood pressure and doesn't want to change his habits, stop drinking, or discipline himself to alter his lifestyle to manage his blood pressure on his own. He feels it's easier to take a pill, and so he continues to foster habits that don't promote his health and well-being, all while subjecting is body to the side effects from the synthetic drug he insists on ingesting daily.

Another example is a woman who has diabetes. Her condition has escalated, and now that she has a pump installed to inject a dose of Insulin, she regularly binges on chocolate cake, candy, and sweets—or so I thought. One day when we talked, she admitted she didn't just start overeating sweets, she never stopped. She said she knows it's what caused her diabetes in the first place, and she also knows that it's what has caused it to progress to this level. Sugar is probably the most addictive substance I know.

Sugar impairs cognitive skills.

We commonly think there are four physical areas of focus to a healthy lifestyle, yet we often fail to remember that the habits of health and well-being must include mind and emotions, which are at the root of a healthy lifestyle. These are the six areas to a healthy lifestyle:

- Mind
- Emotions
- Diet
- Activity/exercise
- Rest
- Hydration

You have all the power you need inside you to see what needs to be done and where to begin—when you are ready (an important caveat). You see, we all know, deep down inside, maybe at a subconscious level, what we need. The conditioning our health care society attempts to instill is that they know more than you. Come in and get a checkup. Come in and tell us your symptoms, and we will prescribe a fix. Yet that fix is not a fix; it's actually just a Band-Aid. It camouflages the symptoms but does nothing to get to the core of the problem to really remove it. When you are ready, you will be open to your awareness and to making the change.

I've been on quite a few unhealthy journeys in my life. Each one was really my avoidance of looking at the core component beneath the bad habits. Almost always, these core components are the emotions that I didn't want to feel. I surely didn't want to deal with, experience, feel, or process the pain, and therefore, I created habits to help me avoid what I most needed to deal with. Maybe this is you too. Don't beat yourself up if this is you. Know that nearly every human being avoids pain. We weren't taught to move through it. Being trapped in habits is our human addiction. Seeing these habits is the superpower of awareness.

This is why the Observer is so helpful. From the Observer self, you can see, even experience, and allow that emotion to do what it came to do all along…move through you. Emotions are energy in motion.

We live in a world of massive conditioning—conditioning you, me, and everyone to focus on the outer world, others, and technology, and thus forgetting our true nature and abilities. We are more than the physical body; we are spirit, a soul, and awareness itself.

The Age of Aquarius is awakening humanity. It's awakening you to your own inner power, and it's showing you where you give your power away to others. It's awakening humanity to more of their human potential. If you haven't seen it, you might search the internet to explore the many medical miracles and healings, like people walking after years in a wheelchair. Advances have happened in sports, with people surfing waves of 50 feet high and free-soloing mountains in times unheard of without any gear. How do you explain the work of Joe Dispenza? Check out a few of the testimonials on his YouTube channel, and you, too, will be surprised by what you find.

HABITS OF BEHAVIOR

If you thought the habits of health were big, intense, and full of learning, take a deep breath and get comfy for this one: The habits of behavior aren't always as easy to spot for the one with the poor behavior. Why? Because your habits of behavior aren't always seen by you; they operate from your subconscious. But these poor habits of behavior are almost always seen and noticed by others.

The aid of a good coach can help you in spotting your blocks, patterns, and behaviors that you don't see and are unconscious to you. The aid of a great coach can shine the loving light of awareness on your shadows and illumine for you what others are experiencing from your behavior. A really great coach will be able to illumine and evoke from you the parts of yourself that are unloved, unworthy, or unskilled. They will also guide you in creating new habits and patterns by first catching yourself in the unwanted behavior and then shifting to a self-created new supportive behavior.

No longer are you limited by your past; in fact, you never were except in your own mind. Awareness to your human behavior can show you your limits and your potential. Look at the Bannister effect. Roger Bannister, an ordinary runner and full-time student, broke the four-minute mile and allowed other runners to move beyond the psychological barrier that a sub-four-minute mile wasn't possible. Now, many runners achieve a time of less than four minutes. Don't let a habit of thought about something hold you back from achieving more.

I worked with a woman who, through a company reorganization, was now managing twice the number of people. Her initial complaint or topic of focus she shared was her current level of overwhelmed and how she was constantly finding fault in her team and then pointing it out to them in ways that were not constructive. She had just been written up for an interaction with one of her staff for the way she spoke to them. As we dove deeper into her thoughts around overwhelm, she was able to see that she tended to shut down when she was overwhelmed. She quickly related her reactions at the office to how she reacts at home with her kids when she is overwhelmed. She said she noticed that when she's had a busy, stressful day at the office, she tends to bring it home with her. Because she doesn't deal with it internally, she begins accusing the kids of everything she sees that is wrong. She noticed how she jumps on her son about the trash cans still down at the curb, his bike in middle of the front yard, and the shoes at the door that she almost tripped over. And these were just the things she could see; she also went on to complain about things she couldn't even see and often made up.

Bringing the conversation back to the office and how she handled overwhelm there, she noticed by not dealing with her own emotional state, she quickly went to finding fault in those around her. In her overwhelm, she would shut down inside and not deal with her inner chaos. Then, in an attempt to ease the explosive energy inside, she would look to find fault in others to make herself feel better. She thought the problem was the additional workload when, in reality, the additional workload triggered a habit that she had created—a habit of avoiding.

Together, we crafted a plan on how to deal with the overwhelm, which also included bringing all of herself to the party when she would engage with others. This quickly resolved her habit of finding fault in others and allowed her to deal with her emotions as well.

It's said a boss's behavior can take good staff and destroy it, causing the best employees to flee and those that stay to lose drive, motivation, and productivity.

*People don't leave bad jobs,
they leave bad bosses.*

Some of the most common unacceptable and unskillful managerial behaviors are:

- Discrimination
- Harassment
- Defensiveness
- Bullying
- Passive or active aggression
- Abusive behavior or talk
- Narcissistic behavior
- Gaslighting
- Belittling

Even putting others down and looking down on others is unacceptable behavior from management in the workplace. The aim of leadership should always be to build up their team and to empower others. When management's behavior causes the employee to feel shamed, belittled, or disrespected, they lose faith and respect in the company and their job. No one wants to work for a tyrant. Times have changed, and the drill sergeant, dominating, and dictating leaders of the past are not welcome in today's leadership roles.

It matters not if the unacceptable behaviors of management happen to be that of an abusive belittler, a covert narcissist, or an uncontrollably passive- or active-aggressive boss, the damage they do is both direct and widespread. Sadly, the damage is greater than just the immediate individual and department. The negativity spreads through the workplace like a contagion. Negative energy and low morale can turn even the most solid of cultures into a toxic environment, causing happy, productive employees to leave the company and ultimately impacting the bottom line.

It's a fact that the damage done by a boss's negative or unskillful behavior first lies in the boss themselves. They have damaged parts or aspects within themselves that they have yet to notice, heal, and repair. This inner work left unaddressed could cost them their job, relationships, and their happiness. The damage their unskillful behavior has on others is sharp and biting. If you are on the receiving end of this, you will fall into one of three ways of receivership:

- The first way you might receive the unskillful behavior is that you feel worthless, wrong, or unacceptable. When this shows up, it is showing you that you, too, have some work to do beneath the scenes. Your work is to notice, heal, and repair those parts and aspects of you that feel unworthy, rejected, or shamed so that you can see if there is any truth to the comments.

- The second way you might receive your boss's negative and unskillful behaviors is to reflect and look within to see if there might be any truth or validity to their words. If there is, you could take ownership and acknowledge that they notice that too. The best approach here would then be to either ask for your boss's ear as you think through your plan of action or ask for your boss's input and suggestions before you reflect on your best plan of action.

- The third way of receivership of this unskillful behavior is to see it as the boss projecting out that which lives deep within themself and to not take it personally. Of course, you first must scan your awareness to see if there is even a residue of truth before you can come to this conclusion.

Only when you are in your center, using all four of your intelligence systems, and being the Observer will you be able to quickly scan for any triggers or residues of truth in those often awkward and uncomfortable moments of experiencing your boss's poor behavior.

Oftentimes when the boss comes down on you, they catch you off guard, meaning they catch you at a time when you were in your head about a project you were working on. Or maybe they catch you at a time when you were worried and a bit overly emotional about something in your life. So, off guard is simply you off of your center. It's you leaning more into only one of your intelligence systems, thus leaving you vulnerable and victim to their words and behavior.

Whether you are reacting or responding to what another says, remember, your response does not need to happen immediately. Everyone has the option to say something like, "You've shared a lot here. I think it best if I reflect on all that was shared. May I get back to you with what I realize?"

Another important point to make here is this: If you are feeling like you have to defend yourself, stop. If you feel you've just been attacked or criticized, do not respond. This never comes out the way you intend it. In fact, defensiveness is one of the unskillful and unacceptable behaviors.

Defensive behavior is a barrier to communication.
~ Gary Chapman

Defensiveness says that from your victimhood, you need to protect your honor. It says, "Let me show you my worthiness." Defensiveness is used to form a sense of self-protection in the face of a perceived attack. Psychological defensiveness includes the many ways that we let ourselves off the hook when we do wrong: misrepresenting or misremembering what occurred, not paying attention to information that is critical, deflecting blame to others, minimizing any harm caused, denying responsibility, or disengaging entirely from the situation.

In your defensiveness, you'll first start out trying to prove the other person wrong. After numerous examples and reasons for why they aren't seeing the whole picture, you'll begin blaming the other for things that had nothing to do with what was said or discussed. Why? First, because you are trying to prove them wrong. Second, because hurt people project that hurt out onto others. In all the hurt, you can't see your own denial, deflection, and dissuasion. If you feel hurt, attacked, or wronged, do not respond from that level of awareness or it will come out wrong and come back like a boomerang to bite you in the rear.

All defensiveness stems from the need to be right and frustration over not being able to control others. ~ Bryant McGill

You will often end up feeling rejected, betrayed, or taken advantage of when you look to find fault in the other instead of looking within. As I work with clients, I find that it isn't what another said so much, as it is about how it made the client feel inside, which means that the real problem isn't being addressed. In trying to make the other person wrong, you are escaping the real issue. The real message for you is in how it makes you feel. It's in your feelings that you will gain the greatest insight and awareness.

You've heard the saying, "Don't shoot the messenger"; in this case, don't focus on blaming the messenger, but look at the message and how it is affecting you.

Herein lies the real work.

The reason it's wise to pause, reflect, and think about it is that this gives you the opportunity and ample time to look at the conversation

by bringing all of you to the party and not just the wounded, triggered, or tiny aspect of you that feels hurt and attacked.

Go easy on yourself as you create healthy habits of behavior. They will empower both you and others.

HABITS OF MIND

Healthy habits of mind have been shared throughout this book and this chapter. The focus in this section will be on the unhealthy habits of mind to help you spot, notice, and change what you may have been previously unaware of.

It turns out that everyone from AARP and WebMD to NIH post and share articles on the bad or unhealthy habits of the mind. Everyone wants to talk about this topic because these unhealthy habits of mind can damage your brain health and cognitive function and, thus, affect your quality of life. These habits can even increase your risk of depression or cause you to feel more anxious or stressed out. Unhealthy habits of mind can suck the joy right out of your life.

Know that there are many more bad habits of mind, so do your own research to further enrich your knowledge. Here are a few:

- **Perfectionist** – Oh, that nagging pursuit of excellence. In one way, it can help you do your best, and in another way, it may cause you to set standards beyond your reach, find dissatisfaction with anything less than perfection, even create a preoccupation with failure or disapproval, and see mistakes as evidence of unworthiness.
- **Guilt** – Unhealthy guilt, and its even nastier sidekick shame, can lead you to beat yourself up for everything or take responsibility for things you shouldn't, causing yourself undue stress and failure to set boundaries with people who want more from you than it's healthy for you to give.
- **Limited mindset** – A limited mindset is a mindset fixed in the belief that there are limitations to what you can accomplish in life. This mindset could limit life's opportunities, relationships, and both personal and professional growth and development. Worry and fear feed here.
- **Overuse of technology** (smartphone or social media) – These devices are awesome. They've become our personal assistants, entertainment, and connection to research, data, and valuable information. They have also become disruptors and triggers

for FOMO—fear of missing out. This overuse may be dangerous to your mental health, promoting anxiety, depression, and lower self-esteem.

In summary, habits are part of the structure and formation of all that you do. All the universe works in symmetry, repetition, and a unified system of calculated processes that go on to repeat themselves. You, too, work in this same symmetry.

> *You have an innate power—your own unique ability to program yourself as you see fit, to set forth the right habits and patterns that will be most supportive in your life.*

HABITS OF HIGHLY EFFECTIVE PEOPLE

This chapter doesn't feel complete without the reminder of the *7 Habits of Highly Effective People*, a self-help book by Stephen Covey. Covey's belief is that the way you see the world is entirely based on your own perceptions. In order to change a given situation, you must change yourself, and in order to change yourself, you must be able to change your perceptions.

Here are the *7 Habits of Highly Effective People*:
- Be Proactive
- Begin with the End in Mind
- Put First Things First
- Think Win-Win
- Seek First to Understand, Then to Be Understood
- Synergize
- Sharpen the Saw

I won't go into explaining them because I believe the book is a great read and one that you'll find worthy of your time.

Intellectually, you know what to do, you know how to drop ten pounds, and yet you do nothing. Until you are shocked emotionally with an unexpected diagnosis or your child begging you to stick around to see them graduate, you continue to supersize your meals. Why? The real change happens when you can identify with that new version of yourself. There is a mental and emotional connection to your identity.

I think my biggest takeaway from my first Tony Robbins event sums this up so well. He said:

The strongest force in the human personality is the need to stay consistent with how we define ourselves.

Think about this for moment and look at your need to remain consistent in how you define yourself to maintain your identity. Make sure that how you define yourself is in alignment with the results you want to achieve. Don't say, "I'm on a diet"; instead say, "I am choosing a new lifestyle for myself." In order for you to become a new version of yourself, you'll need an identity that supports that new version.

INVITATION

Take time to reflect on your habits. When you find one to let go of:

- Be ready to look at your fight to hold on;
- Be ready to look at your fight to let go;
- Be ready to see your need to remain consistent with how you define yourself.

_____

_____

It's in your awareness that your courage to move forward will rise.

Crafting a new order, process, and habit in its place will greatly speed the time required for change. Craft a new way to define yourself that is in alignment with the new you.

Be realistic and choose a habit you can commit to and craft a story that aligns with the new identity of you. To make this easy, choose only ONE change in your Habits of Health and then list the changes necessary in your Habits of Behavior and Habits of Mind for you to achieve the new results. Put reminders on your calendar, Post-its around your home/office, and add any other tools to help remind you during your day.

_____

_____

Enjoy the work you are doing, put a smile on your face, and feel your smile as it radiates inside you.

CHAPTER 26:

YOUR GREATNESS

There is so much greatness in you. You are the only block to your success. You are the only one stopping you from realizing your greatness. No one, and nothing, is stopping you from realizing and being all that you are. Can you see your greatness? Have you embraced your greatness?

Your life offers you free will and a variety of realities to choose from. With a simple shift in your perception, you can be living an entirely different reality. Sounds far-fetched, doesn't it? Allow me to explain and expand on this thought by sharing my story of finding my greatness because we are all just a diagnosis or a story away from our entire reality changing in a flash.

BLOCKED FROM SEEING MY GREATNESS

Late in 2009, after a year of living in pain, three back surgeries, and a grand mal seizure, I was in a pretty dark place. I was still experiencing physical pain in my back. I couldn't sit for more than about 20 minutes without needing to get up and move. I lost my short-term memory and had trouble having conversations with others. Comprehending a long email wasn't happening. I'd read it over and over before calling the client to verify what I thought they were wanting. Not only did I experience a loss of my health and well-being, but I also lost my independence and freedom since, after a seizure, I was unable to drive for six months. Adding just one more worry to the pile, I lost my health insurance. I then thought my COBRA insurance had been canceled on me, but years later found that its time had simply expired. I had no one in my life to count on to help me. I was struggling to live, and I was depressed in the struggles.

I had just started Complete Solutions in 2008 and was seriously contemplating if I was even employable. Would I need to file for disability? Would I ever get back to who I was, or did I need to accept where I was? In my eyes, I was seriously broken and half the person I use to be. Having my freedoms taken away as well as my quality of life was playing havoc on my mental and emotional state.

As I look back and reflect on the many thoughts that consumed me, I see how easy it is for any of us to get stuck in a limited mindset. With loss of your health, your routine, freedoms, and independence, you are forced to take a pause and reflect. It's all too easy to get stuck on the hamster wheel of repetitive thinking and getting off the hamster wheel requires noticing you are on it.

We get what we focus on.

I couldn't stop the never-ending thread of stories that played out in my head—stories that weren't even mine, stories the doctor told me like, you'll always have back pain; you have three vertebrae with no disk material that are bone on bone; you need a fusion; you'll be back in a year or so for another surgery; winters will be hard on you.

Think for a moment and reflect on your life and where you might be retelling a story that isn't yours. Look for any area in your life where you might have a repeating story that limits you.

GETTING A GLIMPSE OF HOPE

Months into 2010, I had a life-changing moment. On a call with my brother, he asked, "Oh sis, when will you tell a different story?" I was immediately defensive; I reacted with, "What, you want me to lie to you?" Things got heated, words were said—hurtful words. I hung up on him, both of us feeling angry, hurt, and bitter. The fact is, I knew he meant well; he was the only one checking in on me, and no one was making him. Later that night, wallowing in my guilt, contemplating my feelings and behavior, I thought about what he might have meant by what he asked, and from the Observer role, it was as if a light bulb went off inside me. I recalled my all-time favorite quote by Norman Vincent Peale:

Change your thoughts and you change your world.

As quickly as that, I dropped into an entirely new reality—one with hope. I could see where I was and where I wanted to be, and I could see that I was the bridge to get me there. It felt as if my darkness had been illumined for me to see. Stepping into the Observer role has the power and potential to shift your reality.

In my new reality, I created a mantra to help me stay focused. I typed out on a standard letter-size Word document the words, "Every day in every way, I am getting better and better." These were the best thinking thoughts I could muster up. I printed out 10 copies and put this message in every room of my home.

I was making progress. I detoxed my body, going on a five-day organic green juice fast, and felt great for the first time in two years. I started to really see results. I was walking every day, morning, noon, and night. I was also doing things for my brain. I knew I needed to start creating new neuropathways and connections. From sudoku puzzles to stepping out of my comfort zone to try new things—even playing video games—I was determined to make changes in my diet, lifestyle, exercise routine, brain-building activities, memory skills, and more.

Success sends a flood of feel-good
hormones through the body.

PURE POSSIBILITY AND YOUR INFINITE POTENTIAL

For the first time in over two years, I really was getting better and better with each day. I noticed my greatness and was determined to never forget it again. I started believing in myself again. It's ironic how when you start to believe in yourself, more of what you want starts showing up, change happens more quickly, and you shift your focus to your progress with gratitude. I started wondering what this next chapter of my life was all about. My first half was being an amazing mom, pursuing and succeeding at a career in sales, and even starting my own cleaning business. I was proud of all that I had created and experienced. Filled with joy and gratitude, I knew the second half of my life would be equally as fulfilling and rewarding as the first half.

In wondering what's next, I got curious about what I wanted and what wanted to come through me. I knew that all that I had experienced would probably be part of my next chapter. I knew my own transformation was not only available for me; it was available for everyone. I knew I'd be sharing the power of transformation to others. This transformation is the greatness that lives in each of us.

As I began to get curious, ask bigger questions, and sit in the space of the unknown to allow the answers to come…I got answers. They came as an inner knowing, like a free download from the universe. Not always immediately, but they did come.

While out on a walk one day, out of the blue, I got the message—the big message of what I was to do in this next chapter of my life. I was to bring spirituality into business. My first thought was, okay, that's BIG. As I sat in the pause, that space between what I had realized and my response, I noticed I wasn't resisting. I was open and receptive. I was both surprised and delighted. It's big enough to grow me. It's so far out of my knowing, I will surely be leaning into my higher self and intuitive guidance for every step along the way. There was no college degree to attain. There was no program or certification to acquire, but yet a lot of learning, developing, and creating to do. And it had a lot of goodness and greatness in it for everyone, not just me. This next chapter was truly about serving others. I felt an acceptance, almost as if it resonated with a part of me that I hadn't met yet.

With an aim so big, like *Bringing Spirituality into Business*, it prodded me to go deeper into what I did to heal, why I did it, what it caused internally, and how it helped. You see, I beat the odds; the doctors' prognosis was a lifetime of pain, but I was pain free and have been for over a decade. How does this happen? I looked to scientifically explain much of what happened and why, which is why I share throughout this book the science, philosophy, medical research, and data that validates spirituality, quantum physics, psychology, psychedelics, and the effectiveness and power we hold within our mind and mental intelligence alone. And I was so curious why the doctors aren't sharing any of this.

At the root of the shift in me was awareness, self-worth, self-love, and believing in myself again. I can't begin to emphasize the value of the Observer.

Unconditional love and acceptance of self is the starting point in the journey to know yourself.

If there were a message for you to tattoo on the inside of your eyelids, it would be this: unconditional love and acceptance of self is the starting point in the journey to know yourself. To truly know yourself is to love yourself. This message alone will allow you to see your greatness.

When you focus on your greatness you elevate everyone around you. ~ Gabrielle Bernstein

Challenges are going to be part of your life; face them, and as you do, you face them in your greatness. Your life is a journey of your growth. All of your dreams will grow you. Every dream teaches us more about ourselves. A challenge is a sign of your growth. You see, when you are confronted with obstacles that challenge you, you're forced to find a way around or through the current situation or circumstance. This is in itself growth.

My journey showed me the value of my Spiritual intelligence that I always have access to. Maybe you are noticing this too. For me, it was about embracing all of my intelligence systems, not one over another, not one without the other. You are meant to blend and unite both your humanness and your spiritual nature into every moment and every experience. I kept getting caught up in the humanness to see my problems, fears, and the blocks in my way. You will too—it's in our human nature—but with awareness, with your Observer self, you can catch yourself in being too focused on a problem instead of the solution and then be able to come back home to your center.

Spirituality is the quality of being concerned about the human spirit or soul as opposed to material and physical things. Spirituality is bringing your focus back home to all that you are. It's acknowledging that there is an energy, a force that has a rhythm, pattern, and repetitive nature to it, and it's found in all things. From the universe and planet Earth to every living thing on this planet—every plant, animal, bird, insect, and human being—everything is a byproduct of this life force energy we call Spirit. The human experience loves to label and discuss, so having gods or naming these powers has been part of our history. You are a spiritual being here having a human experience.

*Give yourself permission to step
into your greatness.*

I had shifted my awareness from life happening *to me* to one where I could see it was happening *for me*. In the *for me* awareness, I saw options, as if life was now illumined and sight was restored. But the biggest shift was the shift to life happening through me, and wow, what a shift that was. Life happening through you requires you know your self-worth and gives you the strength to see the joy in life through good times and bad, sickness and health. Life happening through you is owning your greatness.

I had shifted my reality from the Doom and Gloom (focusing on the pain, problems, and past) to the Current reality (filled with the highs of future potential and the dips of the doom and darkness), and onto the Future Possibility and Potential reality, where all my greatness was found.

I hope you are able to see the many options that life holds for you. Your greatness lies in your ability to illumine what is, who you are, and what you want. You are pure potential, pure possibility, opportunity, and growth. You are where the magic happens. There is greatness in you.

INVITATION

Reflect on your reality and discern if you are living in your Future Possibility and Potential reality.

_____

_____

What might your future reality hold for you? Allow yourself to imagine. When ready, craft a vision for your future, one that allows your greatness to shine.

_____

_____

Make this your aim as this is where the magic happens. Don't focus on the blocks; keep your focus on the end results and enjoy the journey. It's always way better than you could have imagined.

_____

_____

CHAPTER 27:

BUSINESS AWARENESS

This chapter focuses on business awareness and is broken down into three specific areas: organizational awareness, social awareness, and political awareness.

ORGANIZATIONAL AWARENESS

Organizational awareness is the ability to read a group's emotional currents and power relationships, and identify influencers, networks, and dynamics within the organization. Organizational awareness is the capability of perceiving and understanding the different components of an organization, both through its formal elements as well as through the informal patterns that emerge in the organization. It includes the understanding of political, social, and economic issues affecting the organization and its environment.

Organizational awareness is a blend of self-insight, social insight, and mastery.

In a well-written article by Daniel Goleman, published by the Korn Ferry Institute, he calls it "A Sixth Sense for Reading Your Company." Every leader needs to cultivate this sixth sense. Researchers at the University of Toronto's Rotman School of Management found that when it comes to being a change maker in an organization (having this sixth sense), rank in a company's formal hierarchy doesn't matter as much as how well someone is able to read and mobilize the informal networks needed to make change occur.

The leaders who can recognize networking opportunities and read key power relationships are better equipped to handle the demands of leadership. Such leaders not only understand the forces at work in an organization but also the guiding values and unspoken rules that exist among their people. Leaders skilled at organizational awareness can sense the personal networks that make the organization run and know how to find the right person to make key decisions and how to form a coalition to get something done.

Organizational awareness helps guide strategy, structures, and processes to accomplish goals in any organization or network, no matter the setting.

ENGAGING IN THE MISSION

The **mission statement** of an organization is a concise explanation of the organization's reason for existence. It describes the purpose and overall intention. The mission statement supports the vision and serves to communicate purpose and direction to employees, customers, vendors, and other stakeholders.

Leaders can look at how their mission statement relates to the way people operate within their organization. The company's mission—the so-called "why" and "purpose" of the business—may not have much relationship to what people do day-to-day. If that's the case, the leaders who wrote that statement lack organizational awareness and are failing in their responsibility to make sure the company's operations are in line with its mission.

Employees put their focus on what has meaning, and so leaders can direct attention by the goals and mission they articulate. The best leaders display their organizational awareness by capturing and directing the collective energy toward the strategic goals that matter most. These leaders know where that energy seems well directed and where in the organization it could be best utilized—and put their own energy into upping the game as needed.

It becomes a **game changer** when these leaders activate and engage the entire organization in their mission and vision and allow employees to see and realize the valuable role they play and the contribution they bring to the success of all. When coupled with each individual's vision, this is where the real magic happens.

READING THE ROOM

Organizational awareness requires a 360-degree awareness of what's going on; who's doing what, why, and when; and how all the parts come together. **Organizational awareness**—"social flow," social awareness, and even political awareness—is the ability to read the signs, be aware of what is not clearly said, and to understand the unwritten workings within the environment. It is both a necessary and critical capability of any organization, a form of consciousness that the organization develops while adapting to the business strategy and processes.

Organizational awareness begins in the interview and flows into the hiring, choosing the correct candidate to bring forth the missing elements to create a power team and add a beneficial asset to the company. It expands once the new employee is onboarded, established in the new role, and comfortable in their new position and contributions. This is often where many organizations and the leadership may slip up or take their eye off the ball, so to speak. People grow, change, and develop greater aspects of themselves, and thus, their greatest contribution to the organization shifts. When not monitored and managed, these people grow bored with their current position and move on. No one at this level is happy working beneath their capacity. They wish to continue to excel, to perform at their best, and contribute at their highest level. It's human nature.

When people outgrow their role, they will begin by expressing dissatisfaction or a need for more, like more responsibility or a new project. This can be seen by leadership as having a bad day or complaining. Leaders lacking social awareness and good listening skills will miss the small and subtle messages from their team. They'll overlook and dismiss what is said and end up dealing with the turnover when these people decide to move on to fulfill their own needs for professional growth and development and serve elsewhere.

SOCIAL AWARENESS

Social awareness is understanding the perspectives of and empathizing with others, as well as recognizing the massive contribution that comes from diversity: a range in ages, ethnicities, gender, backgrounds, cultures, and contexts. This includes the capacity to feel compassion for others and understand historical and social norms for behavior in different settings.

Here are a few examples of ways to develop social awareness:

- Listen to and consider others' perspectives.
- Recognize the strengths and value in people.
- Express gratitude to others.
- Identify diverse social norms, including unfair ones.
- Recognize situational demands, opportunities, and threats.

NAVIGATING WHAT YOU READ IN THE ROOM

Social awareness typically helps people read situations factually, beyond their own biases, emotions, or assumptions. Your proficiency in social awareness builds on both self-awareness and emotional intelligence skills (self-control and empathy), which will help you see clearly and from multiple viewpoints—think 360-degree awareness.

When leaders are able to recognize the skills, personalities, and strengths of their team, this is only the first step. The next step has the greatest impact. It comes when you have the ability to recognize the level of trust, agreement, and commitment of others. When you are able to identify your allies (high trust, agreement, and commitment) and your opponents (low trust, agreement, and commitment), you will be able to wield greater impact and influence in your professional position and setting in the organization. This is where the real culture of a corporation is manifested.

Various roles may be played (by nature, you'll fall into one, two, or all three):

- **Ally** – Those who are strong allies tend to be your team players and supporters. You'll want to be able to empower, fuel, and partner with your allies.
- **Adversary** – The adversary is generally perceived as one who fights against you every step of the way. You'll want to listen to their point of view, take it into consideration, and respect their contribution.
- **Fence sitters** – The fence sitter remains neutral; they are hard to gauge and are never fully committed. You'll want to engage them and understand their concerns, objectives, and the value they bring to others.

Donalee Gastreich

POLITICS IN THE WORKPLACE

Throughout the years, due to massive growth, we have seen organizations reinventing themselves to become more agile, networked, and less bureaucratic. Despite all these changes, organizations are still political structures. This means that companies still operate by distributing authority and setting a stage for the exertion of power. These political structures also provide opportunities for people to develop their careers and grow within the organization, allowing people to step up the corporate ladder and thus gain authority and power. Those at the top have big roles to play, an impact to make, and may lead with an influence that empowers and engages others to do the same.

The development of careers, particularly at high leadership levels, depends on one's accumulation of the power as the vehicle for transforming individual interests into activities that influence other people. Therefore, learning how to navigate in office politics and build influence is a key success factor, and this is directly linked to your emotional intelligence. To successfully navigate office politics, you'll need to correctly read key power relationships and detect essential social networks. Political awareness helps you understand the forces that shape the views and actions of stakeholders like clients, customers, community, and competitors, and accurately read the organizational and external environment.

Simon Baddeley and Kim James developed a useful model for political skills using two abilities and two dimensions: "Reading," to understand the world around them, and "Carrying," to understand their internal world. They suggested a scale from "acting with integrity" to "playing psychological games," creating four possible states: Clever, Innocent, Wise, and Inept, each of which can be described in terms of an animal (as shown here).

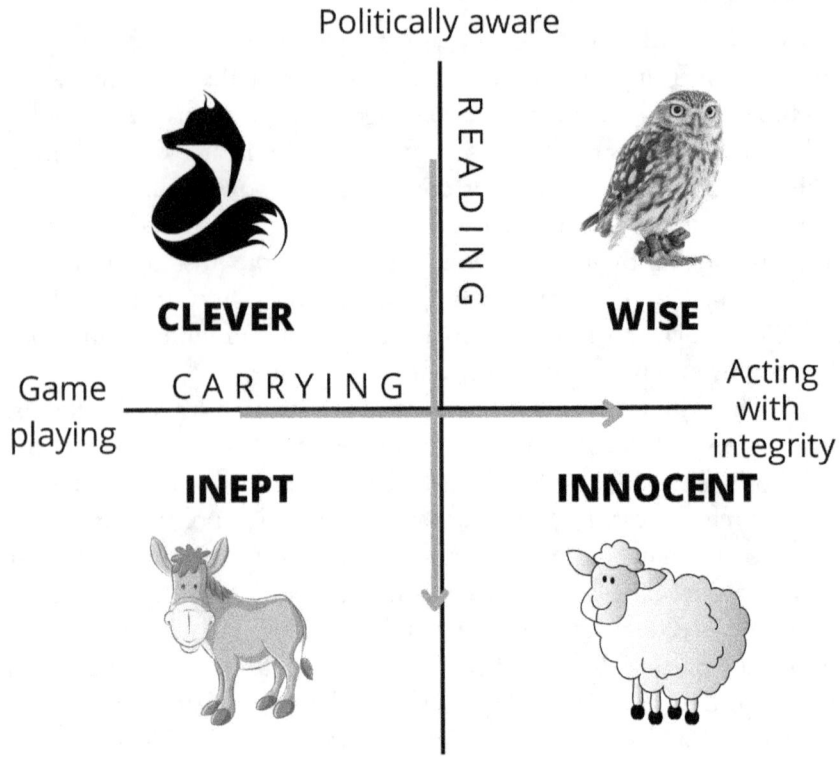

Politically aware

READING

CLEVER   WISE

Game playing   CARRYING   Acting with integrity

INEPT   INNOCENT

Politically unaware

Using the four-box matrix to understand behaviors:

- Where an integrated sense of self resulting from the experience of being either comfortable with one's capability or perception of being on familiar territory meet an unskilled reading of the environment, the result is Innocent behavior.
- Where unskilled reading meets lack of self-insight, the choice is frequently ego-defensive behavior as a way of defending the self in situations that one cannot make sense of or feel good in. We call this option Inept.
- Where skilled reading meets self-serving and defensive ego needs, the resulting behavior is likely to be controlling and manipulative. We call this Clever behavior.
- Where skilled reading meets self-insight and willingness to put oneself at the edge of what is familiar, to risk new options be-

cause the situation calls for one's highest values to be exercised, then the Wise option is displayed.

In the intricate organizational settings, people need the ability to simultaneously understand the world "out there" and their interior world, making sense of both and choosing appropriate behavior. We all have the ability to act in all four ways. The strength of the model lies in understanding how each of us can be Wise one minute and Inept the next. The external world we need to read is in constant flux, and the interior world is equally variable; the interface between the two is crucial in choosing an informed action.

Organizational awareness is a common trait among successful leaders. We only need to look at the great inventors in history to see the workings and success of organizational awareness. Take Henry Ford, for example; he had no college education, left school at 16, and pursued his passion and dream. He had no knowledge of finances, business building, teamwork, organizational flow, or any of the many other components of business. He had one huge advantage over those who fail in business—he knew he wanted and needed to build a team of highly skilled individuals to fill the void of all the skills and talents that he himself lacked. He was great at seeing the value in others. He was great at knowing his strengths and weaknesses and surrounding himself with those who filled the gap. In doing so, he had the greatest respect for those in his company. And it showed. People wanted to be in his company...in a twofold meaning: in his presence, as in friendship, and in his business, Ford Motor Company.

Ford also revolutionized what is known today as focusing on one's strengths, both in the leadership of the Ford Motor Company and the inner workings of his business. The creation of the assembly line gave workers the opportunity to focus on one or two tasks and to do them really well. With repetition, you become masters at the task before you.

*A great leader will see your value and
contribution and empower you.*

INVITATION

Make organizational awareness your organization's aim and your personal focus. Schedule a consultation to lay out a framework to meet your needs, build the skills, expand the awareness, and create the right interactions that fuel the success of your organization. Schedule a time to discuss your needs at *Donalee360.com*.

Develop social awareness and political awareness to greatly enhance your ability to navigate and lead with the power to engage all employees.

- Invest time in developing social awareness:
- Listen to and consider others' perspectives.
- Recognize the strengths and value in people.
- Express gratitude to others.
- Identify diverse social norms, including unfair ones.
- Recognize situational demands, opportunities, and threats.

Invest in leadership training to up-level your leadership team and strengthen the backbone of your organization.

Find your way to a Winner's Circle, a group of masterminds, genius individuals, and highly successful business owners, that will place you in the company of other bright, intelligent, successful executives, business owners, developers, and influencers that will empower you, fill the voids, and strengthen your growth and development. The worst thing you could do as a leader is find yourself on an island, alone or with only a few that constrain, limit, and obscure your vision and awareness.

CHAPTER 28:

MEANING AND PURPOSE

In my lifetime, I've seen and experienced so much of my own evolution. I've seen more change than I could have ever believed possible. Often when something was talked about as a future possibility, I couldn't wrap my head around it. As a 10-year-old in the late '60s, I couldn't envision talking to a screen and seeing the other person before my eyes when my current reality was a corded phone that only allowed audio. As a 16-year-old, I couldn't see sending a document via a phone line across the country in a matter of minutes (what would become the fax machine). As a baby boomer growing up with no central air conditioning, a black-and-white TV, and corded phones, I've seen technology change in massive ways. I couldn't comprehend the vastness of the internet when it was first discussed. Yes, I've seen abundant change in both my inner and outer world.

I've seen how we all grow, change, and evolve. I had the joys and privilege of raising three amazing sons. I've seen and experienced my own change and my sons' changes. The only things constant in life are change, the unknown, and the unfolding of future growth and development.

With our focus on the material world, human beings have lost their connection to themselves and the meaning and purpose of life. The ABCs to master you and your results in life are aimed and meant to bring you back home to yourself and to your purpose in this lifetime.

The meaning of LIFE is to give life meaning.

MEANING

I was told to get a good job, find a husband, and have a family. I was told this is what life is all about. Yet something in me wasn't sure I agreed. Or maybe this wasn't enough for me. I had more questions, curiosity, and an inner need for more meaning and purpose than to simply follow a set of standards that others labeled as normal or expected. Sure, I wanted a best friend and partner, but I really didn't even know myself. And yes, I did want to fit in. But why am I here? Who am I? What is love? How do I fit in this world? I had way more questions than I had certainty, and making those big life decisions from a place of confusion seemed odd. It wasn't until my 30s that I realized I had so much to learn and love about myself. It was also in my 30s when I discovered how many of my dreams were coming true—how much of my life I was living and experiencing, and how I had achieved all my inner wishes and desires.

I've listened to others tell their college-age kids to find a partner to settle down with while in college because it would be difficult later. I've heard friends and family prodding their sons to get a girlfriend and those with daughters to find a boyfriend—as if not having one was a bad thing, as if others were judging them for not being partnered up, as if they couldn't be happy without one, as if life had a series of checklists to complete and this was the next one on the list.

I've seen young adults struggle to find their way. When deciding on the degree to pursue in college, they change their mind numerous times before settling on one. I've seen others go on journeys to find themselves as if they were lost. I've seen the challenges of young adults brought up in a world of materialism, feeling disconnected to life and themselves.

> *The struggle you're in today is developing the strength you need for tomorrow.*

I've seen the struggles of stress in our world, in both the young and the old. People find stress when fighting with a busy, active mind and struggle with negative feelings, all the while wanting peace, calm, and harmony within. Yet they don't know that choosing peace is an option. They go on to tell stories about their stress, how it keeps them up at night and causes them to overeat or indulge in activities that become addictive habits, but the medical society labels them as disease or disorders. With a medical label, you'll now need to a prescription to aid you in dealing with your so-called diagnosis or a treatment to help you overcome it. From depression to anxiety, anorexia to bulimia, alcoholism to drug addiction, cancer, and all the other diagnosed labels given, most stem from self-induced stress. Stress is physical, mental, and emotional tension.

I know this thing called stress oh too well. I used to have a lot of stress—a stressful marriage, stressful relationships—all causing me to blame others and seek ways to avoid the stress that led to unhealthy habits and addictions. I thought all this stress was happening *to* me. I didn't know I had options on how to see it differently and thus to respond to it verses avoid it or numb it.

Today, we are experiencing the biggest disruption to the old ways we have seen since the Great Depression. The Great Depression was the worst economic downturn in the history of the industrialized world, lasting from 1929 to 1939. It began after the stock market crash of October 1929, which sent Wall Street into a panic and wiped out millions of investors, businesses, and people.

With disruption comes opportunity.

The disruption the world is experiencing now is both an outer and inner reality disruption. Inwardly, it's challenging your freedoms, your rights, and your ability to make personal decisions. It's challenging your health and well-being and what you believe is true. It's challenging your mental and emotional health. It's challenging who and what you believe. It's challenging you to do your own research, to investigate, experiment, and explore what is true, correct, and accurate for you. Outwardly, it's challenging how, where, and what we do to conduct business, earn a living, and function in society.

Humanity has been on a search for meaning and purpose. No longer do the young adults feel a need to follow the footsteps of their fathers. We see it in the young adults boldly taking off to see the world without a care or concern for home, family, job, or the ways of past society, bravely exploring their dreams, desires, and curiosities.

We see this search for meaning and purpose in the Great Resignation that followed the pandemic of 2020. People are setting boundaries for themselves, for what they will and won't accept; standing up for

271

their choices and decisions; no longer following the herd mentality; no longer tolerating the mandates of bosses, businesses, and the bullying of society expecting others to think and act as they do.

PURPOSE

Meaning and purpose are found deep within yourself. Your life purpose consists of the central motivating aims of your life—the reasons you get up in the morning, those things that excite you and fulfill you. Purpose can guide life decisions, influence behavior, shape goals, offer a sense of direction, and create meaning. For some people, purpose is connected to vocation—meaningful, satisfying work. But not all will find their purpose in their work. Some may find it in parenthood, a hobby, or an interest that consumes them, like volunteering at a no-kill shelter or working on an organic farm.

Think back to your first dream as a child. Who or what did you wish to become? What did you dream of being as an adult? In this exploration, you will most likely find a thread from that time to your purpose now. Often the childhood dreams and desires are the start to finding one's purpose and meaning in life. Hard to imagine, I'm sure. I know it was for me and all those with whom I have shared this.

My childhood dream was to be a movie star, an actress. As I child, I thought it was about being on TV, making a lot of money, being popular, and getting noticed. As a child, I focused on the outer world and society's ways of what was expected. Only now am I able to see **why** these were my original thoughts. Only now am I able to see the conditioning that enveloped my thinking. Only now am I able to see the true dream that has lived inside me and what I really wanted to experience from it. So often we think our dreams are about having something tangible, like that Christmas wish list made from going through a catalog and picking out the presents we wanted to see under the tree on Christmas morning.

As an adult, reflecting back on what that dream may have meant on a deeper level, I see it completely differently. I see that what I was really wanting was to experience the fullness of all the different experiences that life had to offer. An actress plays various roles. She gets to be a wife, a mother, a sister, a boss, a bad girl, a good girl...you get the picture. I enjoyed pretend, dress-up, and role-playing as a child. It was exciting for me to be a doctor, a nurse, a mommy, and a daddy all in the course of one day. In my mind, each of these roles brought with it a different experience. I was truly wanting the richness of all the experiences that life had to bring; from the addict and the victim to mother, wife, and business owner, I've had the experience that each of these brought.

As I reflect on that dream now, I see that it was also to encourage myself to embrace my fears, to dismantle or dissolve the parts of me that felt limiting. It was to stop playing small in life. That childhood dream was for me to live life big and bold and bravely go for what I want, and not to get to the end of my life and wish I had had more courage and confidence to follow my heart and my dreams.

That childhood dream was my guiding light. Beneath the outward expression of what it looked like to be an actress was a bigger message for me. I am the actress on the screen of my life, the life I create for myself. I get to choose if I want to play the victim. I get to choose if I want to play the hero and experience victory. I get to choose to say YES or NO. I get to wipe the screen clean and start a new story, a new chapter, a new experience. Life is full and rich and rewarding when we live into our meaning and our purpose. I am the actress in the story of my life. I play all the roles I wish to experience, and it is the experience I truly wish for, not what the experience brings me. There is no magic shiny object that will fulfill me when I get there; all my joy, all my satisfaction, is found in the experience of every single role I play.

> *What I've really come to learn is this: You are the lead actor, director, writer, and producer in the movie of your life. If you don't like any aspect of it, change your story.*

What's your purpose? What gives you meaning? According to Viktor Frankl, author of *Man's Search for Meaning,* meaning can be found through:

- Experiencing reality by interacting authentically with the environment and with others
- Giving something back to the world through creativity and self-expression
- Changing our attitude when faced with a situation or circumstance that we cannot change

For Frankl, meaning came from three possible sources: **purposeful work, love, and courage in the face of difficulty**. Love goes far beyond the physical person of the beloved. It finds its deepest meaning in one's spiritual being, one's inner self.

Ralph Waldo Emerson puts it like this:

The purpose of life is not to be happy. It is to be useful, to be honorable, to be compassionate, to have it make some difference that you have lived and lived well.

Once you are able to stop looking outside yourself for the satisfaction and fulfillment you seek, you may be able to find your true meaning and purpose. You see, you have been taught that you should do, have, and become all these things in life and that will complete you, that all these material possessions and achievements will bring you joy, meaning, and purpose. If you are able to find meaning and purpose, true joy and love, it will probably be found within each and every experience. Let me explain. I don't know a single person who can assign their meaning and purpose in life to their title, position, or acquisition of material possessions. Every business owner, CEO, or homeowner may have thought there was meaning and purpose in achieving a certain status, possession, or claim, but the real meaning and message to their purpose came from the impact and service they brought to others through their position or possessions. Most will say that it is the sense of who they have become and the contribution they bring that gives them fulfillment, satisfaction, and reward. And for many, it is what they found within each experience that brought them clarity to their meaning and purpose.

The meaning of life is to find your gift. The purpose of life is to give it away. ~ Pablo Picasso

What I have found in over a decade of coaching hundreds of people out of their pain and suffering and into living a life they love is that it's not about getting anywhere or achieving a set goal. It's more about who you become along the way. It's about the fulfillment and satisfaction of the experiences, the growth, the challenges, the struggles, and overcoming each one. It's about the perseverance, your resiliency, and your dedication and determination to follow your heart and your dreams. It's about leaning into what lights you up. It's about the service and gifts you bring to others, the impact and influence you offer, and the contribution you leave. Maybe you will find greater meaning and purpose in life as you know yourself fully; as you learn of your strengths, gifts, and talents; and as you realize how sharing them with others makes you feel. It's my hope that you will find meaning and purpose in your life, but if you don't, I hope you find peace and satisfaction in all that you are. What if being alive is the meaning and your purpose is to live life boldly, bravely, and beautifully?

It's only by starting in a place of peace that we find our purpose and power. ~ Martha Beck

What would you love? I think your meaning and purpose are as individual and unique as you are, and only you can assign that message and meaning for yourself. For me, I have always had an interest and passion for human behavior. In my experiences, learnings, struggles, and successes, I have grown to better understand human behavior in myself and others. I am here to be the best version of myself and share my gifts with the world, and this is meaning and purpose enough to have me excited to wake up and live another day. Know that you have the power to create a deeply meaningful and wildly passionate life for yourself.

INVITATION

What was your childhood dream? Contemplate this, journal about it, and give yourself time to reflect. Reflect on your childhood dream from both your outer world needs and accomplishments and your inner world—your thoughts, feelings, sense of self-fulfillment—and accomplishments.

_____

_____

What were the underlying feelings, meanings, and joys that that dream had for you? Are you subconsciously living it?

_____

_____

If not, what brings you joy? What do you love most about your journey in life?

_____

_____

Your deepest meaning is found within. Take time to explore and journal. Ask yourself, What would I love?

_____

_____

CHAPTER 29:

PURE POTENTIAL

The pure power and potential that you really want flows through you when you unite your personality and spirit, ego self and divine self, as one in awareness. Your pure potential manifests when you are able to stop seeking one or the other, when you are able to be present in the moment, seeing, holding, and abiding in both your humanness and all the roles you play, as well as your divinity, the underlying connection behind it all, connecting you to all things.

For years I thought I was seeking spiritual growth to be someone different. I thought my spiritual growth and enlightenment would magically allow me to "Be in the world but not of the world." I thought I was seeking some sort of freedom from the corruption, murder, punishment, and pain that I saw on the news and headlines of the paper, or at least a freedom from my personal pain and complaining by others. I would get high seeking the bliss of the spirit world, looking for heaven on earth, the vast openness, unity, and connectedness with all beings. It allowed me to connect with that part of me that didn't judge and didn't focus on all the corruption and chaos around me, but instead could see compassion, love, and a sense of peace and harmony. Looking back, maybe I felt it was necessary to experience both heaven and hell, and getting high was my way of bringing a bit of heaven into a day of hell.

It was what I called, at the time, **balance**. You know, balance between the real world, the world where I was exposed to the toxic behavior patterns that people would habitually project out, where people focus on differences and create a bigger divide, a separation in which others are pushed away, and a different reality, one where peace, love, and unity did exist. Getting high allowed me to push away from all that I didn't want to see, feel, and acknowledge and find that space where we all were one big, happy, and loving family. For some years, I used cigarettes to create a semi-altered state and a momentary break from my life. Years later, I used alcohol to alter my state of mind, get high, numb myself out of the demands, stresses, and busyness of the world to find a space where I could relax, let go of the chaos for a few minutes or hours, and find what I called a bit of balance to my day. I wasn't the only one either. Society had a name for it—happy hour—and it followed the workday, as if we needed that time to shift back into the loving, kind, and happy people we were supposed to be after a day at work.

YOU give the meaning to everything in your reality.

I had a mentor that asked me what I really wanted in life. I replied, "To be happy." His response was, "Then what's the problem?" He reminded me that no one and nothing can steal my happiness. With happiness as my main objective, I was able to see that I was assigning the meaning to everything in my life. I began to observe the meaning I had given things and questioned if I wanted to be right or happy. Choosing happiness as a theme and main objective in my life shifted how I looked upon the world around me. What do you really want in life? Can you choose it and make this your main objective?

Happiness is a choice and not a destination.

The truth is, as long as you are pushing away from anything, you push yourself out of your center, out of the center of the circle of unity, harmony, and your inner power. Time on this planet has taught me much about life. One of my greatest learnings has been how to accept what *is* without pushing away from others and resisting differing viewpoints and attitudes. At your center, you are able to be, do, and connect with all things effortlessly and pleasantly.

Furthermore, whatever you bring to your center will beautifully blossom into your world. You already have brought things into your center. The things that are at the center of your world are the things that you are spending the majority of your time thinking about. As you experiment with this, you'll find that you can only perform at your highest and greatest peak potential when you are bringing your goals in alignment with the things that are at the center of your world.

> *You won't succeed at anything if it isn't at the center of your world.*

You have two variables: what should be at the center of your world and what truly is at the center of your world. By aligning these two together, you will stay centered and your aim will proactively be part of every thought and action you take.

This goes for a new daddy who brings the new addition to the family to the center of his world. This goes for the entrepreneur with a new start-up business who brings that business to the center of their world. This goes for the individual recently diagnosed with a life-changing disease who chooses to bring their health and well-being to the center of their world. This goes for you and whatever is at the center of your world; it is what you will master and what you will create, become, and live.

> *At your center, you are unstoppable, focused, aligned, and empowered.*

The circle is considered a symbol of unity because all the regular polygons are embraced by the circle. It is also the *symbol of infinity*, without beginning or end, perfect, the ultimate geometric symbol.

Your goal is to know yourself, your happy place, that state of being where you feel calm, fulfilled, and empowered; where love, joy, and harmony saturate your inner being, and you radiate and share this energy outward like a radio wave. This is you at the center of your circle. You are the sending and receiving beacon for all you experience. Here you have dominion. Here you create the foundation for your practices of mastery by engineering the plan of action to allow your journey to unfold. Your aim is alignment, preparedness, being in the flow of what is, knowing, trusting, and allowing life to empower and guide you. At your center, you are in total alignment with all of your energy bodies, intelligence systems, and both your humanness and your divinity.

Productivity evolves from your center.

Hermes Trismegistus, who is considered the founder of science, religion, mathematics, geometry, alchemy, philosophy, medicine, and magic, described the circle as thus: The **circle** is a universal symbol with extensive meaning. It represents the **notions of totality, wholeness, original perfection, the Self, the infinite, eternity, timelessness**, all cyclic movement.

Life is a circle; the end of one journey is the beginning of the next.

It is said that Hermes received his divine wisdom in meditative trances. His influence was so impactful, it developed into what is called Hermeticism. The word *hermetic* is defined as complete and airtight.

In science, a phenomenon that is being observed is separated from the soul and the internal value system of the observer. When science observes a phenomenon, it assumes that it is nature; the perceptual is the actual. However, in the modern fields of relativistic and quantum physics, observation affects the process being observed, with a different outcome than if the process was unobserved.

In Hermes wisdom, that which is being studied is a reflection of the observer, and the two are intrinsically linked. This is central to Hermetic philosophy as seen in the phrase, "As above, so below": the universe is a symbolic reflection of what is happening inside ourselves. The quest for knowledge becomes a spiritual journey to return to a state of unity with the divine, known as the "Great Work" of humankind.

All are one. As above, so below.

What does this tell you? Let's break it down like this: In the circle, you are at the center. In this center point, you are whole, complete, infinite, and timeless. You are all things and everything and yet you are nothing...until you say differently.

In this circle lies all of you: all your humanness, mind, emotions, physical body, and all the roles you play in your outer world, along with all the realities of others interacting in your journey. Standing in this awareness means holding multiple realities in your awareness at the same time. You are a multidimensional being. You are multifaceted. You have desire, will, and the potential to experience a variety of realities.

Every time you wish to choose or hold only one reality as true, you push yourself out of the center. You are still in the circle but choosing to experience only one reality, one thought system, or one belief alone.

Every time you resist someone, something in your awareness, you push yourself outside the center. Every time you separate yourself from others or oust another from your circle, your friendship, your love, or your forgiveness, you push yourself outside the center. Every time you think you need to be noticed, forgiven, acknowledged, and accepted, you push yourself outside the center. Every time you see yourself as separate and alone, you are pushing yourself outside the center. Every time you play small, hold back, or resist, you are pushing yourself outside the center.

You are the center of your universe!

Outside the center of the circle, you are disconnected from awareness to your natural and true nature. Away from your center, you seem to struggle, suffer, and seek something from the world. Away from your center, you have momentarily chosen to focus on a particular detail and are not using all of your intelligence systems to serve you in your awareness.

Only at your center are all four of your intelligence systems fully engaged and activated and working together in harmony. At the center of the circle, you are connected to all of you. At the center of the circle, you are fully engaged, activated, and empowered.

The circle represents equality, equity, equanimity, equilibrium, and the equalizing of all parts to equip you with your eternal totality. The circle represents all of you and all of your universe. The circle represents everything everywhere, in all ways and always:

- **All ways** – in every manner possible
- **Always** – perpetually, frequently, repetitively

As within, so without. As above, so below. ~ Hermes Trismegistus

This just might be the biggest secret of life. This quote is one of the seven principles in *The Corpus Hermeticum*. It can be interpreted in a multitude of ways, yet the most suitable meaning, the meaning shared here, would be:

Quoted Phrase	Interpreted Meaning
As within	What we think within ourselves…
So without	…will be expressed or reflected on the world we live
As above	As in heaven (your own mind)
So below	So on Earth (in your body and environment)

If we think good, good follows; if we think evil, evil will follow. Whatever we think and accept (consciously) will be the perceived circumstances of our life.

Take a peek into the life of Napoleon Hill, author of the best-selling book *Think and Grow Rich*, which still ranks among the best-selling business books 85 years after it was first published. Hill was inspired and motivated by Andrew Carnegie to interview and learn from the most successful businesspeople of his time. He dedicated his life to doing just that, and the book is a must-read and one that many motivational leaders recommend rereading every year, so I won't be giving it all away here. What I will say is that this principle of the circle, *As within, so without,* can be seen and expressed in each of the successful businesspeople that inspired the work of Hill. They all had a definite purpose, a desire to succeed, a belief in themselves, and the universe conspiring to make it so.

Quoted Phrase	Interpreted Meaning
As within	What every business leader thought in their mind (what they believed possible) …
So without	…was expressed in their reality, their world (what they created)

INVITATION

Come fully present to this now moment, in awareness, bringing all of you to this party of life so that you can stay curious to how you are called to show up and express yourself fully to connect with one another in a deep, rich, and rewarding way. Follow your breath and allow yourself to drop into your center. Notice where you sense this to be in your body.

_____

_____

From your center, you automatically connect to and have dominion of your thoughts, feelings, and perceptions. From your center, you are balanced and strengthened.

Do you feel stressed? Overwhelmed? Out of control? Create a practice that brings you back to your center. Begin a practice of noticing when you have gotten too far off center and develop the right response to bring yourself back to center.

_____

_____

You have been fully equipped to know yourself more intimately and honestly, to notice the upsets and thoughts that take you off course, out of peace and harmony, and away from your center. Maybe it's a time of day that you find yourself off center. Create a practice that allows you to come home to all of yourself, abide here a while, breathe into the balance and harmony of the body, and feel into your stability, strength, and fully empowered being that you are.

There is greatness in you, and you are here to live it.

CONCLUSION

You are a beautiful and amazing being. You are fully equipped with everything you need to master you and your results. You are here to have dominion over your earth. You are the earth you are here to monitor, manage, and master. You are the center of your universe. At this center, you are fully empowered with everything you need to be the best version of you.

Educate, Engage, and Empower is the underlying theme in *Bringing Spirituality into Business* and the underlying theme of life in general. You learn, apply new learning, and evolve in your life journey. No one knows your journey except you. No one guides your purpose in life but you. Your journey, your purpose, comes from within you, from knowing yourself, growing yourself, and living your life empowered.

You know you've grown in just reading *Bringing Spirituality into Business*. It's been your guide to knowing yourself, growing yourself, and living your life empowered. What's changed and how have you grown? Be sure to measure your changes with the Finish Assessment. It's the same assessment you took at the beginning of this book, and it will show you where you are now in the same 18 topics. You'll be able to see by the numbers you scored exactly what areas have shifted and changed for you. You can find your Finish Assessment in the Companion Workbook or at *https://complete-solutionsllc.com/Bringing-Spirituality-into-Business/*. Scroll to the bottom of the page and click on "Finish Assessment."

After a life commitment to interviewing the most successful businesspeople of his time, Napoleon Hill discovered the benefit of the Mastermind. He found that surrounding yourself with other successful minds is both mandatory and priceless. You can't put a price tag on the valuable resources found in surrounding yourself with other successful, innovative leaders, both in what comes to you through the one mind and to you through the ideas of others.

I trust you've journeyed through this book with a group of other growth-minded people—your own book club, department, or coworkers—or joined me in mine. Reflect on the value you've gotten from meeting with others each week to discuss and share your learning and progress through each chapter. As you reflect, you might be thinking, now what? If this is you, I have the perfect solution to continue to nurture your growth and development and continue to increase and expand into more of your greatness. If you recognize the value in being in a circle of support, and if you are feeling called to encompass yourself in a Winner's Circle mastermind with me, you'll find more information and enrollment at *https://complete-solutionsllc.com/winners-circle/*.

I hope you found value and massive growth in your travels through this book. I hope you are finishing with many golden nuggets that will continue to aid you in your life journey. Come back and reread often, as you will get more from each chapter as you do. Many chapters were filled with more growth than one could embrace the first time through, so do go back and reread, and when following the Invitation at the end of each chapter, be sure to stretch yourself to greater awareness, growth, and success.

Last, if you found this book helpful, please share it.

> *You will only succeed to the level with which*
> *you help others do the same.*

And I ask that you please share an honest review of this book. You can share your review on Amazon or wherever books are sold. I thank you for sharing yourself, your time, and your opinions.

May your journey through life always be rich and rewarding as you remember the ABCs to master you and your results with just one skill, one practice, and one process.

Scan the QR code for **bonus material**.

GRANT ME

Grant ME the mastery of
AWARENESS
to be self-aware
and socially aware

Grant ME the ability
to OBSERVE myself
and who I am
BEING

Grant ME the confidence to value
BEING
over doing

Grant ME the
CURIOSITY
to seek questions
I cannot answer
solutions over problems
serving verses getting
insight above information
and
courage instead of comfort

Grant me the **WISDOM**
to be ME
the best version of ME
to bravely and boldly
accept all of me
my quirks
my weirdness
my strengths
my weaknesses
and own the
beauty and greatness
of all that I am

~ Donalee Gastreich

www.ingramcontent.com/pod-product-compliance
Lightning Source LLC
Chambersburg PA
CBHW071144130626
46553CB00004B/1513